FROM THE MAY FOURTH MOVEMENT
TO COMMUNIST REVOLUTION

SUNY Series in Chinese Philosophy and Culture

Roger T. Ames, *editor*

FROM THE
MAY FOURTH MOVEMENT
TO COMMUNIST REVOLUTION

Guo Moruo and the Chinese Path to Communism

XIAOMING CHEN

STATE UNIVERSITY OF NEW YORK PRESS

Published by
STATE UNIVERSITY OF NEW YORK PRESS
Albany

© 2007 State University of New York

For information, contact State University of New York Press, Albany, NY
www.sunypress.edu

Production by Diane Ganeles
Marketing by Anne M. Valentine

Library of Congress Cataloging-in-Publication Data

Chen, Xiaoming, 1956–
    From the May Fourth Movement to Communist Revolution : Guo Moruo and the Chinese path to
Communism / Xiaoming Chen.
        p. cm. — (SUNY series in Chinese philosophy and culture)
    Includes bibliographical references and index.
    ISBN-13: 978-0-7914-7137-1 (alk. paper)
        1. Communism—China.   2. Guo, Moruo, 1892–1978.   3. China—History—May Fourth
movement, 1919   I. Title.
HX418.5.C45262 2007
335.43'45—dc22   2006027522

10   9   8   7   6   5   4   3   2   1

To my son Michael

Contents

Illustrations

Photos courtesy of the Guo Moruo Museum in Beijing. Used with permission.

Acknowledgments

I would like to thank Chang Hao for the help and criticism he gave me in the process of writing this book. His criticism kept driving me to clarify my thinking and eventually forced me to come up with the scholarship that comprises this work. I am especially grateful for Ezra Vogel's support of this work. I also am grateful to Kirk Denton and Yan-shuan Lao for the help and criticism they gave me in the initial stage of this manuscript. I also appreciate the help and support I received from Jeremy Baskes, Michael Flamm, and Rowena Hernandez-Muzquiz, my colleagues at Ohio Wesleyan. Thomas Wolber, another colleague of mine, deserves recognition for helping me with some of the translations from German. Finally, I would like to thank Dana Foote for her editing of this book.

The author thanks the Guo Moruo Museum in Beijing, China, for granting permission to reproduce the photos in this book.

Introduction

During the second half of the May Fourth period (1915–1925), China saw some of its best brains turn to the Communist cause. Why did these May Fourth intellectuals become interested in Communism? Why and how did China develop from the seemingly Western-style, bourgeois May Fourth movement, which featured, among other things, an urge for individual emancipation, to the collectivist and violent revolution of Communism? An examination of the case of Guo Moruo (郭沫若) (1892–1978), a leading May Fourth advocate for Western Romanticist individualism who converted to Communism in the mid-1920s, may help answer these questions.

First published as a poet in 1919, Guo came to have a significant impact on China's May Fourth reading public with his numerous poems, essays, novels, and translations of foreign works in fields such as literature, art, philosophy, and political theory. After leading the May Fourth movement in introducing and promoting Johann Wolfgang von Goethe's (1749–1832) celebration of romantic love and individuality and challenging China's traditional system of arranged marriage, a symbol of the Confucian social ethics of *lijiao* (禮教), Guo declared his conversion to Communism in 1924, three years after the founding of the Chinese Communist Party (CCP). He then further committed himself to the Communist revolution by participating in the Northern Expedition (1926–1928) in July 1926 and joining the CCP in August 1927.[1] As a highly articulate writer he recorded, step-by-step, his change from a major May Fourth figure to an enthusiastic Communist, providing an important reference for us to understand the intellectual transition in China from the May Fourth movement to the cause of Communism.[2]

Scholars basically agree that the frustration and desperation that some May Fourth intellectuals felt in trying to save China as a nation in the modern world was a major reason they turned to the radical cause of Communism in the 1920s. This study confirms this view, as it finds that a major reason Guo turned to Communism in the mid-1920s was that, inspired by the 1917 Soviet revolution, he came to see Communist revolution as a powerful means to strengthen his nation so it would not only survive suppression and exploitation by Western and Japanese imperialist powers but eventually defeat those powers.

There were, however, other reasons Guo (and, I would argue, other May Fourth intellectuals) turned to Communism, to which scholars have not yet paid enough attention.[3] As this study shows, for instance, while nationalist drive was a major factor in leading Guo toward Communism, his cosmopolitanist ambition to save mankind was also an important driving force behind his conversion to the cause of the Communist revolution. More precisely, his nationalist concerns had always had a strong Confucian cosmopolitanist perspective. It was this traditional, egalitarian, cosmopolitanist perspective that made him feel that he could relate to the Marxist ideal of an egalitarian cosmopolitan world, and it was in the Marxist cosmopolitan revolution that he finally found a modern and an effective way to achieve his Confucian cosmopolitanist goal of harmonizing the world. This book also shows that Guo turned to Communism in the mid-1920s for its emancipation of the individual. Having experienced the so-called May Fourth enlightenment, the essence of which was the pursuit of the freedom of the individual, he could no longer tolerate the exploitation and suppression that he suffered as an individual in China's society in the 1920s and found his solution in Marx's promise of achieving ultimate individual emancipation by completely destroying capitalist society.[4] This finding means that while scholars such as Li Zehou (李澤厚) argue that the Communist revolution in China came to smother the May Fourth theme of enlightenment (qimeng 啟蒙) with the other May Fourth theme of national salvation (jiuwang 救亡), Guo's experience shows that it was actually the inspiration of May Fourth enlightenment that helped lead him (and possibly others) toward the Communist cause.[5] What Guo's case suggests here, in other words, is that China's transition from May Fourth to Communism was not the simple story of national salvation smothering enlightenment, as Li argues. On the contrary, to some extent enlightenment actually cofunctioned with nationalism to lead some May Fourth intellectuals to make the transition from May Fourth to Marxist Communism. This book also points out that Guo turned to Communism for moral/spiritual salvation of the self, which was in fact a Confucian goal that he had never ceased pursuing, even during the high tide of May Fourth's seeming Westernization. By bringing Confucian elements such as the concept of moral/spiritual salvation into Communism, of course, Guo was not merely converting to a modern Western Marxist Communism but instead creating a new brand of Communism that was not only Western but Chinese. This brings up another major reason Guo turned to Communism in the mid-1920s: he saw that in Communism he could create a combination of the best of both Western modernity and Chinese tradition. In achieving this combination, something that he had been searching for since his May Fourth years, he had finally found a satisfactory solution to modern China's intellectual crisis, at the core of which was the fundamental question of whether the Chinese people should rely upon tradition or modern Western thinking for their value system and ideological guidance in a collision between the modern West and their traditional society.[6]

In determining why and how Guo made the intellectual transition from May Fourth to Communism, I examine, in the context of the interaction and collision between Chinese tradition and Western modernity, his experience with and thinking on two basic issues of humanity: the relationships between the self/individual, the family, the nation, and the whole of mankind in the mundane world and the moral/spiritual transcendence of mundane human individuals (or the negation of such transcendence).

To begin with, on the issue of people's mundane relationships, while modern Western influence had already started undermining China's traditional society at the turn of the twentieth century, Guo (as did most Chinese of his generation) at the time was to a substantial extent still brought up with the basic framework of the Confucian orientational order of *xiushen* 修身 (morally cultivating the self), *qijia* 齊家 (regulating the family), *zhiguo* 治國 (managing the state), and *pingtianxia* 平天下 (harmonizing the world). This sequence, to which I will refer as the Confucian model of *xiu-qi-zhi-ping*, starts with an emphasis on the moral cultivation, development, and fulfillment of the individual, a concept that Wm. Theodore de Bary calls "Confucian personalism." As de Bary puts it, this Confucian personalism differs from modern Western individualism in that it sees the individual "as fulfilling himself through the social process and in a moral and spiritual communion with others" and "does not set the individual over against state or society."[7] In other words, the Confucian concern for the individual self's moral/spiritual growth carries a strong collective perspective, specified in the individual's obligations to the collectives of family, state, and world.

The family was the collective with which Confucian individuals should have the closest relationship, hence their first collective task of regulating the family. The importance of the family in Confucian society can also be seen in the fact that two of the Confucian Three Bonds, those between the father and son and between the husband and wife, center on the family. For centuries, the family functioned as the cornerstone of China's traditional Confucian *lijiao* society.

Beyond the family the Confucian sequence further demands the individual's obligation to the state and to the cosmopolitan world. The point to be made here is that the Confucian calling for the individual to strive to harmonize the world gives the Confucian goal of managing the state a constant cosmopolitanist perspective and therefore assigns to that goal a secondary importance (secondary to cosmopolitanist achievement). Partly because of this cosmopolitanist perspective, the Confucian goal of state management is substantially different than modern nationalism, which, as suggested by Benjamin Schwartz, exists when "the commitment to the preservation and advancement of the societal entity known as the nation takes priority over commitment to all other values and beliefs."[8] By the same token, we can say that the Confucian cosmopolitanist concern is also modified by the serious attention that Confucianism gives to state management, to the extent that such concern does not constitute a cosmopolitanism that thoroughly transcends and ignores national boundaries.

The Confucian orientational order of *xiu-qi-zhi-ping* was also part of Guo's upbringing on the issue of the individual human being's moral/spiritual transcendence from the mundane world. According to Confucianism, especially Wang Yangming's (王陽明) mind-heart school of Neo-Confucianism that significantly influenced Guo in the 1910s, not only are regulating the family, managing the state, and harmonizing the world important goals for the individual to achieve in the mundane world, but they are also the means through which the individual cultivates himself in order to achieve moral/spiritual transcendence. This idea of achieving what Yu Ying-shih (余英時) describes as "inner transcendence" through mundane activities is summed up in the Confucian concept of *neisheng waiwang* 內聖外王 (inner sagehood and outer kingliness), part of whose calling is for the individual to strive for transcendental, moral/spiritual sagehood through mundane achievements that would ultimately lead to kingliness.[9]

As this book shows, as a basis of his thinking on both the issue of people's this-worldly relationships and the issue of people's moral/spiritual transcendence, Guo, throughout his May Fourth and early Communist years, to a certain extent carried on portions of the Confucian *xiu-qi-zhi-ping* orientational model, namely, the portions of self-cultivation, state management, and cosmopolitanist achievement. For instance, in 1925, after his announced conversion to Communism in 1924, he wrote enthusiastically that he continued to follow Confucianism as a "perfectly round" and smooth orientational system. He noted that thisworldly Confucianism, with its orientational model, guides the individual to relate himself to the state and the cosmopolitan world without tension, and, transcendentally, it enables people to "freely travel in and out" of the mundane world in their drive for moral/spiritual inner transcendence.[10] The Confucian system, therefore, makes life "meaningful" for people by allowing them to develop "without obstacles in every direction" within and beyond humanity (*sitong bada* 四通八達).[11]

As I argue here, Guo's continuity with Confucian tradition tells us that the May Fourth intellectual movement was not as antitraditional as many perceive it to be. As a major figure of the second half of the May Fourth movement, especially as an influential advocate of Western Romanticism and individualism, Guo's continuity with part of the Confucian tradition suggests that the tradition had survived the seemingly overwhelming impact of Western modernity to an extent that has not been fully realized by scholars and specialists of the May Fourth movement or modern China in general. Further, I argue that Guo's Confucian background was a major factor in his development from a May Fourth intellectual to a Communist. For instance, while modern Western and Japanese nationalist influences were substantial elements in his thinking, the traditional Confucian calling for state management also served as an inspiration for his drive to save and revive his nation, which was an important factor behind his conversion to Communism in the mid-1920s.[12] The Confucian cosmopolitanist ambition also served as a link between Guo's Chinese traditional background and the Marxist version of Western modernity, as his attraction to Marxism partly resulted from his discovery that the Marxist cosmopolitanist ideal was comparable to his Confucian cosmopolitanist dream. Further, his Confucian background directly led to the creation of his version of Chinese Communism, as his Confucian concept of inner transcendence and self-cultivation significantly modified Marxist historical materialism with a moral/spiritual, transcendental perspective and therefore gave his Communist thinking a unique Chinese touch. What is historically important here is that not only did his version of Chinese Communism precede the Maoist version of Communism, to which he himself was to contribute, but the traditional elements in his Communist thinking also could be found one way or another later in Maoist thinking and practice. One can argue, for instance, that behind the Maoists' nationalist drive and cosmopolitanist ambition there were also at work the Confucian goals of managing the state and harmonizing the world. The Maoists' obsession with thought reforms, which was first exemplified by Liu Shaoqi's (劉少奇)*On the Cultivation of a Communist* (*Lun gongchandangyuan de xiuyang* 論共產党員的修養) and then culminated in the "revolution on the soul" (*linghun shenchu naogeming* 靈魂深處鬧革命) during the Cultural Revolution, also strongly reminds us of the Confucian emphasis on moral self-cultivation in Guo's Communist thinking in the 1920s.[13] As the Maoists, later with their Marxist antifeudal and antitraditional image, hardly recognized or admitted much of their continuity with the Confucian tradition, the link between the tradition and modern Marxist/Leninist Communism that Guo publicly and elaborately established in his early Communist thinking provides us with a helpful reference point to better understand Chinese Communism's overall continuity with Chinese tradition.

What Guo and many of his fellow May Fourthians did break with was the *qi* (regulating the family) portion of the Confucian *xiu-qi-zhi-ping* model and a fundamental part of the Confucian *lijiao* society. Largely due to the influence of modern Western individualism, Guo in the early 1920s was finally able to justify his years-long and hard-fought rebellion against a marriage arranged by his parents, which meant that he had justified his disobeying his parents on the marriage and abandoning his arranged wife. In so doing, he successfully broke with the Confucian father-son and husband-wife bonds, which constituted the essence of the Confucian family and two of the crucial Three Bonds, the core of the *lijiao* society.[14] More important, in publicly justifying his rebellion against the arranged marriage, he played the role of a leading advocate of Western Goethean individualism and Romanticism during the second half of the May Fourth movement and influenced a whole generation of educated youth in their battle against arranged marriage and, in general, against the Confucian family and the suppression of *lijiao*.

Through the context of the Confucian orientational model of *xiu-qi-zhi-ping*, therefore, we can see that what Guo (and his generation) did during the May Fourth movement was to break with the *qi* (regulating the family) part of the model while to a certain extent carrying on the *xiu* (moral self-cultivation toward inner transcendence), *zhi* (managing the state), and *ping* (harmonizing the world) parts of the sequence. Their carrying on of the *xiu*, *zhi*, and *ping* parts of the Confucian model, of course, was significantly modified by the fact that, under the impact of modern Western thinking, the subjects of these three parts—the self, the state, and the world—all went through changes in their definitions.[15] In addition, the May Fourthians' break with the *qi* (regulating the family) part also inevitably affected their continuation with the *xiu, zhi*, and *ping* parts of the Confucian model, since the regulation of the family used to be a major task for the individual to pursue in the original Confucian process of self-cultivation, and the Confucian family used to be a major part of the foundation of the traditional state and world. Further, as exemplified by Guo's case, some May Fourthians' preoccupation with their individualist break with the Confucian family and *lijiao* meant that the collective matters of saving their country (*zhi*) and the world (*ping*) were sometimes not their central concern. This said, however, the *xiu, zhi*, and *ping* parts of the Confucian model did to a certain extent survive the May Fourth movement, to the extent that during and after the May Fourth movement in China there continued to be a moral emphasis concerning the self's development, and the Confucian calling to manage the state and harmonize the world had contributed overall to the country's modern drive for national and world salvation.

The carrying on of the *xiu, zhi*, and *ping* portions of the tradition, of course, differed in degrees among the May Fourthians and tended to be a subconscious experience for many of them. In rebelling against the Confucian family and *lijiao*, many May Fourthians came to believe and conveyed the image that they were doing away with Confucian tradition in its entirety. It is on this issue that we find another major part of Guo Moruo's significance in modern Chinese intellectual history: when many of his fellow May Fourthians were just subconsciously carrying on the *xiu-zhi-ping* ideals of the tradition, and their break with the Confucian family and *lijiao* was misunderstood as a break with the whole tradition, Guo publicly and enthusiastically defended and promoted the tradition while helping lead the May Fourth rebellion against the Confucian family and *lijiao*. In so doing, he personified, demystified, and dramatized the essence and complexity of the May Fourth movement as one primarily against the Confucian family and *lijiao* instead of one that destroyed Confucian tradition as a whole.[16]

Scholars have developed various theses in examining the issue of the May Fourth movement's treatment of Confucian tradition.[17] I approach the issue in the context of the Confucian *xiu-qi-zhi-ping* orientational model because, for one thing, this approach highlights in its right proportion the importance of the family in the Confucian tradition and therefore the significance of the May Fourth movement's break with the Confucian family. This break, in my view, was part of the essence of the May Fourth movement. As a side point to help make my argument here, I believe the reason Ba Jin's (巴金) novel *Family* (家) later became so popular is that it had caught the essence of the impact of the May Fourth rebellion against the Confucian family and the *lijiao* society.

The individualist awakening that Guo achieved in his May Fourth battle against the Confucian family and *lijiao* was a major reason he later, in the mid-1920s, became interested in Marxism, specifically in Marx's promise of ultimate individual emancipation.[18] After being awakened by Western Goethean individualism and Romanticism, Guo could not help but feel bitter that China's society in the early and mid 1920s had deprived him of his freedom as an individual. As a result, he became deeply attracted to Marx's promise that after the destruction of the suppressive capitalist society there would be ultimate individual freedom and development for everyone in the ideal Communist society.[19] In other words, it was to a certain extent Guo's May Fourth awakening of individual rights and freedom that had made him extremely intolerant of Chinese society's suppression of his individual development and prepared and led him to be attracted to the Marxist promise of individual freedom, even though, with his continuous Confucian collectivist obligation to the state (and his influence by modern nationalism), it is doubtful that he had fully understood the Marxist concept of ultimate individual emancipation.

Guo in fact was not the only May Fourthian who turned to Marxism for its promise of individual emancipation. Li Dazhao (李大釗) (1889–1927), for instance, wrote in 1921 that he saw no tension between socialism and individualism. In his words, "Truly reasonable socialism allows individual freedom."[20] In 1923, Li further drove home the point by stating that only in socialist/Communist society can one find "free and equal individuals."[21] Qu Qiubai (瞿秋白) (1899–1935) in 1923 also noted that when private property is abolished and socioeconomic classes eliminated in the Communist society, there will be "free development of everyone's individuality."[22] What this tells us is that the May Fourth individualist awakening was actually a reason for at least some of the May Fourthians' interest in and conversion to Marxist Communism. These May Fourthians started their Communist careers with the goal of realizing Marx's dream of individual emancipation. In their eyes, collective and temporary suppression of people's individuality was a necessary part of the Marxist revolutionary means to eventually achieve the ideal society in which everyone will enjoy individual freedom and self-development.[23]

In fact, not only was the May Fourth theme of individualist enlightenment a factor in preparing some May Fourth intellectuals to be attracted to the Marxist promise of individual emancipation, but that theme, which focused on challenging and breaking with the Confucian family and *lijiao* society, was to a substantial extent also popularized by the Communist movement that those May Fourthians later came to lead. After all, while it had been a revolutionary climax of the changes of the Confucian tradition since the early phase of the Transitional Period (Chang Hao's terms), the May Fourth movement's individualist break with the Confucian family and *lijiao* remained by and large a limited urban phenomenon among educated youth. It was the Communists who later popularized among the rural masses a substantial portion of what had been achieved by the urban May Fourth youth. In their collectivist ways, of course, the Communists carried out in their revolution mass anti-*lijiao* social reforms and specifically pushed for individuals' freedom of marriage and divorce and equality between the sexes among millions of peasants. Few can argue, for instance, that "The Marriage of Xiao Er Hei" (*xiao er hei jiehun* 小二黑結婚), a short story highly popular in wartime, Communist-controlled areas in the

1940s, was not a popular version of Guo Moruo and other May Fourthians' struggle against the Confucian family and *lijiao*.[24] In 1945, Mao Zedong (毛澤東) stated that "imperialism" (*diguozhuyi* 帝國主義) and "feudalism" (*fengjianzhuyi* 封建主義), a major part of which was *lijiao*, were the twin "Big Mountains" that the Communist movement aimed to move at the time.[25] What this means is that in their own ways the Communists were carrying on not only the May Fourth's theme of anti-imperialist nationalism but also its theme of anti-*lijiao* emancipation. In other words, there was substantial continuity between the Communists' twin goals of anti-imperialism and antifeudalism and the May Fourth twin themes of nationalism and enlightenment (to borrow Li Zehou's terms here).

It is certainly true that the collectivist ways in which the Communists carried out their revolution worked against individualism. The lack of the development of individualism in post–May Fourth China, however, was not because under the Communists the theme of national salvation came to smother an already existing May Fourth theme of full-scale individualist enlightenment, as Li Zehou argues. At issue here is the scope and nature of the May Fourth enlightenment. As I see it, the May Fourth enlightenment was fundamentally limited in its scope and functioned mostly to inspire May Fourth individuals to rebel against the collectives of the Confucian family and the *lijiao* society. While it further inspired some May Fourthians to follow the Marxist cause of emancipating the individual from capitalist suppressions, this limited May Fourth individualist enlightenment did not lead the individual against the collective of the nation-state, as full-scale, modern Western individualism would potentially do. On the issue of the Confucian tradition, this means that, while damaging the *qi* (regulating the family) part of the Confucian model of *xiu-qi-zhi-ping*, May Fourth individualist enlightenment had left the door open for the continuous functioning (at a certain level) of the *zhi* (managing the state) part (as well as the *xiu* and *ping* parts) of the traditional model.[26] The fact that the May Fourth enlightenment focused on challenging the collectives of the Confucian family and *lijiao* society and did little to interfere with the Confucian individual's obligation toward the collective of the state, I believe, had a direct link to the Communists' later practice of emancipating the individual at the mass level from the suppression of the Confucian family and *lijiao* society, while at the same time commanding the individual's commitment to the Chinese nation. What the Communists did, in other words, was to a substantial extent a logical (though an extreme) development of the May Fourth discontinuity as well as continuity with the tradition. The Communists did not smother or kill an already existing May Fourth theme of full-scale Western individualist enlightenment that would celebrate the individual's independence from the nation-state. Such a theme never took root to begin with during the May Fourth movement, which is a major reason post–May Fourth China has lacked development in the direction of full-scale individualism.[27]

With his acceptance of the Marxist ideal of ultimate individual emancipation from capitalist exploitation and suppression, Guo Moruo in the mid-1920s also came to accept the Marxist/Leninist, collectivist revolutionary means to achieve that ideal as well as the goals of liberating the nation and the cosmopolitan world.[28] He especially found it not difficult to accept the Leninist notion that the Communist cosmopolitanist revolution should start with revolutions in individual nations and with the nation building of these revolutionary nations in order to fight against the threats by capitalist countries, a notion that he could somewhat identify with his Confucian sequence of managing the state and harmonizing the world.[29] He also was strongly attracted to Leninist anti-imperialism theory and practice, as he considered foreign imperialism a major source for his nation's modern-time problems.

The Marxist/Leninist mundane goals of individual, national, and world emancipation, however, were not all that Guo pursued. As a Confucianist, he also insisted on the goal of achieving the individual's moral/spiritual inner transcendence through self-cultivation, hence his combining the Confucian transcendental concept with the Marxist/Leninist elements that he had accepted to create his version of a Marxist/Leninist/Confucian Communism in the mid-1920s. In reaching such a combination, he seemed to have succeeded in obtaining what he had always been searching for since the May Fourth period: a "transcendental perspective" (*chushi de jinhuai* 出世的襟怀), in the form of the Confucian moral concept of inner transcendence, and "this-worldly skills" (*rushi de benling* 入世的本领), in the form of materialistic Marxism/Leninism that provided systematic guidance for economic, political, and social development in this world.[30]

At a functional level, both the Confucian moralism and Marxist historical materialism in Guo's combined Communist thinking provided him with criticism of capitalism: his Confucianism saw capitalism as an awful flooding of human desires for material gains and his Marxism "scientifically" noted that capitalism had begun to hinder further material and social/political development in history. The different approaches with which Guo's Confucianism and Marxism criticized capitalism, however, made them contradict and reject each other: while his Confucianism blamed capitalism for being too materialistic and therefore morally imperfect, his Marxism criticized capitalism for not being materialistic enough (in the sense that capitalism hindered further material development). This means that his Confucianism and his Marxism had to be practiced at the expense of each other: the Confucian moralism, on the one hand, needed to be achieved by suppressing people's material desires and therefore smothering a major incentive to material development; the material development that Marxism required, on the other hand, was likely to be achieved with people's desires for material development, which would definitely jeopardize the Confucian moral cause.

This tension between Confucian moralism and Marxist historical materialism was at the core of an overall predicament in Guo's Communist thinking. On the one hand, he needed historical materialism to "scientifically" prove that the evil of capitalism would phase out in history and that an ideal society is definitely on the horizon, which his traditional Confucianism seemed inadequate in proving. Further, he was not without interest in achieving the material modernity that Marxism required, if such modernity was within reach and could be achieved without the flooding of people's desires. On the other hand, however, he was profoundly troubled by historical materialism's deterministic notion that high-level material development is the prerequisite of Communism, which would deny China the chance of starting a Communist revolution in the 1920s. In order to have a Communist revolution, as he saw it from his Confucian moral/spiritual perspective, a materially underdeveloped country such as China did not have to wait for its material productivity to develop and mature and for a socioeconomic class of industrial proletarians to form and function. As long as people were "awakened" and morally/ "spiritually" ready, or as long as there were already moral/"spiritual" proletarians, he insisted, then Communist revolution should take place and would succeed in China.[31] Material development, after all, was not his primary concern. In fact, as a Confucian moralist, he could live without elaborate material development.

Guo was aware of the tension between his Confucianism and Marxism and made efforts to justify his combining the two. For instance, he tried to prove that Confucius, with all of his moral concerns, was not without interest in material development and material production. He also had tried to convince himself and his readers that there was readiness in Marx to depart from the position of a non-emotional observer of history. Instead of always passively and calmly waiting for material productivity to gradually develop and mature for the Communist revolution, he argued, Marx did show emotions and a willingness to have a revolution first and use the revolution to boost and promote material production.

The gap between Confucian moralism and Marxist historical materialism, however, was too real and too wide for Guo to bridge, and he never managed to escape the tension between the two. In fact, it was in his struggling with this tension that we find a major portion of his historical significance: not only was he one of the earliest and the few among Chinese Communists to be clearly aware of the tension between Confucian moralism and Marxist historical materialism, which was to be a central issue for them during their Maoist revolution, but he also was one of the very few to have publicly expressed profound doubt about the correctness of Marxist historical materialism from the perspective of Confucian moralism. In October 1924, a few months after he announced his conversion to Marxism, Guo wrote that the realization of Communism does not necessarily need "the fullest development of material production" as required by Marxism. As far as he was concerned, a guarantee of "minimum" material life and some pastoral comfort, harmony, and simplicity would be sufficient to make it an ideal Communist society.[32] In making such a statement, he probably was speaking the minds of quite a few early Chinese Communist intellectuals such as Mao Zedong and Yun Daiying (恽 代英) (1895–1931), who had also expressed longing for pastoral ideals but stopped short of verbalizing pastoralist/ruralist doubts about the Marxist requirement for high-level material development.[33] In a larger historical context, Guo was, probably better than anyone else, speaking the minds of millions of Communists who were to conduct the Maoist revolution later in China, with whom he was to literally participate in creating a fair and just Communist society with "minimum" material living during the radical years of the Cultural Revolution (1966–1976).

CHAPTER 1

Toward Individual Emancipation and Personal Moral/Spiritual Salvation

FROM THE MAY FOURTH INDIVIDUALIST REBELLION TO THE MARXIST CAUSE OF INDIVIDUAL EMANCIPATION

A May Fourth Individualist Awakening

GUO'S PAINFUL PERSONAL STRUGGLE AGAINST AN ARRANGED MARRIAGE

Guo was probably the most influential Chinese intellectual in the May Fourth battle against the Confucian family and *lijiao* society on the issue of arranged marriages, and it all started with his own painful struggle against a marriage that was arranged for him by his parents.

Arranged marriages had been a part of the social norms of *lijiao*. Behind the practice of arranged marriages were the Confucian concepts of the Three Bonds and filial piety, which required that the son should always obey his father, and children should always obey their parents. In accordance with these Confucian concepts, the final decision on marriage was made by the parents for their child, and it was to be obeyed by the child, even though the parents might occasionally consult the child when arranging the marriage. In Confucian society, where social connections were highly important for a family to succeed, arranged marriages had unique social functions. A well-arranged marriage, one that matched the social status of two families, could benefit both families, since it enabled them to join force and help each other in gaining power, wealth, and influence. To a great extent, such a marriage was not so much a union of two individuals but rather a marriage between two families. The individuals might find themselves having to sacrifice their happiness for the sake of their families if their marriage worked well for the families but not for themselves, which, not surprisingly, was quite often the case.

When Guo was growing up, arranged marriages were still very much in practice, and at a very young age he found himself in a position of having to react to and deal with this traditional social norm. The first marriage arrangement was made for him before he was ten years old. This marriage, however, did not happen, because the girl died when Guo was fourteen. As Guo later described it, he was actually glad that he had become a "widower." By that time, he said, "I had already read some new [Western] and old [Chinese] novels and had been greatly attracted to the love stories in the old novels and the romance in the new novels. For me, of course, such romance at the time was simply beyond my reach. To dream for such romance was like trying to catch the moon by following its reflection in the water or trying to reach the sky by touching its image in the mirror." However, since he was now temporarily freed from the arranged marriage, he was hoping that somehow a miracle could happen so that he himself could someday have the love and romance that he had read about in the novels.[1] As a result, he kept expressing reluctance in the next two or three years when his parents talked to him about marriage. Because of this reluctance, his parents, who "had been very understanding," had to turn down marriage proposals for him from forty or fifty families in his home region. Some of those families were good matches for his family. Some were even of higher social status than his family. Since there were not too many more families left in the locality that could match his family well, in the following two or three years there were few proposals of marriage for Guo. This, for his parents, meant that he was running out of possibilities for a good marriage, and they naturally became concerned. Their concern seemed to have been confirmed when a neighboring family of some low-life background and poor social image proposed to have Guo marry their daughter, whom he described as ugly and possibly sick with some disease. His mother, in particular, took this proposal as an insult. Further, by the time he was nineteen, his younger brother and a younger sister had both had their marriages arranged. According to social norms, however, their weddings had to wait until he (their older brother) married. His marriage, therefore, became not only an issue of filial piety but also an issue of honoring his Confucian obligations as an older brother to take good care of his younger brother and sisters.[2]

It was with this background that Guo's parents in 1911 hurriedly arranged a marriage to a girl Guo had never met. This time they did not consult him. He was at the time studying in Sichuan's capital city, Chengdu, which is about ninety miles away from his hometown of Shawanzhen. He was simply informed of the marriage decision in October of that year through a letter that his parents wrote to an older cousin of his, who was then working in Chengdu. According to the letter, the go-between for this marriage arrangement was a remote aunt, and the girl was a cousin of this aunt. It was a good match between the two families and, as described by the aunt, the girl "had good looks," "was going to school," and had the modern "unbound feet." The aunt, according to Guo's mother, was trustworthy, thus her description of the girl should be credible. Guo's parents, who themselves had to a certain extent been influenced by social changes at the time, seemed to be making efforts to satisfy Guo's desire to marry a modern woman. It seemed to them that if the girl had unbound feet and was going to school then she should be modern enough for their son.[3] What was beyond them as the older generation, however, was that the arranged marriage itself was fundamentally antimodern. Such marriages, as proven so many times in China's history, could result in personal unhappiness and even tragedy. Guo was somewhat caught by surprise by his parents' sudden decision. He was certainly not excited about this marriage arrangement. Under increasing Western influence, he now dreamed that someday he would have a Western-style romance. He had the fantasy that he would be like a Western prince who ran into a woman of "unrivalled beauty" on a desert island during a hurricane. He had also imagined that he would be like a Western gentleman who "won the love of a beauty at a duel." If such Western-style romance could not happen, then he still dreamed that his marriage would offer a beautiful and poetic experience.[4] With all of the Western influence that he had received, however, he also had been brought up with Confucian *lijiao* ethics through a combination of parental guidance, formal education, and the influence of social norms and popular culture. According to those ethics, he had no choice but to honor his Confucian duty of filial piety and obey his parents' decision on the marriage. Besides, there were simply no other alternatives available to him at the time. Everybody around him was having his or her marriage arranged in those days. It was simply a very natural part of life. Furthermore, there was also the curiosity of the unknown in such a blind arrangement. If the girl was said to be so good, then maybe she would turn out to be an ideal wife for him. What got his attention was that his aunt had mentioned that the girl was as beautiful as one of his (cousin) sisters-in-law. Ever since his childhood, he had secretly admired the beauty of that sister-in-law. If the girl could be that beautiful, then why not marry her.[5] With such mixed feelings, he obeyed his parents on the marriage arrangement.

His wedding took place on March 2, 1912.[6] It was a rushed wedding. After the collapse of the central order of the Manchu Qing dynasty in 1911, Sichuan Province fell into social chaos with numerous bandits becoming increasingly active. Furthermore, the radical change from dynastic rule to the brand new concept of a republic was too confusing a transition for many, who believed that such change would lead to greater chaos in China's society. As a result, some people with unmarried, grown-up daughters were in a hurry to marry their daughters, for they feared that in the upcoming social chaos their daughters would be exposed to the danger of being raped and losing their virginity. Once raped, their daughters would be devalued as unmarried women in Confucian society and would have less chance of enjoying decent marriages. It was against this background that the parents of the girl wrote to ask Guo's family to have the wedding done in a hurry.[7]

Guo was at home during a school break when the letter from the girl's family arrived. This time his parents consulted him. Since the marriage had already been arranged and was therefore going to happen anyway, and since he somehow still had some hope for this marriage, he agreed to the wedding. Years later, when writing an autobiography in 1929, he noticed that his own agreement to the wedding, which amounted to his own agreement to the marriage, had been the thing that he had "repented the most" in his life.[8]

The wedding turned out to be a complete nightmare for him. On the first day of the wedding ceremonies, the bride, whom he and his family had never seen before and had been described as very good looking and with unbound feet, shocked him with a pair of old-fashioned bound feet and, in his eyes, a very ugly nose![9] He was numbed and reluctant to go on with the rest of the ceremonies. Seeing him behaving like this, his mother gave him a talk. First, in an indirect way, she blamed the go-between aunt for having given a misleading description of the girl's feet and looks. Then she went on to say that he should not behave like this at the wedding. "We can ask her [the bride] to unbind her feet tomorrow and, as a man, you shouldn't concern yourself too much about your wife's looks." "If she [the bride] has a good personality and is intelligent," said the mother, "I can teach her some [Confucian] ethics and you can also teach her to read poems and books. As long as she has these it's going to be OK."[10] Guo kept silent. Then the real lecture started. His mother began to blame him for his "lack of filial piety." After working very hard for the arrangement and preparation for this wedding, said the mother, his father was heartbroken to see him looking so miserable. It was not right, said the Confucian mother, for him "as a son and as a human being" to break his father's heart like this![11] This finally and painfully aroused him from his numbness.[12] He was, after all, a Confucian son with a strong sense of filial piety toward his parents, a sense that resulted from longtime moral teachings of *lijiao*. For the sake of not making his beloved parents suffer, who "had already overworked themselves in their lives," he decided with great pain to carry on with the rest of the wedding ceremonies.[13] The whole nightmare of the arranged marriage, however, was simply too much for him to take. Just a few days after the wedding, he found some excuse and left home for Chengdu, thus starting a passive rebellion against the marriage and against *lijiao*.[14]

One major reason behind his rebellion, of course, was the fact that he had been influenced by modern Western concepts of love, romance, and individuality and could hardly sacrifice himself completely for *lijiao* norms. In fact, though the ethic of filial piety still had a strong hold on him, the whole *lijiao* system of traditional life had already been undermined in his surroundings, sometimes by himself. For instance, pushed by his Western-influenced oldest brother, the practice of footbinding, a symbol of women's status in the Confucian system, had already been stopped for some women in his community, including his mother.[15] Under Western influence, the old Confucian authority of teachers also had been seriously challenged at the schools that he had attended. In one of his autobiographies he would later recall such an incident in his second semester of primary school, a quarrel that took place among some students over a meal. In his investigation of the incident, the school principal happened to have slapped a student on the face to show his authority, just as teachers used to do in the traditional education system. Guo and some other students were present when the principal beat the student, and Guo shouted to the principal, "What you did is barbaric! . . . Yes, barbaric!" Other students followed: "You can no longer beat students in such a civilized time!" "You are very inhumane (*taiwu rendao* 太無人道)!" "You have violated us students' human dignity (*renge* 人格)!" The principal was overwhelmed by the students, even though he later managed to give Guo a demerit for punishment.[16] What this incident tells us is that even at a very young age Guo had already been influenced by the modern Western emphasis on humanity and respect for the "dignity" of individuals. To a great extent, it was such Western humanism and individualism that was making him deviate, step-by-step, from the collective norms of *lijiao* society.

It is important to note here that in Guo's resentment and rebellion against the arranged marriage, he was not without a certain amount of sensitivity and feelings of pity and guilt for what he had actually done to the woman he had married, which is consistent with his influence by modern Western humanism. For instance, on his way to Chengdu right after the wedding, he wrote in a poem that he felt "sorry" for the wife that he was leaving behind, whom he believed was thinking of him at home.[17] Years later, when writing his autobiographies, he more than once pointed out that it was she who had been hurt the most in the "tragedy" of the traditional marriage.[18] It was such moral sensitivity on his part that added to the pain and sense of guilt that he later felt for a long time when trying to morally justify to himself and society his rebellion against the marriage.

Once he was back to school in Chengdu, the pain of the marriage helped lead to "a most dangerous period" in his life.[19] He "wildly" abused alcohol and indulged himself in gambling and other "unhealthy" habits.[20] His only hope now was to leave Sichuan and get farther away from his problems. However, his parents could not let him go. For one thing, he completely relied on his parents and elder brothers for his expenses, and they were not rich enough to support his studies away from Sichuan. As a result, he continued his "disgusting" lifestyle in Chengdu for a "long" period of a year and a half.[21] It was not until 1913, after he was admitted into a government-sponsored medical college in Tianjin with a full scholarship, that he was finally able to leave his home province of Sichuan.[22]

Guo left Chengdu for Tianjin in September 1913 to attend the medical college. When he arrived in Tianjin, however, he found that the college did not match his expectations, and so he soon went to Beijing to visit his oldest brother, whom he thought was staying in Beijing at that time. There was, of course, a deeper reason for him to leave the medical school. With his longtime interest in literature and possibly also because of his Confucian idealism and Taoist antimundane mentality, he felt at the time that it was simply too "practical" of an idea for him to make a career in medicine. After all, it was not the study of medicine but a chance to leave Sichuan that had brought him to Tianjin.[23]

Guo's brother turned out not to be in Beijing at the time but was traveling in Japan and Korea. Guo waited in Beijing until his brother returned from abroad in mid-December. Not long after his return, the brother decided to send Guo to study in Japan. Since his brother could only support him financially for half a year,

Guo would have to study hard in Japan so that he could qualify for a scholarship from the Chinese government in half a year. Guo had no idea if he could succeed in getting such a scholarship in such a short time. However, the chance to go to Japan, something that he had long dreamed about, made him very excited. Accompanied by a friend of his brother's who happened to be traveling to Japan, he left Beijing on December 28, 1913, and arrived in Tokyo on January 13, 1914, thus starting his study and life in Japan.[24]

After "desperate" hard work, in June 1914 Guo passed the entrance tests for a one-year preparation program designed for Chinese students at Tokyo First Higher School.[25] After that program, which lasted from September 1914 to the summer of 1915, he was assigned to the Sixth Higher School in Okayama to major in premedicine, a major that he now chose for himself.[26] After three years of study, in the summer of 1918 he graduated from the Okayama school and was admitted to the Medical School of Kyushu Imperial University at Fukuoka, from which he was to graduate in 1923.[27]

Throughout his first years in Japan, from 1914 to 1919, his struggle against the arranged marriage and Confucian *lijiao* and the pain and guilt he felt over this struggle seemed to have overshadowed many other aspects of his life. First of all, away from home in Japan, a foreign country distant from China and more Westernized than China, he was provided with a real opportunity to rebel against his nightmare marriage. In the summer of 1916, about two and a half years after he arrived in Japan, he fell in love with Sato Tomiko (1897–?), a Japanese Christian girl whose father was a Protestant minister. Tomiko was at the time working as a student nurse in a hospital in Tokyo after graduating from an American missionary school. A friend of Guo happened to have stayed in Tomiko's hospital for treatment of tuberculosis before he transferred to and died in a sanatorium. Guo had just finished his first year at the Sixth Higher School and was in Tokyo visiting his sick friend during the summer break. After the friend's death, when handling the friend's funeral affairs, he went one day to Tomiko's hospital to ask for an X-ray taken when his friend was under treatment. The nurse he talked to about the X-ray was Tomiko. Hearing of the death of Guo's friend, Tomiko broke into tears and spoke with him to share his sorrow over his friend's death. About a week later, when mailing the X-ray to Guo, Tomiko enclosed a long letter in English in which she used "a lot" of Christian language to console him over the pain of losing his friend. Guo was greatly moved by Tomiko's sympathy and loving personality and felt attracted to her. He then started a regular correspondence with her. Before long, he persuaded her to move from Tokyo to Okayama in December of that year, and the two soon started living together as common-law husband and wife.[28]

Guo's relationship with Tomiko brought him the love and romance that he had long desired. However, it also caused him tremendous suffering and a strong sense of guilt. For one thing, after learning about his living with Tomiko, Guo's parents stopped writing to him until after Tomiko gave birth to Guo's first son in December 1917. Even when they resumed correspondence, his parents still

refused to accept Tomiko as their legitimate daughter-in-law. They would insist
on addressing her as his "concubine" (qie 妾) and calling their sons "concubine kids"
(shuzi 庶子).[29] The main issue here was again filial piety and other Confucian lijiao
ethics. Judged by lijiao, Guo's living with Tomiko was against the marriage formally
arranged for him by his parents and therefore showed his lack of filial piety to his
parents. In China's traditional system, it should be noted here, men's extramarital
sexual desire could be accepted in the form of their taking on concubines in addition to their legal wives. Guo's oldest brother, for example, had at least temporarily
taken on a woman as a concubine.[30] With such an accepted practice in the lijiao
system, Guo could have, to a certain degree, made up for his lack of filial piety by
nominally staying with his marriage arrangement while simply living with Tomiko
as some kind of a concubine. Guo's desire, however, turned out to be too modern
for the old wife/concubine format to accommodate. With his modern thinking, he
now wanted love, romance, and, most importantly, personal freedom in finding and
enjoying his romantic love. The old wife/concubine lifestyle did not interest him
at all. As he later described it, he was "most heartbroken" and "most sick" when his
parents called Tomiko his "concubine" and called his sons with Tomiko "concubine
kids."[31] As far as Guo was concerned, the old, arranged marriage was completely
over, and Tomiko was now his beloved wife.

It should be noted that Guo's having a son with Tomiko had made up a little
bit for his misbehavior in the eyes of his parents, since infertility, especially to be
without a son, would be an even greater offense against filial piety in the Confucian culture. As Guo later put it, Tomiko's giving birth to a son was a major reason
his parents eventually "forgave" him and resumed their correspondence with him.[32]
Guo's modern desire for love and romance and his insistence on dishonoring his
arranged marriage, however, had and would always put him in profound and irre-
solvable conflict with his parents.

Guo agonized tremendously over his parents' disapproval of his conduct. He
simply could not bear to see his parents be hurt like this. Yet with modern Western influence, he could not overcome his desire for personal happiness. He also felt
guilty for what he had done to his wife back in Sichuan. According to Confucian
ethics, not only should a wife obey her husband, a husband also had responsibili-
ties to his wife. Brought up with such traditional concepts, he still found himself
in certain ways connected to his arranged wife. During this period he sometimes
received letters from his wife, and in the letters that he wrote home to Sichuan he
also from time to time referred to her.[33] In fact, in a letter that he wrote home on
July 20, 1915, in the tone of a typical Confucian husband, he even asked his wife
to "take good care of" his parents for him.[34] With all of the Confucian obligations
and connections that he felt toward his parents and his arranged wife, he suffered
greatly in rebelling against the arranged marriage. During this period and later he
"had decided several times" to write to his Sichuan home to "ask for a divorce" from
his arranged wife, but every time he was stopped because he was certain that his
divorce request would greatly anger his parents, and such anger was very likely

to kill them in their old age. He also was afraid that asking for a divorce would "surely" drive his arranged wife to commit suicide, because she had "an old-fashioned mind" of the ethics of *lijiao*, which considered it a great disgrace for a woman to be divorced by her husband. If his arranged wife committed suicide, he felt that he would really "be guilty of murder." After all, he also felt sorry for her because she, like him, was trapped in this marriage as a victim.[35]

Thus began one of the most painful and tortured periods in Guo's life. As he later recalled, 1916 and 1917 were "the most confusing and dangerous years" for him. Sometimes he "wanted to commit suicide." Sometimes he wanted to be a Buddhist "monk."[36] In 1916, he wrote the first of his suicide poems:

> I went out of home to commit suicide,
>> there was the lonely moon moving in the sky.
> Bitter wind had frozen my soul,
>> regret over my sin had torn me apart.
> Where to go in this vast world?
>> I sighed with every step I took.
> I have so far had no achievements,
>> and ended up being a nothing between heaven and earth.
> Since it is so hard to drag on like this in the world,
>> it shouldn't be a difficult decision to die!
> Yet I can't help thinking of my family and country,
>> and came back to live in this world with pains.
> When I returned home and saw my love,
>> she was all in tears. [37]

It should be remembered that 1916 was the year he fell in love with Tomiko, and 1917 was their first year living together. The end of 1917 also seemed to be the point at which his parents refused to write to him because of his living with Tomiko.[38] In other words, instead of fully enjoying his newfound love and romance with Tomiko, he was haunted by the ethics of *lijiao* and tortured by a strong sense of guilt and immorality. On May 25, 1918, after his parents resumed correspondence with him, he wrote the following in a letter to home:

> Dear father and mother:
>
> Since I have committed such a sin [living with Tomiko] and can not atone for it and have thus made you greatly worried and concerned, I really regret and could do nothing but cry everyday in my heart. After receiving my brother's letter the other day that blamed me, I have tried several times to write home. But every time I tried I could not even write a single sentence because I felt very ashamed and could find no excuses for myself. Today I have just received a letter from Yu Ying [his arranged wife]. It describes how you have been hurt by me and this has made me suffer even more.[39]

Later in 1918, after living with Tomiko for about two years and when their first son was about one year old, he wrote another poem expressing his wish to die:

> I remember it was seven years ago,
>> my Seventh Sister was still a child.
> She and I were both homesick,
>> and we both cried until we collapsed.
> But now I am alone far away from home,
>> and I have cried with so many tears.
> I have lost my soul and now only have an empty body,
>> I regret that I have not died to finish my misery.
> I have a motherland but it amounts to nothing,
>> since the country is constantly suffering from wars.
> I have a home but I can not return to it,
>> my parents are there sick and old.
> I have my love but she has already been ruined,
>> like a bird without its nest.
> I have a son who is only one year old,
>> and it takes a lot to take care of him.
> I thus have a life which is not happy,
>> so I often hope that I can die soon.
> Overwhelming sadness and regret is tearing me apart,
>> and I have cried from morning till night.
> I have such profound sadness in my heart,
>> which is hard to end even if I die ten thousand times.[40]

Clearly this poem demonstrates his depression, sense of guilt, and regret that because of his rebellion against his arranged marriage he could not go back home to see his beloved parents. As he later elaborates in an autobiographical novel in the 1920s, he was afraid that if he went back home he would have to confront his parents and his arranged wife about his marriage. Such a confrontation, he worried, would anger his parents and might cost them their lives. As he saw no functional solution to the situation, the only thing left to do was to avoid going home and pay the price of not seeing his parents.[41] To his great regret, indeed, he was never to see his mother alive again.

One thing that needs mentioning is that Guo in this poem refers to his "Seventh Sister," to whom he did not otherwise seem to pay special attention among his siblings.[42] One reason he thought of this younger sister in this 1918 poem was probably because he had heard that this sister was being married that year.[43] Guo was strongly against the marriage arrangement for his sister, clearly because it reminded him of his own misery and made him very worried about his sister's future. The sister's marriage arrangement was first mentioned by Guo in a letter that he wrote to home on July 20, 1915. In that letter, which gives major attention to his sister's marriage arrangement, Guo notices that he had heard that his mother was going to visit a family to see if they and their son matched Guo's family and sister. "I cannot say that I agree [with this decision by mother to visit the family] and yet I cannot say that I disagree," said Guo in the letter. "It's hard to understand the marriage system in our country. . . . Since father and mother despite their old age are willing to make a trip for their daughter, how dare I as a son say any-thing differently [on my sister's marriage arrangement]? After all, as the saying goes: 'marriages were determined in our previous lives and we cannot do anything about them in our current lives'; 'if you happen to be married to a chicken then live your life with this chicken and if you happen to have married a dog then live a life with this dog.'" Guo goes on in the letter, however, to say that his Seventh Sister is still too young and is in no hurry to be married. "If mother has not yet made the trip [for the sister's marriage arrangement]," Guo asks, "could mother and father please first try to learn more about that family and see if their son is good for my sister? Not only could this prevent my sister from potential misery, it will also reward [our] parents' efforts to work for their children's happiness. . . . With all said, however, I believe that if mother thinks a person is good [for my sister] then he must be good."[44]

This 1915 letter clearly demonstrates the dilemma in Guo's thinking between his love and filial piety for his parents and his reservations about the marriage that they were arranging for his sister, the kind of dilemma that he had known so well. His parents were very angry at this letter and "severely blamed" him for it. Guo's sarcastic description of the possibility that his sister's arranged marriage might not turn out to be a happy one also led to his sister's several attempts to commit suicide, which was to a certain extent another example of the sometimes life-and-death seriousness of arranged marriages in Confucian society.[45] On November 7, 1917, Guo wrote the following in a letter to home, further petitioning for his Seventh Sister:

> I remember that my brother mentioned in his last letter that Seventh Sister was to be married next year. I am afraid that she is still too young and such early marriage will be most harmful to her still growing body. The system of early marriages in our country is really no good. To reform it, people should start with their own families. . . . My opinion is that my Seventh Sister's marriage could still wait for another two years.[46]

Guo's concern and sympathy for his Seventh Sister's arranged marriage is clearly because her marriage had reminded him of his own matrimonial misery. As a Chi-nese saying goes, "An ill person tends to sympathize with those who suffer from the same illness as his" (*tongbing xianglian* 同病相憐). It is no coincidence, therefore, that Guo mentions his Seventh Sister in the previously quoted 1918 poem, which is mainly an expression of the pains caused by his arranged marriage. In fact, several years later in the 1920s, when he wrote an autobiographical novel, Guo would once again be reminded of his Seventh Sister's experience when mentioning the pain of his own arranged marriage.[47]

Guo's depression and sense of guilt was a major factor that shadowed his family life with Tomiko and their first son during this period. There were, however, other factors. For instance, after he started living with Tomiko as common-law husband and wife, especially after their first son was born in December 1917, Guo gradually became somewhat disillusioned with family life. The tedious and trivial daily routines in the household and the tiring work of taking care of his infant son were anything but romantic and colorful. Tomiko, whom he used to find so attractive, now seemed to have lost her "mysterious" beauty of "purity" and simply turned into an ordinary housewife.[48] To be sure, Guo did sometimes find happiness and joy with Tomiko and their child, and this was shown in some of the poems that he wrote during this period. However, he also had from time to time written poems to indicate that life in his family was not happy. In a poem written in 1918, for instance, he began to describe Tomiko and his son as "burdens" for him.[49] Then, in early 1919, he wrote the following poem:

> It is a cold day in spring,
>   I feel very depressed and unhappy.
> I have profound sadness beyond description,
>   but I have to force a smile for my son.
> The son is in my arms sick,
>   he does not talk yet and can only babble.
> My wife [Tomiko] looks as miserable as withered grass,
>   she is doing laundry at the well.
> I look into the vast sky with tears,
>   the sky is full of depressing clouds.
> I want to fly but I have no wings,
>   I want to die but I can't move, as if I am paralyzed.
> It is I who have ruined my wife and child,
>   my heart is aching as if thousands of arrows are piercing it.[50]

Guo and Tomiko also were despised by their neighbors when they first started living together. When Tomiko came from Tokyo to stay with Guo in Okayama at the end of 1916, the two somehow believed that their relationship could be kept as that between a brother and a sister, and Guo actually told his neighbors (landlord) that Tomiko was his sister. However, it was not long before they became common-law husband and wife. As Guo recalled, once his neighbors (landlord) found out about this, they showed contempt for them. This reaction by the neighbors was in fact very natural, considering the fact that Japanese society, even with substantial Western influence, was still very much controlled by Confucian and other traditional Japanese values. For Guo, as a morally sensitive person, his neighbors' (landlord's) attitude of course added to his sense of immorality and guilt.

Guo's depression through his rebellion against the arranged marriage, in addition to his exhaustion from overwork at school, helped lead to a serious health problem. By the summer of 1915, he had begun to suffer from severe neurasthenia. His symptoms at the time included irregular and rapid heartbeats and serious chest pains that made it hard for him to walk even slowly. He also was suffering from insomnia. He only managed about three or four hours of sleep each night, and in his limited sleep he was "constantly" bothered by nightmares. He also seemed to have "completely" lost his memory. For some time he found it very hard to memorize anything he was reading. It also was from this time on that he began to complain that sometimes he had severe dizziness and his head "burned like a furnace."[51] Though the severity of his neurasthenia did not seem to have lasted long, some of its symptoms did stay with him, and he was to complain about them in some of his later writings.

JUSTIFYING REBELLION AGAINST *LIJIAO* IN PUBLIC

In struggling to justify his rebellion against *lijiao*, Guo in his early years in Japan desperately sought help, guidance, and comfort in his intellectual environment. During the worst days of his personal crisis, he first found Sir Rabindranath Tagore (1861–1941) to be his "spiritual teacher."[52] The first time he read Tagore was in early 1915, when he was in his second semester of the one-year preparatory study at the First Higher School in Tokyo.[53] He was then living with a relative, who also was studying in Japan. One day this relative showed him mimeograph copies of some English poems written by the Indian Hindu poet, who as a winner of the Nobel Prize in literature was at the time very popular in Japan. The poems were *Baby's Way, Sleep-Stealer, Clouds and Waves,* and *On the Seashore.* Guo was immediately attracted to these poems. He was "surprised" to find that they were easy to understand and that their prose style differed from other English poems he had read and the old style Chinese poems with which he was so familiar. As he later described it, reading these poems by Tagore "especially" made him "feel purified, refreshed, and free from mundane worries." Tagore's poems, he said, made him "joyful" with something "beyond their poetic beauty." "From then on," he had become a "worshiper" of Tagore and developed an "indissoluble bond" with the poet's works. He had thus started "eagerly" looking for Tagore's books to read.[54] Because of their popularity, however, Tagore's books were usually sold out the moment they reached book stores in Tokyo. It was not until after he graduated from the preparatory program in Tokyo in the summer of 1915 and went to the Sixth Higher School at Okayama that he was finally able to purchase a copy of Tagore's *The Crescent Moon.* Then, in the fall of 1916, he "suddenly" found Tagore's *Gitanjali, The Gardener, The King of the Dark Chamber,* and *One Hundred Poems of Kabir* at a library in Okayama. The discovery of these books made him really feel that he had found the "life" and "fountain" of his life. Every day, as soon as school was over, at about two or three o'clock in the afternoon, he would hurry to a "very quiet and dimly lit" reading room at the library and read these books facing the wall in a corner. "From time to time," with "tears of gratitude," he would try to memorize the books' contents. Reading these works, which conveyed Hindu moral and spiritual messages, he "enjoyed the happiness of Nirvana" and felt a "quiet and pure sadness rippling both inside and outside of" him. It was usually not until evening that he could finally tear himself away from these books and walk back slowly to his "lonesome" dorm.[55]

Through Tagore, especially through his *One Hundred Poems of Kabir*, Guo came to be attracted to Kabir (1450?–1518), a major religious figure in India's Hindu tradition. Tagore's works also had made him interested in and "fond of" the philosophy of the Upanishads, the Indian classic that gives spiritual and moral teachings on human souls and the world soul.[56] As Guo later wrote, he had "reveled in" Tagore's poems for about two or three years and had read "almost all" of Tagore's early collections and dramas.[57]

Soon after his interest in Tagore started in early 1915, Guo also became attracted to the moral teaching of China's Neo-Confucian master Wang Yangming (1472–1528), whose thinking also had been influential in Japan. In September 1915, the time when he was suffering from neurasthenia, "in the depths" of his "soul" Guo felt a desperate "need for spiritual cultivation" and bought himself the *Complete Works of Wang Wen Cheng Gong* (Wang Yangming) at a used book store in Tokyo.[58] From then on he started a routine of reading ten pages of Wang's works every day. Every morning after getting up and every night before bed he also practiced thirty minutes of "quiet sitting," a method of self-cultivation taught by Wang's mind-heart school of Neo-Confucianism.[59] Thanks to Wang's teaching and the quiet sitting, Guo soon began to see "remarkable" improvement in his health. Within two weeks, both the quantity and quality of his sleep began to improve, and his irregular heart beating had become less serious.[60] Further, "spiritually," he found that he had been "thoroughly" enlightened by Wang Yangming to a "world of wonders." While the world in his eyes had been nothing but a "dead and flat picture," Wang's philosophy now brought the world "alive" and "three-dimensional" and thus enabled him to clearly and "thoroughly" comprehend this world.[61] As he later noted, even though he had been "fond of" reading the *Zhuang Zi* (莊子) before, he could hardly understand Zhuang Zi's thinking. Now, through the teaching of Wang Yangming, who had been influenced by Taoist philosophies, he had begun to really appreciate and understand the thinking of Zhuang Zi.[62] The enlightenment that he had found in Wang's Neo-Confucian philosophy also had contributed to his interest in the metaphysics of Lao Zi (老子), Confucius, Indian philosophers, and various thinkers of "early modern European" schools of idealism, especially Benedict Spinoza (1632–1677). In his words, Wang Yangming's teaching had started his discovery of a clear and "solemn" world of metaphysics.[63]

Based on Guo's writings later in the 1920s, what Wang Yangming's teaching and career provided for him during this period probably also included an inspiration for "the expansion of the self" and an encouragement for the individual to "fight against" his "evil environments."[64] In the middle of his lonesome struggle against the *lijiao* society, Wang's message of Confucian personalism could to a certain extent help serve as a support for him. Zhuang Zi also might have helped him in coping with *lijiao*. In a sense, Zhuang Zi's teaching of transcending mundane concerns and freeing oneself from established society could help him numb his pain and find some temporary escape from the heavy moral pressure of mundane *lijiao* ethics.

For a while Guo also became interested in Christianity, and one of the factors contributing to his interest was very possibly Tomiko's influence over him.[65] In fact, together with Wang Yangming's Neo-Confucianism, Zhuang Zi's Taoist philosophy, and Tagore's Hinduist messages, Christianity had at least for a while served to meet his needs for spiritual and moral comfort and guidance. In 1916 and 1917, the time when he was tortured the most by his sense of guilt and immorality as a result of his falling in love and then living with Tomiko, he had made it a daily routine to practice quiet sitting and "read Zhuang Zi, Wang Yangming, and the New and Old Testaments" as his spiritual and moral lessons. It also was during this period that he read many of Tagore's works. As Guo put it, the need for religion was a result of people's "loneliness and pains," and the pain in his life at the time had suppressed his "liveliness" as a young man and pushed him to ponder metaphysical and moral issues covered in Eastern and Western philosophies and religions.[66]

Despite some effect and comfort on Guo, however, the moral and spiritual messages of Wang Yangming, Zhuang Zi, Tagore, and Christianity had in a way made it even harder for him to justify his rebellion against *lijiao*. He had turned to these messages for help and guidance largely because he had been tortured by his sense of guilt and immorality as a result of dishonoring his arranged marriage and living with another woman. These moral and spiritual messages, however, told him basically that he should purify his soul and keep away from human desires. In other words, all of these philosophies and religions from which he was seeking help were largely telling him that he was morally wrong in following his human and mundane feelings and desires and living with Tomiko as a married man. Wang Yangming, for example, especially emphasized in his works the moral importance of practicing filial piety and "ridding oneself of human desires," such as men's desire for women.[67] Using Wang's teaching to ease his sense of guilt, which was largely a result of his living with Tomiko and disobeying his parents, Guo was to a great extent actually adding fuel to the flames. It is not at all surprising, therefore, that with all of his efforts to seek spiritual and moral help, he had never ceased suffering from his strong sense of guilt before 1919.

The breakthrough started for Guo in September 1919. On the eleventh of that month, *Xue Deng* (學燈 *Lamp of Learning*), the literary supplement of Shanghai's *Shi Shi Xin Bao* (時事新報 *The China Times*), started publishing his new-style vernacular poems and thus triggered an "outburst" of his poetry and other writings from September 1919 to the first half of 1920.[68] He began to be known in China as a modern poet and writer.[69] This success fundamentally changed his life. The publication of his work was recognition and encouragement not only of his new literary style but also of the thinking and feelings that he expressed in his writings. With such encouragement, he went through a period of what he later referred to as the "emancipation" of his "feelings."[70] In other words, through his published writings, he finally found an outlet for his "pent-up feelings" over his "personal and national problems."[71]

It was largely starting with *San Ye Ji* (三葉集 *Cloverleaf*), a collection of letters between Guo and two friends, Tian Shouchang (田壽昌 also known as Tian Han 田漢) (1898–1968) and Zong Baihua (宗白華) (1897–?), that Guo openly expressed feelings over his personal crisis and struggle and with the help of his friends found in the Romanticism and individualism of Johann Wolfgang von Goethe (1749–1832) the justification that he had needed for his rebellion against *lijiao*.[72]

In a letter dated mid-February 1920, in *San Ye Ji*, he told Tian about his love story with Tomiko. After describing in detail how he had met Tomiko and how they started living together as brother and sister, he wrote:

Alas! Brother Shouchang! I was after all too confident in my weak soul! Shortly after living together with Tomiko, my soul completely collapsed! I ruined my Tomiko! . . . If my sin were merely the violation of the sacredness of love, or more directly, merely having sex with Tomiko, then my sense of guilt would not be as strong as it has been. The truth is that I have another painful experience which is really hard for me to tell. In 1913 I was married according to my parents' arrangement. . . . Shortly after my wedding I left home and finally came to Japan in January 1914. After the marriage I already had a profound flaw in my heart, which was beyond cure. Then, unexpectedly, I met my Tomiko. When we started as friends I was already a married man and she knew that. And it was because I trusted myself as a married man that I felt that I could safely live with her as brother and sister. Alas! I ended up ruining her! . . . I have written so much in this letter to you, and I feel that I am really like a convict waiting for his death sentence. You said that we should make known our character, but my character is almost too bad to be known. . . . I am literally the quintessence of sin.[73]

To Guo's great relief, not only did Tian understand and accept his confession but in his reply Tian also encouraged and justified his rebellion against *lijiao* by citing the example of Goethe:

. . . I do not consider what you have done as your personal sins. Instead, I see them as sins of all mankind, or at least of those who feel strongly for romantic love. Further, they are sins that are more likely to be committed by geniuses . . . Goethe had at least nineteen lovers in his life. . . . If we talk about sin, then Goethe in his later years was really "the quintessence of sin." . . . My radical opinion is that what you have done is very natural. Even though you were married—married, as you said, according to your parents' arrangement—once you fall in love with [an]other woman you already have less and little love, if not no love at all, for the woman to whom you are married. Once that happens, your marriage is no longer a marriage in its complete sense. No! It should no longer count as a marriage. Such being the case, it's completely alright for you to follow the idea of "you go your way, we go ours." . . . If someone should prosecute you for your sins on the Day of Judgment, I would bravely step forward and serve as your apologist![74]

Tian's citing of Goethe's example here is of great significance for Guo. Thanks to his education in Taisho, Japan, which carried a tendency to favor German culture and German thinking in the learning from the modern West, Guo by now already had substantial knowledge about Goethe and had become a worshiper of his life, works, and thinking.[75] In an earlier letter in *San Ye Ji*, for instance, he had admired Goethe, with all of his achievements as well as the qualities of a "Mephistopheles," "devil," and "dog," as one of only two all-around "geniuses" in human history and "the best of all human beings."[76] Naturally, Tian's comparing his rebellion against *lijiao* with the Romantic experience of Goethe was liberating for him in trying to get rid of his sense of guilt and immorality. If Goethe could live as a free soul and did not hesitate to break social and moral norms, then why couldn't he?! If Goethe was celebrated for having desires of the "flesh," love, romance, and the qualities of a "Mephistopheles," "devil," and "dog," then why should he be ashamed of the same qualities in his life?![77] With great excitement and deep gratitude, Guo, in his reply to Tian, wrote that Tian's words had made him "really feel like a convict who had been awaiting his death sentence but was eventually pardoned."[78]

As Tian Shouchang had, Zong Baihua also helped free Guo from his pain and sense of guilt. In a letter to Guo in late February, Zong wrote:

> In all fairness, it should not be considered a grave sin if a man and a woman live together as a result of their pure and serious love for each other. Further, since you have the sincerity to confess and the vigorous improvement of yourself, your sin is merely Mephistopheles in your mind, something that can help make you improve your character! I am very glad to see that you have developed sincerity and the courage to confess thanks to the influence of Western literature, such as the influence of Rousseau and Tolstoy. It shows here that this is something unique to Western literature, something that Eastern literature lacks.[79]

Zong's help for Guo also can be seen in his preface to *San Ye Ji*, where he sets aside all other issues that the collection of letters covers and focuses solely on the issue of rebelling against arranged marriages, as raised by Guo's case:

> Readers! Why do we want to publish this small book [*San Ye Ji*]? . . . Our purpose is to raise a serious and urgent social and moral issue for you to discuss and judge in public! . . .
>
> This issue is a very comprehensive one. Generally speaking, it is "the issue of marriage." More specifically, it covers a) the issue of the freedom of romantic love; b) the issue of the system of arranged marriages; c) the issue of free romantic

love under the system of arranged marriages; and d) the issue of whom to hold responsible for the serious consequences of the conflict between the system of arranged marriages and free romantic love....[80]

Clearly, as far as Zong was concerned, the single, most important purpose of publishing *San Ye Ji* was to direct the public's attention to problems caused by the conflict between the Western concept of free romantic love and China's long-established system of arranged marriages, a system under which Guo had been victimized.

The help from Zong Baihua and Tian Shouchang meant a lot to Guo. Zong was then editor-in-chief of *Shi Shi Xin Bao's Xue Deng* and editor of *Young China* monthly (*shaonian zhongguo* 少年中國), both influential publications at the time.[81] Tian was also known to the May Fourth reading public for his published works.[82] Further, both Zong and Tian were members of the Young China Association (*shaonian zhongguo xuehui* 少年中國學會), an influential organization of May Fourth intellectuals that was founded in 1919 by such major figures as Li Dazhao.[83] As active and influential members of May Fourth intellectual circles, Zong's and Tian's understanding, sympathy, and support for Guo's rebellion against his arranged marriage were certainly important to Guo.

What was of greater importance to Guo was the success of *San Ye Ji*. After its initial publication, the book sold very well and was reprinted several times.[84] This, among other things, signaled that the May Fourth reading public was sympathetic toward his rebellion against the arranged marriage and against *lijiao*, and it accepted and supported his and his friends' justification for his rebellion. Greatly encouraged, in May 1921, one year after the initial publication of *San Ye Ji*, he further emancipated his thinking and made his first explicit written attack on *lijiao*.[85] It was in Guo's preface to a new edition of *Romance of the Western Chamber* (*Xixiang Ji* 西廂記), punctuated and edited by himself, that he made the attack:

> ... *Xixiang Ji* is a triumphal song and memorial tower for the victory of a lively humanity over the lifeless *lijiao*. ...
>
> Our nation has always taken pride in its *lijiao* and kept especially on guard about the relationship between men and women. Sexual desire has been regarded as a flood or wild beast, and young men and women have been treated as criminals.... The great China, which has been proud of its *lijiao* for thousands of years, has actually been nothing but a huge hospital of millions of patients with suppressed and abnormal sexual desires.... Nowadays, sex education has gradually started; the awakening of young men and women to their individuality has taken place like the eruption of volcanoes; and the old and unreasonable system of *lijiao*, which has done nothing but drive people to sexual abnormality, has already been quickly burned to ashes like withered branches and dead leaves caught on fire.[86]

Then, in the summer of 1921, soon after writing the preface to *Xixiang Ji*, Guo started translating Goethe's *The Sorrows of Young Werther* into Chinese. His translation of the German classic, which features a celebration of romantic love and individual freedom, was to a certain extent an expression of his own conflict between his romantic love with Tomiko and Confucian *lijiao*. The translation turned out to be another great success for him. It was published in April 1922 and was to be reprinted at least fifteen times by 1932.[87] Among other things, the success of the translation was to reassure him that China's modern reading public was in favor of and enthusiastic about the Western Goethean concept of romantic love and individuality, the concept on which he had relied as a major basis for the justification of his rebellion against his arranged marriage and against the Confucian family and *lijiao*.

To a great extent, Guo in his struggle against *lijiao* was rescued by the May Fourth movement. First of all, if China had not been in the midst of the May Fourth's (seemingly) overall attacks on Confucian tradition, or if there had not been the May Fourth's enthusiasm for Western concepts such as individual freedom and celebration of romantic love, his rebellion could hardly have received the kind of reception it did. Also, without the overall atmosphere of the emancipation of thinking, Zong Baihua and Tian Shouchang might never have been able to fully develop and express their modern ideas and provide Guo with the understanding and encouragement that he had badly needed from friends. Finally, without the May Fourth vernacular movement, there might never have been the modern poet Guo Moruo. It was the vernacular movement that had made it possible for Guo to discover himself in modern poetry and literature and "emancipate" his feelings as a modern writer.

In turn, it should be emphasized, Guo contributed significantly to the May Fourth's attacks on the Confucian family and *lijiao*. Through publicizing his personal rebellion, he took the lead in China in the early 1920s in influencing the reading public in their fight against *lijiao*'s arranged marriages and became the May Fourth's leading advocate of Western Goethean Romanticism and individualism. The fact that both *San Ye Ji* and his translation of *The Sorrows of Young Werther* sold so well shows that he had made a significant impact on the May Fourth's reading public. What was most inspiring for his fellow May Fourthians was the bold display of his Western individualism against the Confucian *lijiao* society. Though not without tremendous mental suffering, he had publicly dishonored his arranged marriage at the expense of his parents and wife, who in this case personified the Confucian family and *lijiao* society for him and the public and to whom he was expected to carry out the Confucian social obligations of a son and husband. In so doing, he set an example for the May Fourth's public in asserting himself in a Goethean Romanticist and individualist manner against Confucian social norms and rules (the Confucian bonds between the father/parent and son/child and between the husband and wife).[88]

While justifying his disobedience to *lijiao* with Western Goethean Romanticism and individualism, Guo also managed to interpret Confucian personalism to the extent that it also sounded favorable to his assertion of his individuality against the Confucian family and *lijiao* society. Confucius, he wrote, considered people's individuality a "natural expression of God" and "developed his own individuality to extreme [perfection]—in depth and scope."[89] "The Confucian thinking of our country centers upon individuality," he also stated.[90] He specifically managed to find in Confucius's life an example of romantic love and individual freedom. Confucius, he said, "wanted to see" the beautiful woman Nanzi (南子). When editing *The Book of Songs*, Confucius did not leave out those poems that talked about love and sex, which he probably "loved" to read. Confucius was in favor of "freedom of love," as he did not forbid human desires. Further, as Guo believed, Confucius himself "practiced freedom of divorce."[91] All in all, as with Goethe, Confucius was "human" and had developed both his soul and flesh into "perfection" and was thus "the best of all human beings."[92] Obviously, such a Confucius would have little problem with Guo's seeking romantic love and asserting himself against the arranged marriage.

Guo's interpretation of Confucius here was certainly radical and unconventional. To a great extent, he was reading into Confucius's life and thinking of his own modern Western concepts of "freedom of love" and "freedom of divorce," the opposite of the Confucian ethics of *lijiao*. However, with the thinking of Confucius having been interpreted and reinterpreted so many times in China's history in order to suit the different needs of different times, one cannot simply disregard Guo's interpretation as total nonsense. Though his interpretation was against those of most of the previous interpreters of Confucianism, which, among other things, had over the years formed the essence of *lijiao*, the purpose of Guo's effort is actually not that different from those of previous interpreters: what he was doing was drawing and elaborating on some facts in Confucius's life and sayings and making these facts work for his own needs and for those of his May Fourth generation.

This brings up a major difference between Guo and many of his fellow May Fourthians (despite their shared anti-*lijiao* radicalism): while subconsciously still carrying certain elements of the Confucian tradition, the others publicly attacked *lijiao* and Confucianism in general; Guo, on the other hand, tried to get rid of *lijiao* by proving that *lijiao* is against the true meaning of Confucianism. Under the name of upholding Confucianism as a whole, therefore, he stole *lijiao* out of Confucianism and at the same time openly justified his continuation with parts of the Confucian tradition.

Under Western influence, it should be mentioned, Guo also interpreted traditional Taoism with an individualist approach. In "On Chinese and German Cultures," he writes that Lao Zi, like Nietzsche, based his thinking on "the individual" and "strove for positive development." Lao Zi was against "established ethics," which "completely trammeled the freedom of the individual." Such a Lao Zi, of course, also sounded in favor of Guo's individualist rebellion against the established Confucian social norms.[93]

Guo's Western-inspired individualism was for a while also reflected somewhat in his view on the social functions of literature and the arts. In September 1920, for instance, he published two letters to his friend Chen Jianlei (陳建雷), one of which contained the following poem:

Spring Silkworms

Silkworms!
you are spinning silk. . . .
No, it is poetry you are spinning![94]
How is it that your poetry is so fine?
so charming?
so delicate?
so pure?
so . . .
Alas, my vocabulary isn't enough to describe you,
Silkworms!

Silkworms!
I want to ask you:
is your poetry premeditated?
or is it unprompted?
is it artificial?
or is it a natural flow?
Do you make it for others?
or simply for yourselves? . . .
Silkworms! Alas, why don't you answer me?
Silkworms!
I believe that your poetry
is spontaneous;
and it is a natural flow;
you are creating your "palace of art,"
and you are creating it for yourselves . . .
Isn't that right? Silkworms!

Silkworms!
I believe that
you are also unselfish:
you do not mind making sacrifices,
you do not mind others' taking your silk.
Musicians play various music,
with strings made of the silk they take from you;
Young girls embroider the Madonna,
with the silk they take from you.
The Madonna, the musicians' music,
are all from your silk [poetry],
but to have your silk [poetry],
the musicians and girls have to come and get it themselves.
Isn't that right? Silkworms!
Why don't you answer me?[95]

In this poem, he conveys the idea that, like silkworms spinning silk for themselves, a poet writes poetry primarily for the purpose of spontaneously expressing and satisfying himself. However, even when making such an individualist literary point, he still manages to express the social consciousness that, like silkworms' silk, the poet's works benefit others and society.

In his letter to Chen Jianlei, he further elaborates on the idea expressed in the poem: while emphasizing that pure and genuine artworks can only be achieved by artists when they are without the utilitarian purpose of benefiting others, he does acknowledge that "all pure and genuine artworks benefit the society and help people."[96]

In "My Opinion on Children's Literature," he also makes the following argument:

> On the issue of literature there has been a controversy recently between utilitarianism and aestheticism, i.e., between "art for society's sake" and "art for art's sake." In my opinion, it all depends on the angle from which you look at the matter. On the one hand, literature does have its utilitarian side. Those antisocial and misanthropic works in literature, [for example], have profound effects on social reforms and on the improvement of human nature. With those effects in consideration, we cannot say that literature is not "social art." On the other hand, if a writer is overcautious and lets utilitarian concerns restrain him when writing his works, then his works are bound to end up being shallow and unable to move readers. Such shallow works are not even art. If the works are not art, then we do not even have a point in arguing whether they are "social art" or "non-social art." In short, I believe that the balanced and reasonable thing for us to do is: when looking from the angle of literary creation [writing], follow aestheticism; when looking from the angle of the appreciation of literary works, follow utilitarianism.[97]

From the May Fourth Individualist Awakening to a Marxist Radical Approach to Individual Emancipation

Unfortunately, the joy of Guo's triumph over *lijiao* did not last long, and his celebration of Romanticist individualism was soon to be frustrated in China's capitalist society in the 1920s. To a substantial extent, it was the contrast between his May Fourth individualist anti-*lijiao* glory/excitement and the ill treatment that he increasingly felt as an individual in the society that helped radicalize him in his attitudes toward society. As he painfully found out, he had been too awakened individualistically during the May Fourth movement to tolerate the exploitation and suppression of him as an individual in the society, hence his eventual conversion to the Marxist, radical collective approach to destroy the old society in order to achieve individual emancipation.

At the core of Guo's frustration with the society was the financial difficulty and uncertainty that he increasingly experienced in the early and mid-1920s while trying to make a living in his beloved literature. Throughout most of the previous periods in his life, his livelihood had been basically secured for him, even though he seldom had much money. First, in his early years in Sichuan, he was comfortably supported by his parents. Then, from 1914 on, he had relied on his Chinese government scholarship for regular financial income, even though in early 1914 he had to work very hard to qualify for that scholarship. Problems did not occur until 1921, when he decided to give up his medical studies and go back to China to make a career in literature. From April to September of that year, he worked in Shanghai for the Tai Dong Book Company (Tai Dong Tushuju 泰東圖書局), leaving Tomiko and their two sons back in Japan.[98] Soon after he started working for Tai Dong, however, he became increasingly frustrated by the way the company treated him. Tai Dong, to be sure, published many of his works. It was Tai Dong, for instance, that first published in August 1921 his book *The Goddesses*, which was a landmark on the route to establishing him as a major modern Chinese poet.[99] Further, Tai Dong also had promised him that it would publish the journal *Creation* (*Chuang-zao* 創造) for his Chuangzao She (創造社) (the Creation Society, July 1921–1929), a promise that came at a time when he and his friends had great difficulty finding a publisher in Shanghai willing to publish the journal. For this, he was "grateful."[100] However, despite the beneficial roles Tai Dong played in his literary career, he had considerable bitterness about his relationship with the publishing company, which, for one thing, never signed any contracts with him and never gave him a regular salary. During the four months he worked for Tai Dong, he edited at least two books (*The Goddesses* and *Romance of the Western Chamber*) and cotranslated one book (Theodor Storm's *Immensee*) for the company to publish.[101] Further, for those books and other projects, he had to take care of the proofreading and go to the printing house by himself.[102] For all of his work in those four months, however, Tai Dong's payments to him, apart from free room and board, seemed to be no more than a total of 203 yuan (元) and two ship tickets, which were given as Tai Dong's gifts for his two trips to Japan (a round trip from late June to mid-July and a one-way trip in September 1921).[103] Not only were Tai Dong's payments to him shabby, but they also were given to him in a manner that hurt his sensitive ego. For instance, he never seemed to have gotten used to the idea of receiving free room and board as part of his payments. Such an arrangement, as he later more than once noticed, made him feel like a "hanger-on" (*shike* 食客), receiving "free meals" from Tai Dong.[104] Further, given as gifts, the 203 yuan and ship tickets did not look like the payment that he deserved for his hard work. Instead, they looked like some alms that Tai Dong gave him out of its kindness and generosity. Once such gifts were given to him, even though they were less than what he deserved for payments, he was supposed to be grateful for Tai Dong's special treatment. In fact, Guo was sometimes made to feel that he did not even deserve these gifts.[105] Needless to say, Tai Dong, in its noncontractual relationship with Guo, always had the right not to be so kind or generous and not to give him any gifts. This ambiguous relationship with the company, as Guo later described it, made him feel that he was somewhat "like a slave" and somewhat "not like a slave."[106]

Guo also was frustrated with Tai Dong's slow progress in helping him with the literary journal that he and his friends had been planning.[107] After Guo's arrival in Shanghai in April 1921, Tai Dong had initially demonstrated an intention to let him replace the editor of a literary journal that the company had already been publishing. Guo seemed to have counted on turning this into his ideal journal, and he even started informing his friends of his anticipated editorship of this journal.[108] Tai Dong's intention, however, never materialized, as the journal's editor at the time refused to be replaced by Guo.[109] As a result, Guo had to work hard to start a brand-new journal, which turned out to be *Creation*. Even though Tai Dong came to promise that it would publish *Creation*, preparation for this new journal dragged on for some time.

Guo's frustration with his inability to produce his literary journal and the awkwardness and financial uncertainty that he had experienced in his relationship with Tai Dong made him increasingly realize that "it seemed too much" for him "to have dreamed of making a living and supporting a family by having a literary career in Shanghai." In part as a result of this, despite his love for literature and his reluctance to study medicine, he decided to return to Japan to continue his medical studies, as it now seemed to him that he would have more "security" in "making a living" in the medical profession.[110] At least going back to medical school would enable him to continue to receive the Chinese government scholarship as a regular financial income for his family. He went back to Fukuoka in September 1921.[111] While attending medical school, he continued his literary activities, including his contributions to *Creation Quarterly*.[112] Except for the summer break of 1922, which he spent in Shanghai, he stayed in Japan until he graduated from medical school in March 1923.[113]

By the time of his graduation, however, it had finally become obvious that medical practice was not something that he wanted to do or could do. For one thing, with his love of literature, he had simply little interest left for medicine. Further, with his hearing impairment, it had become clear now that he could hardly function well as a medical doctor, even if he had wanted to.[114] It should be mentioned that though he could hardly make a good doctor, the opportunity existed to make a good living in the medical profession in China. Even before his graduation, his oldest brother, obviously through connections, had already arranged for him to work as a doctor in a hospital that belonged to a local Red Cross in Sichuan. Not only did the Red Cross offer him a good salary, but it even sent two people to Shanghai in early 1924, about a year after his graduation, to help him relocate to Sichuan and deliver to him a handsome amount of money (1,000 *liang* 兩 silver) to cover the expenses of the relocation. He firmly turned down the Red Cross job offer. In addition to his unwillingness to practice medicine, he did not take the job because he simply could not afford to go back to Sichuan. As he noted in one of his autobiographical novels, going back to work in Sichuan would make it inevitable for him to meet his Sichuan family and thus confront his parents and his arranged wife on the issue of his arranged marriage.[115]

Unwilling and indisposed to practice medicine, and with his government scholarship terminated after his graduation from medical school in March 1923, Guo found himself struggling again to support his family with a literary career.[116] After all, it was literature that he had loved. To pursue this, he returned to Shanghai in April 1923 to continue work with Tai Dong, taking Tomiko and their children to China for the first time.[117] The problem was that Tai Dong continued to treat him and his Creation Society friends with awkward financial arrangements. As part of these arrangements, he and his family, after their arrival in Shanghai, shared with Cheng Fangwu (成仿吾) a house that was provided by Tai Dong.[118] Guo, however, still did not receive any regular salary from Tai Dong, nor did his friends Cheng Fangwu or Yu Dafu (鬱達夫).[119] Each time they needed money, they had to ask Tai Dong for it, which made them feel as though they were somehow begging. To make matters even worse, according to Guo, Cheng and Yu were so reluctant to endure the humiliation and awkwardness of such begging that they often asked him to do it on their behalf. As a result, from time to time Guo had to ask Tai Dong for money not only for himself but also for his friends. Being at least as equally reluctant as his friends, he sometimes simply chose not to ask Tai Dong and ended up short of money. The problem was so serious that there were often times when he could not even afford bus fares.[120] As he later recalled, he felt that "the lack of money" was "the most painful thing" for him and that he was living the life of a "slave and beggar."[121]

Despite Tai Dong's poor treatment of them, it should be noted, Guo and the Creation Society were not without reasons to stay with the company. As Guo later wrote, he and his friends wanted to freely "express" themselves, "write on impulse," and "speak out bravely." With its somewhat liberal policy, Tai Dong happened to be among the few publishers that were willing to publish writers like them at the time. In other words, while being enslaved by Tai Dong, Guo and his friends had actually also "used" Tai Dong for their own purpose.[122] A related point is that Guo's problem of financial difficulty and uncertainty was actually partly a result of his insistence on having his literary career with the freedom of expressing and developing himself and his refusal to compromise to adapt himself to society. For one thing, if he could compromise and return to Sichuan to take the job with the Red Cross, he would have lived with a very comfortable income. Further, he was not without opportunities to make a better living in Shanghai's literary circle. Commercial Press (*Shangwu Yinshuguan* 商務印書館), for instance, twice offered him decent payment if he sold his works to them. He, however, never accepted the offer. Not only was he reluctant at the time to sell his works for a living, but he did not like the fact that Commercial Press did not allow much freedom for writers to express their opinions.[123]

When Tomiko went to Shanghai with Guo and their children, she believed that life was going to be better for them now that Guo had graduated from college.[124] However, she was soon disillusioned, as they frequently suffered from lack of money.[125] She had become very worried about raising and educating their children under this difficult and uncertain financial condition.[126] One specific problem at the time was that they could hardly afford the medical expenses for treatment of their third son's digestive disease. Because of their financial problems in Shanghai, and probably also because of her difficulty at the time in adjusting to life in China as a Japanese, Tomiko often "quarreled" with Guo and wanted to go back to Japan.[127]

With Tomiko's persistence, Guo finally agreed to let her leave for Japan with their three children in February 1924. He and Tomiko seemed to be struggling with several plans. First, going back to Fukuoka, Tomiko was planning to get by first by borrowing some money from her friends there and then finding a job to make a living.[128] Second, with her previous nursing experience, Tomiko was thinking of taking several month's further training in obstetrics in Japan and then returning to Shanghai to find a job, most likely as an obstetrical nurse, so that she could help with the family income.[129] Third, Guo was seriously planning to go to Japan himself to join Tomiko and their children in May 1924, when he and his friends would have stopped their publication of *Creation Weekly* at its first anniversary.[130] Partly as a result of his frustration with this financial insecurity, Guo seemed to be pondering going back to Kyushu Imperial University at Fukuoka to study physiology.[131] On the practical side, he was hoping that as a student he would again get a scholarship from the Chinese government, which would at least be a stable income for his family.[132] As a student, he also would likely benefit from free medical coverage for his children at the school hospital, which would be a major relief from their financial burden. In Japan, it should be pointed out, he also would expect much better doctors and medical care for his children than in Shanghai.[133]

Whatever he and Tomiko were planning, her leaving Shanghai in February 1924 marked a major crisis in his life. Right after she left, he wrote in an autobiographical novel in February that he felt very depressed and "lonely" and was once again thinking of committing suicide.[134] What was most painful to him in her departure was his sense that he had failed miserably in his efforts to support his family with a literary career in China. "Those who side with me say that I have talent and those against me also bitterly attack me as a talent," he writes in anguish. "But what talent do I have and where is it? I feel so ashamed! . . . I can't even provide for my dear wife and children and have to let them go to find a living by themselves."[135] In China, he laments, literature was "not worth a penny," and a literary writer like him had "no hope at all" of making a decent living.[136] Frustrated over his life and literary career, he had become profoundly alienated from both society and the literary world. In March 1924, after reading a letter from Tomiko on how miserable she and their children were in Japan, he wrote the following to her in another autobiographical novel:

> We have been abandoned by happiness. . . . We have been deprived of everything and we have lost everything. Is there any need for us to keep living! . . . We have

worked our blood out, but for what? For feeding big and small capitalists and for raising our children so that they will live a life as miserable as ours! We are so pathetic. Our blood is so cheap! What is art! What is literature! What is fame! What is career! They look gilded but they actually hitch you up as a dog. I want them no more. I don't want to be a so-called artist at the expense of my human- ity. All I want is to be a man without disguises, even if it means that I have to beg for a living, even if it means that I will die abroad.... I will soon join you [in Japan]. When it really becomes impossible for us to survive, we will kill our three sons and then the two of us will hold each other tightly and jump into Hakata Bay to die![137]

In the same autobiographical novel, he also notes that he was bidding adieu to the world of arts where Beethoven and Goethe lived, a world that he used to love so much but to which he now felt he did not belong. Now with his mind made up to join Tomiko in Japan, he writes in the novel: "Leave! Leave! I will leave and die abroad!"[138]

His crisis, it should be noted, was also added to by his frustration with China's literary circle at the time. First, though he and his friends had developed the Cre- ation Society into an influential literary group, tension did gradually arise between him and these friends, especially Yu Dafu. In the late summer or early fall of 1923, for example, he and Yu ran into a confrontation over whether or not Yu should take a teaching job at Beijing University and thus leave Shanghai.[139] He was wor- ried that Yu's departure would weaken the Creation Society's ability to keep pub- lishing Creation Quarterly, Creation Weekly, and Creation Daily. To Guo's surprise, Yu, with obvious resentment against him, said that he would rather see those pub- lications stopped.[140] Yu did leave Shanghai for Beijing and, as Guo had worried, his leaving did substantially weaken the work of the Creation Society.[141] Further, Guo's frustration also was a result of his tension and conflicts with Hu Shi (胡 適) (1891–1962), Lu Xun (魯迅) (1881–1936), the Literary Research Society (Wenxue Yanjiuhui 文學研究會), and some other literary figures at the time. Cop- ing with various criticisms from those people, he was "sad" and "lonely" and felt that China's literary circle was like a "desert."[142] As he wrote during his crisis in early 1924, the "harsh" criticisms against him in the literary circle and the "hostility" that he felt from "everyone" around him were among the major factors that led him to thoughts of suicide.[143]

He left Shanghai for Japan on April 1, 1924, not only prepared to give up his literary career for physiological study but also determined to leave China for good.[144] Apart from his practical financial need for obtaining a scholarship, he wanted to study physiology at Kyushu Imperial University because he believed that he had a true interest in such scientific study. As he more than once noted, he was at the time planning to "devote" his life to natural science.[145]

His plan, however, was never carried out, as he never received the Chinese government scholarship needed for his scientific study.[146] Luckily, at the end of

April 1924, not too long after his arrival in Japan, he received 300 yuan from the Chinese government as his relocation fee to return to China after his graduation from medical school in Japan, money that he should have received the previous year upon his graduation. With that money, he and his family did get by fairly well for about a month. Three hundred yuan, however, did not last long, especially when most of it had to be used to pay off his previous debts. As a result, after May 1924, he and his family again found themselves struggling with serious financial problems. To survive, they had to pawn their winter clothes, quilts, and some of his books and buy their daily supplies of rice and groceries on credit. Paying rent for the house in which they were living was a major problem. Unable to come up with the rent, they were finally evicted in June 1924, and the whole family had to move to a small, shabby room above the warehouse of a pawnshop.[147]

Despite his previous frustration with his literary career, he had no choice but to make another stab at writing for a living. Unlike before, Guo now started to directly "sell" his writing for money.[148] The idea of having to sell his work for a living, however, was very painful for him to get used to. As he later described, he had been brought up with the concept that selling one's writings was "the lowest" thing a literary person could do, a concept that recalls Taoist and Confucian morals. Selling his work for money was a shameful thing, something that he would never do if there were still other ways of making a living.[149] Needless to say, the fact that Guo swallowed his pride and actually sold his writings shows how desperate he and his family were in their struggle for daily survival.

Guo stayed in Japan until November 1924, struggling to make ends meet by selling his works to publishers back in China. During the summer of 1924, he once ended up without much income and had to work as a storekeeper for the pawnshop over which he and his family were living.[150] Finally, after several months of "abject poverty" in Japan, he decided that his homeland China would be a better place for him to survive after all. In mid-November 1924, therefore, he returned to Shanghai with Tomiko and their children.[151]

Except for teaching part time at Da Xia University from April to May 1925 and full time at Zhong Hua Xue Yi University in the fall of the same year, which did not give him long-term, regular income, he continued to freelance and to suffer from financial insecurity.[152] In December 1924, for instance, he noted that "it is suicidal to be a literary writer in modern China."[153] In May 1925, he wrote that he was so poor that he was almost starving.[154] In February 1926, one month before he left Shanghai for Guangzhou, he lamented that in China a writer like him was worth even less than a prostitute.[155]

It was in the worst moment of his personal crisis in 1924, when he felt most painfully society's oppression and exploitation of him as an individual and its suppression of the development of his literary talent, that Guo began to be desperately attracted to the Marxist ideal of ultimate individual freedom and development in Communist society. When he went to Japan in April of that year, he had borrowed from a friend a copy of Kawakami Hajime's (河上肇) *Social Organization and Social*

Revolution and planned to read and translate it. Other than satisfying his interest in Marxism, he wanted to read and translate the book because he needed to sell his translation for money in order to help his family survive their financial crisis.[156] It took him about two months, from April to May, to translate Kawakami's book, and it was in the process of reading and translating that book that he became a believer in Marxism.[157] In a letter to Cheng Fangwu on August 9, 1924, one of his major writings on his conversion to Communism, he tells his friend:

> Translating [Kawakami's] book marked a turning point in my life. It was this book that awakened me from half sleep. It was this book that showed me the right path when I was hesitating at crossroads. It was this book that saved me from the shadow of death. I am very grateful to the author [Kawakami]. I am very grateful to Marx and Lenin.... I have now become a thorough believer of Marxism! Marxism is the only truth of our times.[158]

Specifically, he tells Cheng in the letter that Marxism makes him believe that Communist revolution will lead to a society in which "the free development of each is the condition for the free development of all" and in which people enjoy "free and thorough development of their individuality."[159] Feeling bitter that he could not freely develop his individual literary talent in his time, he yearns for the "free and thorough development" of "great literary talents" in Marx's ideal society. "In today's world," he writes to his friend, "we are unable to become pure scientists, pure literary writers, pure artists, or pure thinkers. To become those, we not only need to have certain talent but also have to have certain material support." In pre-Communist societies such as China's, that material support is the privilege of either those who have "rich fathers" and are themselves "aristocrats" or those who are protégés of rich people and "dependents of aristocrats." The "big and small stars in Renaissance Italy," Newton (1642–1727), Goethe, Tolstoy, and Tagore, he notes, were some of those privileged people who were lucky to have the material support to develop their talents. While "admiring" the achievements of those "lucky" ones, he lamented that people like him, who are poor and without material support, could expect nothing but "to die of hunger and diseases" before they could develop their talents! "Throughout human history," he said, few "genuine talents" have actually had the opportunity to "freely" and "thoroughly" develop themselves. "I have now realized," he tells Cheng, "that the reason for our (and perhaps all Chinese youths') common depression and weariness is that we have not had the luck to develop ourselves, nor have we found a way to let all people freely develop themselves." With this deep resentment against the old society's deprivation of his and others' individual development, he now longed for the paradise described by Marx. Though he and his friends probably would not live to see the future new society, he told Cheng, they should make efforts to achieve that society and let later generations enjoy it. This, he felt, was "the only thing" they could do as people who themselves had been deprived of "freedom" and individual development by their times.[160]

In his June 1924 "Appendicitis and Capitalism," Guo again admires that in the ideal Marxist society there will be "all-around development of the individual."[161] In his November 1925 "Marx Enters Confucius's Temple," he also states that the Marxist ideal that he pursues includes the ultimate development of people's "individuality."[162]

As Guo increasingly committed himself to the Marxist/Leninist cause, his complaints about his misfortune as an individual in the old society were replaced with an urge to fight for the collective cause of Communism at the expense of his own individual freedom. In his November 1925 "Preface to *Collected Literary Essays*," for example, he claims that as one of the few "awakened" people he now feels the obligation to "sacrifice" his own "individuality" and "freedom" in order to help the masses win their individuality and freedom. It is "improper," he emphasizes, for a few to talk about their own individuality and freedom when the majority of the people have been deprived of such things. "If we talk about developing individuality, then it has to be the development of everyone's individuality. If we strive for freedom, then it must be the freedom for all people."[163] In his 1926 "The Awakening of Writers and Artists," he further writes that to be able to enjoy "individuality" and "freedom," a person first needs to fight against what prevents him from being a free individual. Hence the person (living in his time) should join the Communist revolution to fight against the society that suppresses people's individuality and freedom, even though joining the collective revolution means that the person will have to "temporarily" give up his individual freedom.[164]

The Marxist/Leninist revolution was not expected to bring any immediate financial benefits for Guo and his family and therefore would not solve their financial crisis at the time. What Marxism/Leninism would do for him in this regard, then, was liberate him as an individual from the pain that he had suffered in coping with the crisis. Specifically, it would free him from a dilemma. Previously, with his May Fourth Goethean/Confucian/Taoist mentality, he, on the one hand, was too moralistic and too proud to kowtow to money and tended to restrain his material desires, to be indifferent toward material matters, and to stand aloof from the mundane world. On the other hand, he found that he and his family simply could not do without money for daily survival, and he had to put up with Tai Dong's manipulating him over money matters and sell his writings for money. The result was his sense of awkwardness, humiliation, and agony. Now, as a Marxist/Leninist revolutionary, he no longer had to kowtow to money or to the old society in general. Instead, he and others were to destroy that society once and for all so that people would never again be enslaved by the evil of money. This, interestingly, would ultimately satisfy his Confucian contempt for money. Hand in hand, Marxism and Confucianism worked here for him.

In accepting the Marxist collectivist approach to individual emancipation, Guo had in his words "thoroughly changed" his "previous thinking, which was deeply colored with individualism."[165] By around 1924, he had clearly given up his May Fourth Goethean Romanticist approach to and Taoist preoccupation with individual freedom. At the same time, he also went through a change of emphasis in his reading of Confucian personalism. His May Fourth celebration of what he saw as Confucius's attention to people's individuality was now less and less visible, and there was a new focus in his thinking on Confucian teachings on people's collective obligations and on cultivating and fulfilling oneself through the collective causes of managing the state and harmonizing the world. In "Wang Yangming: A Great Spiritualist," for instance, he sees Wang, his quintessential model of self-cultivation other than Confucius himself, as reaching the ideal of sagehood not only by excelling in Confucian scholarship but also by ultimately contributing to state management with outstanding civilian statesmanship and military leadership.[166]

Consistent with the shift of emphasis from individualist to collectivist concerns in his thinking, Guo also had changed his previous view that literature was primarily a way of expressing the writer's self, and that social function was a casual and secondary concern for the writer in his literary writing. Along the line of his realization that ultimate individual emancipation could only be achieved via Communist collectivism, he now believed that "true, pure literature," which writes on individuals' "pure and innocent" love and romance, would be made possible only after Communist revolution succeeded with the help of, among other things, the social and political function of revolutionary "propaganda" literature. While he did not see revolutionary literature as his ideal of literature, he accepted it as an "unavoidable," "transitional phenomenon" and, maybe more importantly, as part of the necessary means to achieve his Communist ideals. In his August 1924 letter to Cheng Fangwu, he writes that as an oppressed person living in an age that requires revolution and propaganda, he has no choice but to write and promote revolutionary literature that expresses the feelings of "the oppressed" and functions as a "sharp weapon" of revolutionary "propaganda."[167] In his March 1926 article "The Awakening of Writers and Artists," he also writes that the time has passed for Romanticist literature that features "individualism and liberalism." "What we need now," he claims, "is a literature whose form is realism and whose content is socialism."[168]

Though a radical jump, Guo's shifting in a few years from an individualist emphasis to a collectivist dedication was not illogical, at least not from his perspective. While clearly a result of the personal and situational crises that he was facing, ideologically such a transition was made fairly smooth for him by both Marxism and Confucianism. The Marxist promise of individual emancipation, for instance, enabled him to bridge his May Fourth pursuit of individual freedom with his new commitment to Communist collectivist revolution. With its concept of a nonconfrontational and even harmonious relationship between the interests of the individual and those of the nation and the world, Confucian personalism also provided him with a channel to travel without much difficulty from individual concerns to collective consciousness.

STRIVING FOR PERSONAL MORAL/SPIRITUAL SALVATION: FROM A MAY FOURTH CONFUCIAN FOCUS TO A COMMUNIST CONFUCIAN BATTLE

A May Fourth Focus

From the May Fourth period to his early Communist years, Guo never changed his Confucian goal of striving for inner transcendence over moral imperfection, which from his Neo-Confucian point of view resulted mostly from various human desires. His focus of attention, however, changed from guarding against overflooding of sexual desires during the May Fourth period to targeting against human material desires as a Confucian Communist in the mid-1920s.

A MAY FOURTH ELABORATION ON THE CONFUCIAN CONCEPT OF INNER TRANSCENDENCE

In his 1923 "The Traditional Spirit of Chinese Culture," Guo elaborates that through successful self-cultivation one can achieve moral/spiritual transcendence and become comparable to "God." When this happens, one's "wisdom and ability" will be so developed that they match "the great functions of heaven and earth," and one will become "as great and benevolent as God" and turn into "the light of eternal truth." After transcendence is achieved, one will no longer need to make efforts to cultivate and purify oneself, because cultivation and purification will then take place naturally and effortlessly, just as in the case of God.[169]

Personifying for Guo the achievement of inner transcendence was Confucius. As one of only two "all-around geniuses" who had ever existed in human history (the other being Goethe), Confucius (as did Goethe) embodied for Guo the ultimate development of both human "soul" and "flesh" and, above all, "the best of all human beings."[170] Interestingly, while Guo claimed that he did not see Confucius as a dehumanized religious icon, the enthusiasm with which he worshiped the "human" Confucius somehow reminds us of the Liao Ping (廖平) (1852–1932) school's enthusiasm to religiously idolize Confucius.[171] After all, Guo had been significantly influenced by Liao's *jinwen* (今文) school of thinking in his early years in Sichuan.[172]

The discussion here of Guo's May Fourth Confucian concept of inner transcendence requires some attention to his pantheism at the time. According to Guo, his interest in pantheism had started in his first years in Japan before 1919. People who had influenced him with pantheist thinking included Tagore, Kabir, Spinoza, and Goethe.[173] In the preface to his translation of *The Sorrows of Young Werther*, he especially mentions that one of the major attractions he finds in Goethe is Goethean pantheism. Interpreting Goethe's thinking, Guo writes: "All nature is nothing but the expression of God. I, too, am nothing but the expression of God. I am god and all nature is the expression of me." It is the ultimate meaning of man's life to "pursue" the "eternal happiness of being identical with God."[174] Under the influence of the modern concept of pantheism, he also came to interpret Confucianism and Taoism to be pantheistic. In "The Traditional Spirit of Chinese Culture," for example, he describes Confucius as having an "active and pantheistic worldview." That world-view involves the belief that "noumenon" (ben ti 本體), which "contains everything" in the universe, not only "is God" but also "day by day . . . progresses unconsciously" toward "kindness" (shan 善). Further, this "noumenon" (God) "makes laws" (lifa 立法) for "everything," and its "existence and function . . . is beyond the measurement" of people's "perception." This pantheist thinking of Confucius, Guo says, "is very beautiful." As for Taoism, he once wrote that he felt that he could "suddenly see things thoroughly and in a clear light" when he discovered that the Taoist thinking in the Zhuang Zi, which had been a "favorite" of his, was similar to the pantheism of Spinoza, Goethe, Tagore, and Kabir. In his 1920 poem Three Pantheists, he also writes that he "loves" Zhuang Zi for his pantheism. He, however, never elaborated on what he saw as Zhuang Zi's pantheist thinking.

The point to be made here is that while somewhat intertwined with each other, Guo's Confucian concept of inner transcendence differed substantially from his pantheism. It is true that he was not without ground to interpret Confucius's thinking as pantheistic, for according to his favorite Neo-Confucian teaching of Wang Yangming, the concept of principle (li 理), which is identified with the mind-heart (xin 心), does carry Godlike features and could be identified with every-thing in the world.[175] Despite such a Neo-Confucian pantheist tendency, however, Confucianism at least in two ways functioned differently on him than pantheism. First, while his pantheism led him to believe that humans, as everything else in the universe, naturally carry certain divine traits and are somehow identical to God, his Confucianism insisted that the human individual has to work extraordinarily hard to cultivate himself in order to travel the significant distance from his moral imperfection to being a sage, who, though linked to God and perhaps comparable to God as far as this-worldly functions are concerned, is not necessarily a god per se. Second, even though it somehow turned out to have helped him challenge lijiao (as elaborated later), Guo's pantheism with its belief in the divinity of everything tended to be more accepting of and optimistic about reality than his Confucian concept of inner transcendence, whose faith in people's potentials in ultimately reaching sagehood was based on a profound critical consciousness about the exist-ing moral flaws of human individuals and their society. In this regard, compared to his Confucian transcendental concept, his pantheistic optimism about the world was more consistent with his overall poetic romanticization of life at the time.

Whatever the differences between them, both his Confucian concept of inner transcendence and his pantheism were a result of his years-long search for the meaning of life. This search, whose worst moment was the mid-1910s, when he was painfully coping with his arranged marriage, centered on the relationship between his life in this world and the other world of eternity and divinity. As discussed pre-viously, in the mid-1910s, Guo went through great pains to decide whether to give in to the overwhelming pressure of lijiao and suppress and smother his this-worldly desires for love, romance, and individual freedom or to radically break with *lijiao* and enjoy the happiness of this world. He often found himself tortured with this question: "Should I follow all my instinctive desires and stick to this world, or should I negate all those desires and pursue the other world?"[176] After sometimes seriously thinking about committing suicide or becoming a Buddhist monk, he finally decided, largely inspired by Goetheanism, to celebrate his this-worldly happiness against the *lijiao* suppression and came to emotionally and profoundly denounce Buddhism's negation of this world.[177] In "On Chinese and German Cultures," for instance, he criticizes that Buddhism, with its "negation of this world" and "pursuit of the destruction of one's self," has polluted China's original culture and spirit.[178] Buddhism's damage to Chinese civilization, he writes, is comparable to "Hebraism's damage to medieval Europe" and "capitalism's damage to contemporary Europe."[179] While abandoning what he saw as the Buddhist negative linkage between this and other worlds, he found in both the Confucian transcendental concept and pantheism positive ways of connecting this-worldly life to eternity and divinity and thus achieving the spiritual and moral meaningfulness of life by transcending its physical and material existence. The Confucian concept of reaching sagehood through self-cultivation, for example, provided him with a channel to transcend life in this world through the moral and positive experience, appreciation, and improvement of that life. With its belief in the divine nature of everything in the universe, pantheism certainly further bridged for him the gap between people and divinity and, in contrast to Buddhism, it did so with a full appreciation of people's this-worldly life.

Combined with a celebration of humanity that he shared with many of his fellow May Fourthians, Guo's Confucian transcendental concept and his pantheism also contributed to a tendency in his thinking to apotheosize man and his power.[180] When he talked as a Confucianist about man's potential of cultivating himself to match God in functions and when he expressed pantheistically that he was god, he clearly saw no limit in what man could do and achieve. His apotheosis of man can be further seen in his 1920 poem Pyramids:

> Create! Create! Create with all your might!
> The creative forces of man can rival those of the gods.[181]

He also took pride in what he saw as the deification of man in China's ancient tradition. In "The Pompeii of Chinese Intellectual History," an unfinished article that was published in May 1921, he speaks highly of the ancient Chinese belief that it was "man" who "created all the million things and man himself was god."[182] In ancient Chinese thinking, he praises, "Heaven (God) was people and people were Heaven (God)."[183]

A FOCUS ON REGULATING SEXUAL DESIRES TO ACHIEVE INNER TRANSCENDENCE

For Guo, to achieve the goal of reaching inner transcendence, self-cultivation has to be practiced so that one develops the three essential Confucian virtues of *ren* ｛ ⸱

(humanity), *yong* 勇 (courage), and *zhi* 智 (wisdom). Of the three, *ren* was the most important for him.

Guo saw *ren*'s essence in Confucius's teaching of *keji fuli* 克己复禮 (restrain oneself and go back to ethics).[184] In "The Traditional Spirit of Chinese Culture," he writes that Confucius's life philosophy features an emphasis on one's "self restraint." Confucius, he says, was "absolutely" against "complete lack of restraint" and "unlimited indulgence" of any instinctive desires. One can "never see the light of truth" when "distracted by various desires," Guo emphasizes in the article. Confucius, he elaborates, not only worked to use "proper methods" to "musically regulate" his own "instinctive drives and sensual pleasures" but also taught others to do the same.[185] Possibly influenced by the thinking of Wang Yangming, Guo also interprets the Confucian concept of *gewu* 格物 (investigation of things) as "regulating sensual desires with proper methods."[186]

The human sensual desire with which Guo was preoccupied, especially before 1919 but also during the early 1920s, was the desire for sex. In fact, a major part of his moral crisis as a result of his rebellion against the arranged marriage was the sense of immorality that he felt in desiring for and living with another woman as a married man. For a long time before 1919, this sense of immorality was reinforced for him by both the Confucian ethics of *lijiao*, which pressured him to honor his social obligations in the marriage arrangement, and Wang Yangming's Neo-Confucian teaching on the inner restraint of sexual desire, hence the overwhelming torture for him to cultivate himself: not only should he control his sexual desire but he must also control it to the extreme of obeying a marriage arrangement that he could hardly bear. This torture was stopped for him in the early 1920s, when he finally broke with the Confucian family and *lijiao* and managed to detach his Confucian moral self-cultivation from the *lijiao* requirement of regulating the family, which had demanded that he cultivate himself by observing the father-son and husband-wife bonds and, accordingly, honoring the marriage arranged for him by his parents. In 1920 he was already able to separate *lijiao* from what he saw as true Confucianism: in *San Ye Ji*, on the one hand, he openly and publicly defied *lijiao* and, on the other hand, he enthusiastically worshiped Confucius in general, even though at the time he still had to tiptoe away from the Confucian concepts of self-restraint and *li*, which had always been closely related to *lijiao*. By 1923, then, he was further clarified in his thinking to be able to clearly and comfortably verbalize a separation of *lijiao* from what he saw as Confucius's concept of *li*. In "The Traditional Spirit of Chinese Culture," for instance, Guo states that *li* in Confucius's thinking "is not at all the established ritual ethics" of *lijiao*. Confucius's "*li*," he says, refers to people's "inner" morals, something similar to Immanuel Kant's (1724–1804) concept of ethics.[187] In other words, internalized now, *li* for Guo only functions as an inner requirement for people to properly regulate and control their human desires and does not go to the extreme of *lijiao*, which suppressed people's romantic feelings and desires by, among other things, imprisoning them in arranged marriages with the Confucian father-son and husband-wife bonds.[188]

The separation of *lijiao* from *li* now enabled Guo to see his relationship with Tomiko as a modern romance and justifiable rebellion against *lijiao* and no longer as much of a case of indulgence of sexual desire against the inner moral requirement of *li*. Freed from the sense of guilt and immorality imposed on him by *lijiao*, Guo came to focus on the inner cultivation of regulating his sexual desire, which he still saw as being at least potentially sinful. It is true that under the influence of Goethean Romanticism he, in *San Ye Ji*, interpreted Confucius with a humanistic approach and depicted Confucius as a man with human sexual desire and an advocate of freedom of love and divorce. In fact, in contrast to his 1923 acknowledgment and advocacy of the Confucian emphasis on restraining one's desires, he seemed to be carried away in 1920 in *San Ye Ji* by his obsession with what he saw as Confucius's human desire and did not give (and possibly intentionally avoided giving) attention to Confucius's concept of self-restraint. However, even in *San Yi Ji*, which was written at the peak of his humanistic emancipation, he never went as far as unconditionally endorsing sexual desire. This can be seen in the interesting way by which he and his friends came to justify his rebellion against *lijiao*. Through their communications collected in the book, Guo, Tian Shouchang, and Zong Baihua largely justified his rebellion with the fact that the "sins" and "human desire" that he had displayed in his actions against the ethics of *lijiao* were no different than those displayed by celebrated Western figures such as Goethe, Rousseau, St. Augustine, and Tolstoy. As Tian put it, there are hardly men who are born perfect, and the best of human beings are those who confess their sins and improve themselves.[189] Since Guo had the courage and sincerity to confess his "sins" and "human desire," as Rousseau, St. Augustine, and Tolstoy had, he was alright. What is significant here is that he and his friends never said loudly and clearly that his desire for a woman (Tomiko) was completely good in itself. For them, such desire, no matter how excusable, still more or less fell into the category of "sins," something that still needed to be controlled and conquered in order for a person to be a perfect human being.

Guo's moral attitude toward sexual desire also can be seen in his March 6, 1920 letter to Tian Shouchang, which also was collected in *San Ye Ji*. In that letter, he tells his friend about a book written by Arishima Takeo, a Japanese writer who had been substantially influenced by Western and especially Christian thinking. What Guo "likes best" in Takeo's book is a story that to him symbolizes, among other things, a "fierce battle" between the "pure soul" and the "sham," "filth," "degeneration," and "darkness" of the world of "desires of the flesh."[190] The way in which he describes the story clearly demonstrates his own contempt for the indulgence of desires of the flesh and his admiration and longing for the purification of the soul. He explicitly compares himself in the letter to a character in Takeo's story who experiences the painful struggle between sexual desire and the "pure soul."[191] In fact, to best sum up his own battle against desires, Guo chose the following quote from Goethe's *Faust* as his preface to *San Ye Ji*:

Two souls, alas! reside within my breast,
and each is eager for a separation:
in throes of coarse desire, one grips
the earth with all its senses;
the other struggles from the dust
to rise to high ancestral spheres.

If there are spirits in the air
who hold domain between this world and heaven—
out of your golden haze descend,
transport me to a new and brighter life![192]

Later in 1921, when he, upon his arrival in Shanghai, expressed strong disgust at the "loud and lascivious" "flesh" and the "short sleeves of women" on the streets of the city, he once again clearly displayed his contempt for sexual desire.[193] Interestingly, such a negative impression of the modern city reminds one of Old Mr. Wu (in Mao Dun's [茅盾] [1896–1981] novel *Midnight* [*Ziye* 子夜]) who, coming to Shanghai for the first time from the conservative countryside, was dizzied on the city's streets by women's flesh revealed by modern clothing.

Overall, with his contempt for the flooding of sexual desires and his conscious effort to restrain his own desires for sex, Guo was clearly drawing a line, for society and for himself, between the pursuit of romantic love and the indulgence of sexual pleasures. To some extent, one can argue that the Neo-Confucian teaching on restraining sexual (and other) desires had helped prevent him from going to the extreme of indulging his sexual desires while he was emancipating himself from the *lijiao* suppression of these desires. His critics, both of and after his time, may think otherwise. As far as he himself was concerned, however, he was consciously making a serious effort not to step over his Confucian moral line on the issue of sex.

Guo's repeatedly expressing in public his attitude against the flooding of sexual desires also had served to help justify morally to the public his rebellion against *lijiao*. By simultaneously celebrating his love with Tomiko and laboring to criticize the indulgence of sexual desires, he was conveying a message to the public that he was not a lustful man, and his living with Tomiko was for nothing but pure romantic love. The fact that he had to work so hard to morally justify his act to the public, of course, shows that he had felt serious moral pressure from the public. What this suggests is that while it was as anti-*lijiao* as Guo was, the May Fourth reading public also was as Confucianistic as Guo was on the issue of guarding against the indulgence of human sexual (and other) desires.

From a historical perspective, Guo's May Fourth, Neo-Confucian emphasis on restraining sexual desires reminds us of the prevailing moralistic attitudes against these desires during the Maoist Cultural Revolution. (Despite Mao's alleged private lifestyle, under his leadership there was a strong puritanical, moralistic atmosphere against sexual desires during the Cultural Revolution.) In other words, linking

Guo's May Fourth thinking to the Maoist movement, we find that the Neo-Confucian moralistic emphasis against human sexual (and other) desires not only survived the so-called anti-Confucian May Fourth movement but actually reached a peak during the Maoist years of Communist revolution.

Another human desire that Guo wanted to restrain during the May Fourth era was the desire for what he considered excessive material enjoyment and gains, even though the fight against this desire was not his priority at the time. Primarily Confucian (Neo-Confucian) in origin, it should be mentioned, his criticism of material desires also recalls the Taoist tendency to transcend the mundane world and Goethe's Romanticist casualness over material matters. One of the examples of his attitude against material desires is seen in his "On Boycotting Japanese Goods." In this article, as mentioned previously, he argues that many of the goods that China had imported from Japan fall into the category of what he calls "luxuries." He criticizes that the Chinese had imported these "luxuries" because they had a bad habit of indulging in luxury and extravagance. What is interesting is that his long list of "luxuries" ranges from seafood, tea, refined sugar, medicine, and canned food to toys, makeup, soap, textile, leather, and glass products.[194] His main argument, of course, is that some of those products could be replaced with products made by China's own industries. However, the fact that he literally defines so many otherwise commonly needed products in modern life as "luxuries" reveals his philosophy of minimum material living, something that he was to express again in some of his later writings.

His indifference to material matters also can be seen in his attitude toward money. For instance, in about early February 1920, Zong Baihua, on behalf of *Shi Shi Xin Bao*, informed him that the newspaper was to send him some money as payment for some of his poems that it had published. With his low income at the time, he certainly needed this money to support his family. He certainly also deserved the money, as it was the payment for the publication of his works. In a letter to Zong written on February 15, 1920, however, he earnestly asks Zong not to pay him the money. "None of the works that I have sent to you deserves payment," he says to Zong in the letter. "Besides, it was not my intention to ask for payment for these works."[195] Another example was the money issue in his relationship with Tai Dong when he was working for the book company in Shanghai. Even though he badly needed money and did not feel comfortable at all with Tai Dong's financial treatment of him, he never openly talked this over with the company as it seemed too mundane and too materialistic for him to talk about money. Not to talk about money, unfortunately, did not solve his real financial problems. As a result, he was torn between his need to support his family and his pride in not discussing money with Tai Dong. This, in a sense, contributed to the awkwardness that he felt in his relationship with Tai Dong. Such awkwardness was one of the factors that contributed to his frustration in his literary career and his overall depression at the time, which would eventually help lead to his conversion to Communism.

His contempt for material gains also was shown in the antimaterialist and antiprofit-making tone of his criticism against capitalism and in general against what he perceived to be the darkness of China and the world. In "On Chinese and German Cultures," for instance, Guo strongly indicates that it was the "self-profit-ing" and "selfish" (*woli* 我利, *liji* 利己) nature of capitalism that had made it an evil system and caused the disaster of the First World War.[196] People's desires such as those for "material gains" and "possession" are the ultimate reason for "all the anxiety, chaos, and fighting of mankind," he comments when interpreting the Taoist con-cept of *wuwei* 無為 (inaction/letting things take their own course).[197] In the article he also mentions "the current chaos of the stifling of material desires" as a major problem in China.[198] In October 1923, he again remarked that in China's "chaotic" times there had appeared "countless" "evil talents" of "profit-making."[199]

Other than *ren*, Guo also was in pursuit of the Confucian virtues of *yong* (cour-age) and *zhi* (wisdom). For him, *yong* meant that one should first not "deceive" one-self about one's own moral weaknesses and flaws and should learn to be ashamed of them. One should then be "determined" and "make efforts" to get rid of these weaknesses and flaws in order to reach the courageous goal of achieving sagehood. Further, as typical with the collectivist connotation of Confucian personalism, he believed that *yong* also requires that one should go beyond the mere concern of oneself and be willing to devote oneself to and even sacrifice oneself for the cause of "saving fellow human beings all over the world."[200]

To achieve *zhi* meant for Guo that one should "constantly strive" to excel by energetically learning and "absorbing" all knowledge, which is one's "food of life." To learn and to become wise is the way to "enrich" one's life. "A man of wisdom is never in two minds," he said, quoting Confucius.[201]

Shifting the Focus

When Guo came to struggle desperately through the personal crisis of his financial difficulty in the mid-1920s, the restraint of sexual desires seemed to have become too irrelevant an issue in his life and thinking. It is also true that with the victory of his romantic love over *lijiao*'s suppression by the mid-1920s, the issue of romantic love versus indulgence of sexual desires was no longer a pressing one, because he no longer had to morally justify his rebellion against *lijiao* and it no longer seemed a priority for him to concentrate on balancing romantic love and indulgence in sex-ual pleasures in his Confucian moral self-cultivation. As he grew more and more resentful of capitalist society's exploitation and oppression of him, he began to focus his Confucian attention on fighting against human material desires, which he now saw as the source of the evil of capitalism.

A COMMUNIST WITH A CONFUCIAN TRANSCENDENTAL PERSPECTIVE

In 1924 Guo found in Marxism the promise of the individual's socioeconomic emancipation in the material world. Material life, however, was not everything for him. As a Confucianist, he continued to believe that in order to live a fully mean-ingful life, an individual should strive not only for freedom in the mundane world but also for moral/spiritual salvation, which for him lay in achieving Confucian inner transcendence.

By the mid-1920s Guo had gone through a change from his May Fourth transcendental combination of both pantheism and the Confucian concept of inner transcendence to a single focus on the Confucian thought, as he gave up pantheism and Goethe around late 1923 and early 1924.[202] To a great extent, his abandoning pantheism, which by acknowledging divinity in everything tends to be optimistic about the world, and his focusing now on the Confucian concept of inner transcendence, which features a profound awareness and criticism of the moral imperfection of people and their society, were consistent with his overall transition from a May Fourth romanticization of life to a bitter realization of the harsh reality around him.

It was through his expressed admiration of the life and thinking of Wang Yangming that Guo in the mid-1920s elaborated on his continuous belief in and pursuit of Confucian inner transcendence. First of all, he was attracted to the fact that Wang, in search of the meaning of life, traveled from the Buddhist negative transcendental approach to life to the Confucian positive attitude of inner tran-scendence, a path similar to his own during the May Fourth period.[203] When describing Wang's intellectual journey in "Wang Yangming: A Great Spiritualist," he takes the opportunity to once again criticize Buddhism. Both the Mahayana and Hinayana branches of Buddhism, he writes, start with a negation of "the reality" of this world. As a religion that "extremely despises" the physical/fleshly aspect of human life, Buddhism is "absolutely" unacceptable for "normal people" and there-fore was naturally given up by Wang. Consistent with his now-changed attitude toward Taoism, which will be discussed in more detail in chapter 4, Guo points out that Wang arrived at the Confucian concept of inner transcendence also via dissatisfaction with Taoism. Though not as negative about this-worldly life as Bud-dhism, Taoism failed to provide Wang with a true meaning of life, because Lao Zi's "life philosophy" is "fully calculating" and leads to "selfishness."[204] In contrast to the Buddhist negation of this world and the Taoist "selfish" approach to life, Confu-cianism teaches people to morally transcend their this-worldly life by starting with a positive experience and improvement of that life, which includes full interaction with and contribution to their social and political collectives. Under the concept that all are one in the universe, Confucianism requires that people morally cultivate themselves so that in this-worldly life they could achieve the goals of "regulating the family, managing the state, and harmonizing the world," and transcendentally they would be able to live up to their potential of being identified with the whole universe and "eternity" (dadao 大道).[205] Only through following this Confucian thinking, says Guo, will one be able to "freely" travel between this world and the transcendental beyond and thus make life meaningful by merging it into eternity. It was in this Confucian thinking that Wang Yangming finally found his meaning of life, and it was in achieving the Confucian inner transcendence that he excelled and reached sagehood.[206]

As a sage, Wang came to "revive" Confucianism and in effect turned out to be the "only" person after Confucius to have "truly embodied the spirit of Confucianism."[207] According to Guo, Wang's saying that "the mind-heart is li," which is "Heaven" (tian 天), "the way" (dao 道), and "noumenon" (benti 本體), best summarizes part of the essence of the Confucian concept of inner transcendence.[208] The mind-heart's linkage through li to the transcendental beyond (the Heaven, the way, and noumenon), however, is only a potential insofar as the mind-heart (the li of/within the mind-heart) is marred and blocked by one's various human desires. To realize that potential and reach transcendence, then, one needs to work hard to clear one's mind-heart through self-cultivation. Having successfully struggled against and conquered his "enemy within" (xin zhong zei 心中賊 his own human desires) and having fought courageously against hostile and "evil" environments, Wang himself set a perfect example for purifying the mind-heart and achieving the greatness and "brightness" of transcendence.[209]

It is important to note that while both serving as his guidance on the development of the individual, Guo's Confucian concept of inner transcendence, which stresses people's transcendence from their human and material desires, and his Marxist concept of individual emancipation, which derives from Marx's emphasis on high-level material development, differed substantially from each other. The difference between the two was part of an overall tension between Guo's Confucian and Marxist thinking, which will be discussed elaborately later.

A FOCUS ON FIGHTING MATERIAL DESIRES TO ACHIEVE INNER TRANSCENDENCE AND UPROOT CAPITALISM

While enthusiastically advocating the Communist collective revolution as the way to realize his Marxist ideal of socioeconomic emancipation of the individual, Guo in the mid-1920s continuously stressed the need to use self-cultivation as the means for the individual to reach the moral/spiritual goal of achieving Confucian inner transcendence.

To cultivate oneself was for Guo to follow the teaching of Wang Yangming, who emphasized the "the unity of knowledge and action." According to Guo, Wang taught that with the knowledge that human desires are "the absolute evil" and the "Heavenly principle" is "the absolute kindness," people should strive to rid themselves of "human desires" and keep the "Heavenly principle" by taking the actions of "quiet-sitting" and "tempering" themselves through "doing things" (shishang molian 事上磨煉). The purpose of "quiet-sitting" is for the individual to reflect inward into his mind-heart to get in touch with his transcendental potential of linking to the "Heavenly principle." Based on his own personal experience, Guo writes that "quiet-sitting" is an "extremely effective" "means" for one's self-cultivation. As just a means, he also points out, "quiet-sitting" is not in conflict with the spirit of striving and fighting that a person needs in his life. The purpose of "doing things," which in many cases is social and political by nature, is for the individual to not only culti-vate himself in activities but also to collectively help his fellow human beings with their cultivation and development. This, according to Guo, ensures that a person does not get "lopsided" or self-centered in the process of Confucian cultivation.[210]

Guo's discussion here of cultivating oneself, and in the meantime contribut-ing to the cause of collective progress, is consistent with the Confucian concept of achieving "inner sagehood and outer kingliness" (*neisheng waiwang*). While that concept had long been embedded in his thinking, however, during much of the May Fourth period Guo tended to pay more attention to its individual-oriented aspect: the goal of reaching "inner sagehood."[211] It was not until now, when his May Fourth Romanticist celebration of individualist development had been brutally frustrated, that he came to put more emphasis on taking action and fighting for public and col-lective causes, which was along the lines of "outer kingliness," the collective-oriented aspect of *neisheng waiwang*.[212]

Guo's attention now to achieving both inner sagehood and outer kingliness was best seen in his focusing on fighting human material desires for personal inner transcendence as well as for the Communist collective cause of anticapitalism. This focus was expressed in his admiration and interpretation of the life and thought of Wang Yangming.

According to Guo, Wang had correctly understood the Confucian teaching on restricting "human desires" (*renyu* 人欲), which Guo continued to consider the essence of the virtue of *ren*. Not only did Wang understand the Confucian teach-ing, but he had literally followed the teaching and achieved the restriction of his own human desires, of which Guo now emphasized the desires for material mat-ters and gains.[213] In successfully restricting his desires, Wang had conquered his "enemy within" and achieved the Confucian personal inner transcendence.[214]

To a certain extent, Wang's success in restricting his material (and other) desires might have served as an inspiration for Guo. Overwhelmed by his financial crisis in the mid-1920s, Guo was fighting a constant and desperate battle to keep pursuing his literary career, to maintain his intellectual integrity, and not to give in to the pressure of his material needs or the suppression of the society. This being the case, on a day-to-day basis Wang's example in restricting material desires might have functioned as a support system for Guo in coping with the lack of security and certainty in his material life.

The real importance of Wang's Neo-Confucian teaching on restricting mate-rial desires, however, did not lie for Guo in its helping him through the daily dif-ficulty of his material life. That help, in fact, amounted to very little in reality. The brutal truth was that no matter how hard he tried to follow the Confucian teach-ing and restrict his material desires, he could not survive the exploitation and sup-pression of the material world of capitalism, which did not seem to allow him to have any human material desires at all. As he sighed in 1924, it was hard even to have his family's very basic material needs met in the capitalist society.[215] For Guo, the real importance of Confucian teaching lay in the fact that it could join forces with Marxist/Leninist Communist theory in the historic battle against capitalism, which he considered the ultimate source of many personal crises such as his own. As a Confucian Communist, he saw a link between Wang Yangming's Neo-Confucian moral criticism of human material desires and the Marxist/Leninist socioeconomic cause of anticapitalism. The "evil" (e 惡) of human material desires that Wang criticized, Guo elaborates, is the same as people's "selfish desires" (siyu 私欲) or their "impulses for private possession" (zhanyou chongdong 占有衝動). People, he writes, have desires to take private possession of the material goods in this world. Wang targeted these desires in his famous teaching of "ridding" oneself of "human desires" and "keeping the Heavenly principle" (qu renyu er cun tianli 去人欲而存天理).[216] As human desires equal people's desires for private possession, Guo emphasizes, Wang's teaching to eliminate human desires, interpreted from a socioeconomic perspective, actually leads to the conclusion that private ownership should be "abolished" and public ownership should be established. This being the case, the Neo-Confucian concept of Wang Yangming "runs parallel to" the Marxist/Leninist theory of anticapitalist social revolution.[217]

By stretching the concept of restricting human material desires to a criticism of private possession and private ownership, Guo obviously went beyond the Confucian concept of self-cultivation into the sphere of social reform and revolution, which was consistent with his increasing commitment to the Communist cause. What is really interesting here about such Confucian Communist thinking as Guo's is what it suggests: not only should people carry out the modern collective revolution of Marxism/Leninism to tackle the socioeconomic and political institutions of capitalism, but, as these institutions are based on the desires for "private possession," people should also strive individually in the traditional Confucian manner to restrict their own material desires to thoroughly and fundamentally uproot the evil of capitalism. The Neo-Confucian battle against human material desires, in other words, now serves a double purpose: to achieve the individual's inner transcendence and to reach the collective goal of eliminating capitalism.

To put this in historical perspective, Guo's 1920s' Confucian Communist thinking of uprooting capitalism by restricting and eliminating people's selfish material desires strikingly preceded the Maoist practice later during the Cultural Revolution. During that radical movement, in which Guo was a participant, many in China were enthusiastically engaged in a moral battle to "fiercely fight any single impulse of selfish desires" in their own mind-hearts (hendou sixin yishannian 狠斗私心一閃念). This battle, under the guidance of Mao's theory of continuous revolution, was to carry the Communist revolution to another level after the destruction of the socioeconomic political institutions of capitalism and achieve the ultimate victory over the evils of capitalism (and feudalism and "revisionism").

CHAPTER 2

Toward National Salvation

The desperate urgency that Guo came to feel to save China from the hands of imperialist powers was another reason he turned to Communism in the mid-1920s.

Guo was not without passion and concern for his motherland before the mid-1920s. In fact, in contrast to his May Fourth individualist rebellion against the collective of the Confucian *lijiao* society, during the May Fourth period Guo never turned his back as an individual against his nation as a symbol of collective identity. In this regard, he remained by and large a Confucianist in practicing Confucian personalism and fulfilling the collective obligation of the individual toward the nation, in other words, following the Confucian sequence of self-cultivation and managing the state. The influence of modern nationalism, of course, was also a factor in contributing to his concerns for his nation and his passion for the cause of saving his nation in the modern world.

The passion and concerns for his country, however, were secondary in his thinking during the May Fourth period, because he was then preoccupied in his individualist rebellion against the suppression of *lijiao*. By the mid-1920s, things changed. He had by then claimed his individualist victory over the Confucian family and *lijiao* and, unbearably, he began to see his celebration of individuality brutally frustrated by the exploitation and oppression of the capitalist society. As a result, he went through a profound change in his thinking from an individualist focus to a focus on collective causes. It was with this new collectivist awareness that he came to reflect upon China's national crisis in the mid-1920s, and he concluded that his nation was in desperate need for a radical Communist revolution in order to survive in the modern world.

MAY FOURTH LOVE AND CONCERN FOR THE MOTHERLAND

Guo's feelings for his motherland burst forth in his writing when he began to be published in 1919. In the works that he published between late 1919 and April 1921 (when he returned to China from Japan), he many times passionately expressed his excitement about and high expectation for May Fourth China's seemingly promising changes. As he later put it, "after the May Fourth [incident] China appealed to me as a very beautiful girl with promising signs of progress. I had simply fallen in love with her."[1] In *Good Morning*, a poem published in January 1920, he writes the following eulogy to May Fourth China[2]:

> Good morning! My youthful homeland!
> Good morning! My newborn fellow Chinese!
> Good morning! My mighty Yangtze River in the south!
> Good morning! My frozen Yellow River in the north!
> Yellow River! I hope the ice in your chest will soon melt!
>
> Good morning! Ten-thousand-li Great Wall![3]

As he noted later, in his long poem *The Nirvana of the Feng and Huang*, published in January 1920, and in his *The Rebirth of the Goddesses*, published in February 1921, he was also expressing his "strong longing for China's national rejuvenation."[4] *The Nirvana of the Feng and Huang*, he said on another occasion, "symbolized" the rebirth of China.[5]

His love and hope for his country during this period were probably best seen in the following poem, written in early 1920:

> *Coal in the Grate*
> *—My love for my country**
>
> Ah, my fair young maiden,
> I shall not betray your care,
> Let you not disappoint my hopes.
> For you my heart's delight**
> I burn to such a heat.
>
> Ah, my fair young maiden,
> you must know of my former life.
> You cannot shrink from my coarseness:
> only in such a breast as mine
> could burn a fire so bright.
>
> Ah, my fair young maiden,
> certain it is that in my former life
> I was a trusty pillar
> buried alive for years on end:
> not until today do I see the light of day again.***
>
> Ah, my fair young maiden,
> since I see the light of day again
> I think only of my native home:

for you my heart's delight**
I burn to such a heat.[6]

With his love and expectation for May Fourth China, Guo in 1920 was already thinking of going back to his home country. "After the May Fourth [incident]," he later recalled, "young people in China were driven by their desire for knowledge and vied with each other in rushing abroad. . . . At that time, however, I was thinking of running back to China and thus running to the embrace of my lover [China]."[7]

It should be mentioned that though before his return to China in April 1921 he was mainly excited about May Fourth China, he did occasionally show that he was to a certain extent aware of the dark side of the reality in China. For instance, in his *The Rebirth of the Goddesses* he refers to the civil war at the time between warlords in southern and northern China. With the goddesses in the poem as his symbol of hope, he wants to build a new China, "a China of beauty," on the ruins of the ugly wars between the warlord forces.[8] His awareness of the ugly side of China's reality, however, was superficial, a fact he was soon to discover when he finally went back to his country in April 1921.

His ship arrived in Shanghai on April 3, 1921, an experience he would later describe in the following terms:

> My ship sailed into the mouth of the Huangpu River and the scene on the banks of the river was indeed beautiful. . . . This was the homeland that I had longed for in the past few years and this was the lover for whom I had a burning desire. This, after all, was the place where my soul could be comforted. I leaned on the ship's rail and fell into a trance: I badly wanted to jump into the embrace of my lover—the center of the Huangpu River.[9]

On that day, he also wrote a poem to describe his feeling:

Estuary of the Huangpu

Peaceful village,
land of my fathers,
so green those grassy shores,
so straw-pale the flow of the water.

I lean on the rail and look into the distance:
level like an ocean is the great country,
but for a few heaving willows
not a hill or cliff hinders the view.

The little craft ride up and down,
the men might be in a dream.
Peaceful village,
land of my fathers.[10]

This peaceful and beautiful illusion, however, was soon shattered by the semi-colonial reality of Shanghai. As the ship sailed along, the picture of beauty soon changed before his eyes into an ugly scene of the "noise of factories, coal smoke, steam whistles, cranes, and cigarette commercials.... If those factories were owned by the Chinese . . . , or if I were not born a Chinese in China," he later said, "I might have enjoyed those things as scenes of modernity. Unfortunately, I was a Chinese, just like those beggarlike coolie brothers who were moving about on the banks of the river. . . . Nobody could keep dreaming with his eyes closed when seeing his fellow countrymen groaning under the whips of foreigners, unless he was a running dog of those foreigners. The beautiful scenic picture was ruined by those foreigners!"[11]

He was further depressed after he landed in Shanghai: the people he saw on the streets of the semi-colonial city, the Chinese men and women with their "malnourished faces" and somewhat Western-style dresses, looked in his eyes like "walking corpses" and caused him great repugnance. He felt that he had arrived in a "foreign country."[12] On April 4, one day after his arrival in the city, he wrote the following poem:

My Impression of Shanghai

I have been awakened from my dreams!
    Alas! The sadness of disillusion!

The corpses that are idling about,
    the flesh that is loud and lascivious,
the long robes of men,
    the short sleeves of women,
I see human skeletons everywhere,
    I see streets full of coffins,
people rushing aimlessly,
    people walking aimlessly.
My eyes are weeping with tears,
    my stomach is throwing up
I have been awakened from my dreams.
    Alas! The sadness of disillusion![13]

Then, on April 8, he and his friend Cheng Fangwu, with whom he had returned to China, went on a trip to visit the tourist attraction West Lake in Hangzhou, which is not very far from Shanghai. On their train to Hangzhou they shared a second-class coach with some Westerners, a few Japanese, and a group of Chinese who looked like Shanghai politicians and were accompanied by prostitutes. He found the Chinese in the coach, especially the two prostitutes, very annoying. They were loudly eating, drinking, smoking, teasing, playing poker, and gambling. The Western passengers, in contrast, were all "quiet" and seemed to be seriously reading some documents. As for the Japanese, they were making conversations among themselves and were sometimes looking "very scornfully" at the Chinese politicians and their prostitutes.[14] He was greatly disgusted by his fellow countrymen's behavior before the foreigners and wrote the following in a poem to express his feelings:

> Alas! My rather pathetic fellow Chinese!
> Some of you are just gambling like crazy,
> Some of you are wildly smoking,
> Some of you are drinking cup after cup,
> Some of you are eating dish after dish,
> Some of you are just loudly laughing,
> Some of you are just loudly talking.
> Look please!
> Those serious Westerners over there
> are concentrating on reading their manuscripts!
> Those arrogant Japanese
> are over there laughing at you!
> Ah! My eyes hurt! They hurt!
> My bursting tears are about to break my eyes!
> My rather pathetic fellow Chinese![15]

What he witnessed on the train reminded him of the larger picture of the reality at the time in China's politics and the humiliating status that China had in the international community.[16] Overall, during his several months' stay in China from April to early September 1921, he was disillusioned and depressed by the reality in his country. "Wherever" he went in China, he "felt decadence and oppression" around him.[17] Among other things, he found it difficult to do his literary work under such depressing conditions, and that was one of the reasons he finally decided to go back to Japan in September 1921.[18] His profound disillusionment with China's reality also contributed to the fact that, around 1922, he became increasingly interested in "political issues" in order to tackle China's warlord darkness.[19] His criticism of the warlordism and his political interest is well documented in his writings. In September 1922, for instance, he wrote a series of poems criticizing various "politicians, warlords, bureaucrats, Guomindang [Nationalist Party] members, and educators" in China.[20] In May 1923, he also wrote the following in an article:

> China's political career is now on the verge of bankruptcy. The tyranny of beastly warlords, the stupid actions of shameless politicians, and the oppression by greedy foreign capitalists have made our Chinese nation bleed and cry so hard that our blood and tears are flowing like the Yellow and Yangzi Rivers.
>
> We are exposed to the horrible disasters of wars and chaos and are being tortured by the huge claws of the poisonous dragon of capitalism. We long for peace, we dream of ideals, and we are thirsty for the spring of life. . . .

China's current situation is leading us to two different paths:

First, the path of staying away from the dirty reality, escaping from life, and secluding ourselves in mountains and forests and staying friends with nature;

Second, the path of total struggle, of fighting against the evil society as a valiant fighter of life.

Our spirit teaches us that we should choose the second path.[21]

Since Japan was then the closest threat to China and probably also because Guo himself was studying in Japan and therefore closely feeling the tension between China and Japan, his concerns and worries for his country also were displayed in his anti-Japanese writings. His October 1919 article "On Boycotting Japanese Goods," for instance, was a response to the boycott of Japanese products that had been going on in China as part of the nationalist movement since the May Fourth incident. In that article, he writes at length to explain to his fellow Chinese people that a long-lasting boycott of Japanese goods should and could be carried out in China. First, he notes somewhat sarcastically that since China's armed forces were only good at killing Chinese people and could not defend the country against the Japanese, boycotting Japanese goods turned out to be "the only weapon" for the Chinese people to use in their fight against the Japanese.[22] The Chinese people could live without Japanese goods and therefore could afford to carry on their boycott. He notes also that among the Japanese products consumed in China, three quarters were actually unnecessary "luxuries" and only one quarter were "necessities."[23] He points out that China had consumed so many of those luxuries because the Chinese had a bad habit of indulging in luxury and extravagance. Living without those "luxurious" Japanese products, therefore, was not only possible but would actually help cure their bad habit. As for the Japanese-made "necessities," he argues that China could also do without them since they could be replaced with China's own products or products made by Western countries. Seeing it as a feasible and "vital" way to save China, Guo strongly urges his fellow Chinese to continue boycotting Japanese goods.[24] To encourage his countrymen and to further express his patriotic feelings, he also writes a poem at the end of the article:

As a young man I have worries and concerns
    as deep as the sea,
waves of blood are beating my chest
    and I am about to burst into tears.
Let's start everything with ourselves,
China is us and we are China.[25]

In another article published in October 1919, Guo argues against those Japanese who, with their imperialist interest in China, advocated a closer relationship between China and Japan on the theoretical basis that the Chinese and Japanese shared one language and were of one race. He makes a great effort in a scholarly style to prove, step-by-step, that the Chinese and Japanese languages are different from each other and the Chinese and Japanese peoples are of different races. Further, he suggests that in order to enjoy a friendly relationship with other countries, a country such as Japan needed a policy of "benevolence and justice," and it did not matter that much whether or not it shared a language with others or belonged to the same race as others.[26]

At the end of 1919, Guo also wrote the poem *Ode to the Bandits*. As he later noted, the poem was written to protest the Japanese media's use of "bandit students" to describe China's students who had been playing active and leading roles in the anti-imperialist and anti-Japanese movement in China since the May Fourth incident.[27]

Further, in a letter written in March 1920, he tells his friend Zong Baihua that he had been upset when he saw in Japan at an industrial fair how the Japanese treated Taiwan and Korea as their colonies. What was most unbearable for him was that the Japanese at the fair had set up a section on China's Manchuria and Mongolia that they treated as Japanese colonies.[28] He tells Zong that he felt that what the Japanese were doing at the fair with Manchuria and Mongolia was "humiliating" to China. "Do you think that we should report this to our embassy in Japan and demand that the Japanese close down their section on Manchuria and Mongolia at the fair?" he asks Zong. "Studying here in Japan," he continues, "we are actually reading books by Western foreigners and being bullied by Eastern foreigners [the Japanese]."[29]

In April 1921, he published his article "Coal, Iron, and Japan," in which he points out that Japan depended on China's coal and iron in its development of militarism. To frustrate that militarism, he urges China to cut the supply of coal and iron to Japan. At the same time, he writes, China should make good use of its own resources and develop its own coal and iron industries.[30]

His anti-Japanese feelings were sometimes exacerbated by his continuous unpleasant experiences with the Japanese communities around him when he was living in Japan. In September 1922, for instance, he painfully recounted how Japanese children in his neighborhood had frequently bullied and beaten up his oldest son because he was half Chinese. Partly as a result, his son had developed some psychological problems.[31] In October 1924, Guo described vividly and emotionally how he had been discriminated against and humiliated as a Chinese by a Japanese family from whom he had tried to rent some rooms.[32] Some time later, he also noted that he had "fully experienced various ill-treatment" by the Japanese during his stay in Japan from April to mid-November 1924.[33]

Despite Guo's overall patriotic and anti-Japanese (anti-imperialistic) attitudes before the mid-1920s, he was not without occasional awkwardness in his relationship with his nation, which can be traced to his being influenced by Western individualism. There was, for instance, the conflict between his personal literary interest and the national fashion to study science. On the one hand, ever since his early years in Sichuan, he had been developing a passion for literature. On the other hand, as a patriotic Chinese, Guo shared the popular belief at the time that it was science, not something as impractical as literature, that could revive China in modern times. In fact, when he first went to Japan he was "determined" to "overcome" his own literary tendency and major in medicine, a discipline that was "practical learning" and could be of help in China's modern drive for national wealth and power.[34] Partly due to Western individualist influence, however, he became increasingly assertive about his personal literary interest and eventually chose literary writing over medicine, which, in a sense, did make him somewhat less patriotic.[35] Guo, it should be noted, was not without interest in science. It was just that his interest in science was the result of the influence of a patriotic fashion and was not as deeply rooted as his literary interest, which was based on his personal love for literature.[36] Another example here was the fact that as soon as the crisis of the Twenty-one Demands incident was over, despite his strongly demonstrated patriotism during that crisis, he deeply regretted that he had made his trip back to China, which had taken him ten days and had cost him financially. He was criticized for this trip by his family, especially his oldest brother.[37] In a letter to home, written on June 1, 1915, Guo had this to tell his parents:

> I went to Shanghai once when the Sino-Japanese negotiations were at a tense moment, because at the time it seemed that China and Japan were going to war against each other. I stayed in Shanghai for just three days and then returned to Japan. The whole round trip took me ten days and I deeply regret that I made this mistake of acting rashly. Oldest Brother has also written to criticize me.[38]

After his Sichuan family also blamed him for his costly trip, he wrote the following in a letter dated July 5, 1915:

> It is just as my younger brother pointed out in his letter: the reason I committed the mistake of going to Shanghai is that I was too naive and blindly followed others. I am so ashamed and regret it so much! I regret so much and am so ashamed! I hope that my younger brother will help me ease our Parents' anger over my mistake. It took me ten days to make the trip to Shanghai and back and it was obviously a waste of time. However, I was lucky in that there was no school during these ten days and I didn't miss any lectures. In addition, these ten days also gave me some experiences and lessons. In a material sense, I have inexcusably wasted money by making this trip. In short, even though I am wildly arrogant, from now on how dare I be careless and rash and get my parents and brothers worried again?[39]

One more example was an event that took place in the Chinese student community in Japan. In May 1918, in their protest against a Sino-Japanese military convention that demonstrated Japan's imperialistic interest in China, Chinese students in Japan started a strike.[40] Some of these students also organized an "anti-traitor club," which was aimed at Chinese students with Japanese wives. As Guo later described it, this club was very active at the time. It asked those Chinese students to divorce their Japanese wives immediately. If they failed to comply, it threatened to "treat them with violence." "Quite a few" Chinese students in Tokyo did divorce their Japanese wives. Despite the pressure from the Chinese community, however, Guo kept living with Tomiko. By then he had already lived with her as his common-law wife for a year and a half, and their first son was already five months old. However patriotic he was, he simply found that his love for Tomiko and their family life, for which he had suffered so much to obtain and justify, was too precious for him as an individual to give up. This naturally made him a "traitor" in the eyes of his fellow patriotic Chinese students. Luckily for him, the "anti-traitor club" was not as active where he lived in the countryside as in Tokyo, and he was thus spared the "violence" that the club had threatened.[41]

The Chinese students' strike lasted for about two weeks. Then a decision was made within the Chinese community that all of the students should return to China as a further protest against Japanese imperialism. As Guo later remembered, some of those who had money did return to China, while he had to support his wife and son with his limited scholarship money and could not afford to go back. Not being able to perform the "patriotic" act of returning to China, then, made him a double "traitor" among the Chinese students. With his sensitivity and pride, this discrimination against him within the Chinese community had greatly added to his depression and pain. As he later described it, being treated as a "traitor" had made him "weep with many tears."[42]

THE MID-1920s: DEDICATION TO SAVING CHINA THROUGH COMMUNIST REVOLUTION

As Guo became increasingly ready to focus on collective (national and world) issues around 1924, one major event caught his attention: the crisis of China's textile industries since the end of the First World War. During the war, Western powers were busy fighting each other and their economies were being ruined. As a result, there was at that time less Western economic interest in China, fostering a relatively favorable environment in which to develop China's native industries. Soon after the war, however, those powers found the time and energy to return to China and increasingly threatened the country's newly grown native industries. A noticeable fact in this regard was that since 1922 part of China's textile industry had been crushed by overwhelming foreign competition.[43] When Guo went to Japan in April 1924, that is, before he read Kawakami Hajime's version of Marxism, he "had already heard that China's textile industries had the tendency of going bankrupt."[44] Then, when he returned to Shanghai in November of that year, he noticed that "all the new cotton mills [in Shanghai] had closed down one after another."[45] This textile industry crisis profoundly added to his doubt about China's chance of successfully developing its own capitalist economy in the modern imperialist world.[46]

Analyzing China's situation with his recently acquired Marxist/Leninist perspective, he writes in 1925:

> Under China's current conditions, is it at all possible for individual capitalism to develop in our country? In other words, is it possible for China to develop a few tycoons to compete against big, foreign capitalists? . . . You economists who sing the praises of individual capitalism: please open your eyes and look at the reality! Most of China's textile capitalists have failed! All the cotton mills that were newly built and prospering during the world war have closed down one after another! . . . If we still lived in the times of Adam Smith, or if our China were isolated from the outside world, or if the war in Europe [WWI] had lasted for over a hundred years, or if we Chinese could keep boycotting Japanese goods for over a hundred years, then, with the free growth of the seeds of individual capitalism in our vast and resource-rich China, we might in a hundred years reach where Britain and America are today . . . Regrettably, however, our China has started too late in its development and those Europeans have ceased fire too early in their fighting for [the world] market! . . . [47]

> Just exactly what is the status of we Chinese in today's world? Our China now is an important market for capitalist countries throughout the whole world. Then what is the situation of the capitalists in the capitalist countries? They have already been as well developed as giant trees with "bronze-colored branches and rocklike roots." Those towering trees are now growing over our China. How could our saplings [beginning capitalists] compete with those trees? . . .

> Here is a big lesson for us!: individual capitalism has no hope of developing in today's China, even if such capitalism is "in best accordance with the nature of humanity"![48]

The May Thirtieth incident also made a huge impact on Guo, helping bring home to him the painful reality of China's oppression by foreign imperialist powers and the urgency for the country to fight back against those powers. On May 30, 1925, Chinese students and masses gathered in Shanghai's foreign concessions to protest the killing of a Chinese worker by the management of a Japanese cotton-weaving factory in Shanghai. Foreign police at the concessions opened fire on the protesters, killing at least ten and wounding several dozens. This incident greatly angered the Chinese people and triggered a nationwide movement in China against foreign imperialism. Guo happened to have been at the scene of the incident in Shanghai shortly after foreign police opened fire on the protesters. Even though he arrived at the scene after the bodies of the killed had been moved away and the blood on the street had been washed off, he was still in time to witness foreign police beating and intimidating the protesters and bystanders. He himself was once also threatened by the police. As he later said, the brutality of the foreign police against his fellow Chinese angered him so much that he thought several times of fighting the police himself.[49]

Soon after the incident on June 16, 1925, he wrote the following in his article "Roar with Rage for the Tragic May Thirtieth Incident":

> My fellow Chinese, we should know that the imperialists' inhumane oppression of us started long before the May Thirtieth [incident] and, apart from the martyrs of the May Thirtieth, there have been many of us Chinese murdered invisibly by those imperialists.... We should have awakened a long time ago. It is the May Thirtieth's martyrs who have sounded the alarm for us and have quickly awoken us. We should realize that it is now a critical moment for our Chinese nation.... Let's quickly take real action to save our country.[50]

In a speech to a Shanghai college in August 1925, he further noted that the May Thirtieth movement's slogan "down with imperialism and abrogate all unequal treaties" was "most significant" at the time. "Nowadays," he said, "imperialists are really our major enemy. To save ourselves, we have to defeat them."[51] Guo also was deeply touched and encouraged by the heroic struggle that the Chinese people put up against foreign imperialists during and after the May Thirtieth incident. His drama "Nie Ying," for instance, was directly inspired by the story of a young college student who was wounded in the incident and was cared for by his sister in the hospital. Guo finished writing the drama within two weeks after the incident and with his active involvement the drama was soon performed by some Shanghai college students as an effort to support the Shanghai workers' anti-imperialist struggle.[52] In his "Roar with Rage for the Tragic May Thirtieth Incident," he also writes optimistically:

> The brutal killing of our numerous fellow Chinese by the British in the tragic May Thirtieth incident has stirred up our people's morale to an unprecedented level. With this high morale of our people, weeping our blood out in grief and indignation over the tragedy, we see the light of hope and feel that our Chinese nation still has a bright future. Having always been called a sleeping lion, our country is now really awake.[53]

Guo during this period also was further exposed to the darkness of China's warlordism. In December 1924 he visited some rural areas in Jiangsu and Zhejiang provinces. The visit was arranged by some of his friends for him to participate in an investigation of the disastrous results of a war fought between some warlords in the areas earlier that year.[54] As he later recalled, the visit not only let him see the damages caused by the war but also helped him "deeply realize" how "destitute" people were and how "severely" peasants were being "squeezed" by their landlords in rural areas in southern China.[55]

The problem of China's warlordism, as Guo saw it, was nothing but a by-product of foreign imperialism. Imperialist powers financially supported China's warlords, and those powers provided the warlords with their arms and ammunition.

Further, the "lackey soldiers" of the warlords also were a result of foreign imperial-ism. The imperialist powers had "suppressed" and "exploited" China and had crushed the country's native handicraft industries by dumping their products on its market. This had made many people in China "fall to poverty" and "lose their jobs." Some of these people had further become "vagrants" and in order to survive joined warlord forces to fight for limited resources.[56]

To add to Guo's resentment against foreign imperialism and the darkness of warlord China, there also came the March Eighteenth incident.[57] On March 18, 1926, about five thousand Chinese held a meeting in Beijing to protest a Japanese attack on China's Dagukou Fort at Tianjin earlier in the month and subsequent imperialist demands made to the Chinese government by Japan and some other foreign powers. In its cracking down on the protesters, China's warlord govern-ment killed at least forty and wounded over one hundred. In a speech to students at Guangdong University on March 30, 1926, Guo reflected on the incident, which had taken place when he was on his way from Shanghai to Guangzhou:

> Those martyrs in Beijing have died! However, their spirit and their contribu-tions to the history of revolution truly merit our remembrance. They have made two contributions to the history of revolution: First, they showed us that we rev-olutionaries are not afraid of dying in the struggle against evil forces. . . . Second, [their struggle and death] has made people see the real nature of the treasonous warlords and therefore people will fight against those warlords . . . The Beijing martyrs have died! Those of us who are still alive should strive to complete our national revolution! . . . We should work to make the Northern Expedition hap-pen. We should know that in the situation of today's China it is no use simply getting rid of one or two warlords or imperialists. [To save China], we must completely overthrow all the evil forces and go through thorough reforms! To achieve that, the national government has to send troops north . . . to fight into Beijing, seize back all political powers and return them to the people.[58]

To save China from imperialism and warlordism, Guo now firmly believed that a Communist revolution had to take place in the country. As will be elaborated on in the next chapter, he had concluded with his newly learned Marxist/Leninist theory that modern imperialism was the extension and "internationalization" of capitalism. To defeat imperialism and save China, therefore, the country needed to participate in the global Communist battle to thoroughly uproot capitalism and imperialism. Since warlordism in China was a by-product of foreign impe-rialism and the elimination of warlordism therefore depended on the defeat of imperialism, a Leninist anti-imperialist revolution was also a must for the country to rid itself of the evils of the warlords.[59]

Ready to commit himself to the cause of saving his nation through Com-munist revolution, Guo took action. In late February 1926, an opportunity arose for him to go to Guangdong, which had long attracted him as a center of revolutionary activities.[60] Being offered the position of dean of the School of Liberal Arts by Guangdong University, he left Shanghai on March 18, 1926 to take the job.[61] Soon after arriving in Guangdong, he became involved in the revolutionary movement there and applied to join the Chinese Communist Party.[62] Though for some reason the party did not immediately accept him, it did give him the assignment of joining the Northern Expedition as chief of the propaganda section of the political department of the revolutionary army.[63] He joined the expedition in July 1926. It was in the middle of this military campaign, which he joined as a first step in China's Communist revolution, that the Communist Party accepted him as a member in August 1927.[64]

Figure 1. Guo Moruo's father and mother

Figure 2. Guo Moruo in 1897 with his parents and siblings in their hometown. Guo Moruo is the first child from the left in the front row.

Figure 3. Guo Moruo in 1910 in middle school in Chengdu

Figure 4. Guo Moruo with the faculty and students of the Medical School of Kyushu Imperial University at Fukuoka, Japan. Guo Moruo is the second from the left in the second front row.

Figure 5. Guo Moruo and some of his fellow Chinese students in Japan. Guo is the second from the right.

Figure 6. Guo Moruo in 1919–1920

Figure 7. Guo Moruo and his Creation Society colleagues.
Guo stands in the middle.

Figure 8. Guo Moruo, Tomiko, and three of their children in 1923

CHAPTER 3

Toward the Liberation of Mankind

While saving China was an urgent matter for Guo, he was by no means converting to Communism merely for the sake of saving his nation. Ever since his early
years and certainly during the May Fourth period, he had always had in his mind
a Confucian cosmopolitanist ideal of harmonizing the world that transcended his
concerns for his nation.[1] What came to strongly attract him in Communism was,
among others, the cosmopolitanist paradise that Marx had promised. With great
excitement, Guo in the mid-1920s came to believe that the Marxist cosmopolitanist ideal was identical to his Confucian cosmopolitanist dream of Great Harmony (*datong*). The achievement of the Marxist ideal, therefore, would mean the
modern achievement of his traditional goal. Most important, the modern social
science of Marxism/Leninism seemed to have made it within reach to eventually
achieve a cosmopolitanist world of Communism. As demonstrated by the success
of the 1917 Soviet revolution, there finally seemed to be a powerful and an effective means—the Marxist/Leninist revolution—to realize step-by-step for Guo the
traditional Confucian dream of *datong* in the modern world, hence his conversion
to Communism.

A MAY FOURTH COSMOPOLITANIST IDEAL OF *DATONG*: A PASTORAL/PRIMITIVE PARADISE

The Datong *Ideal*

Guo's May Fourth cosmopolitanism can be seen in his 1920 poem *Good Morning*.
While greeting his May Fourth motherland with love, Guo in that poem also passionately expresses his greetings to a world way beyond the boundary of his nation:
a world that ranges from vast geographic areas around the globe to people and historical figures in other cultures.[2] In April 1920, he also wrote the poem *The Lessons
of the Cannons*, in which he imagines that once in a dream he had a conversation
with Russian novelist and thinker Count Leo Nikolaevich Tolstoy (1828–1910). In

this dream conversation, he affirms his faith in Tolstoy's cosmopolitanist idea that "the whole world is our family" and "all mankind is our kinsfolk."[3] Further, in August 1921, he wrote the poem *A Wild Song for Revolution of the Universe* where instead of merely talking about a revolution for his motherland, China, he enthusiastically praises and advocates a revolution of the whole "universe."[4]

Guo's May Fourth cosmopolitanist concerns were specifically demonstrated in his sympathy toward the oppression and exploitation that many peoples suffered at the hands of imperialist powers and his criticism of the evil and destructiveness made manifest by the First World War.

He felt strongly for oppressed peoples all over the world whose experiences in one way or another reminded him of the Chinese people's struggle and suffering in his own time. For at least two weeks in October 1920, for instance, his attention was occupied by the hunger strike of Terence MacSwiney, a leader of the Irish Republican Army who had been arrested and imprisoned by the British government since the middle of August 1920 and who for seventy-three days refused to eat while incarcerated until he died on October 25 of that year. From October 13 to 27, closely following the Japanese media's coverage of MacSwiney's condition in prison and his eventual death, Guo wrote "with hot tears" the four-part poem *Victorious in Death* to express his admiration for MacSwiney's patriotism and heroism and his anger over the British government's treatment of him.[5] The major portion of the poem's last part, written on October 27 after MacSwiney's death, reads as follows:

> The mighty ocean is sobbing its sad lament,
> the boundless abyss of the sky is red with weeping,
> far, far away the sun has sunk in the west.
> Brave, tragic death! Death in a blaze of glory! Triumphal procession of a victor!
>   Victorious death!
> Impartial God of Death! I am grateful to you! You have saved the MacSwiney
>   for whom my love and reverence know no bounds!
> MacSwiney, fighter for freedom, you have shown how great can be the power
>   of the human will!
> I am grateful to you, I extol you; freedom can henceforth never die!
> The night has closed down on us, but how bright is the moon.[6]

Another event in October 1920 also caught his attention. At an international convention in Tokyo, an elderly Korean Christian pastor was rudely cut short in his speech when he talked about the suffering and misery of his fellow Korean people under the colonial rule of the Japanese. Guo was greatly angered by this incident and wrote the poem *A White Sheep amongst Wolves* to express his feelings. In the poem, he describes the Korean pastor as a peaceful sheep and refers to the international participants at the convention who had improperly treated the Korean pastor as a group of wolves who represented the imperialist powers at the time in the international community. With great emotion, he cries that the imperialist powers, the "wolves" of the international community who were bullying others, should be dealt with by "bombs," "rifle[s]," "swords," and violence.[7]

The First World War was a major world crisis that caught Guo's attention, and he started reflecting on the disaster of the war soon after its ending. In his 1921 article "Coal, Iron, and Japan," for instance, he takes time to point out that, in his opinion, the result of the war was simply a case of "having one tyranny replaced by another." The victors of the war, as he describes them, were nothing but another group of "robbers" in the world.[8] Then, in May 1923, as early as a year before announcing his conversion to Marxism, he already concludes in "On Chinese and German Cultures" that World War I was "a natural result of extreme capitalism." "A thinker with foresight [Marx] had already asserted categorically before the war that capitalism was bound to bring disasters to mankind." "After the breakout of the war," Guo continues, "a great practitioner [Lenin] further acted quickly to overthrow capitalism as the evil cause of the war." "Marx and Lenin," he notes, "are after all great figures who we young people should admire and worship."[9] As discussed later, it was partly along this line of reflection on the war that he would develop his interest in Marxism and Leninism and eventually decide on Communism as the solution to what he saw as a world crisis caused by the evil of capitalism.

To save the world (which included not only all oppressed countries but also peoples of the West) from its sufferings and crises Guo, before 1924, held the goal of reaching an ideal that would be modelled after an ancient society that he believed to have existed in China before the Three Dynasties of Xia (twenty-first through sixteenth centuries ? B.C.), Shang (sixteenth through eleventh centuries ? B.C.), and Western Zhou (eleventh century-771 B.C.).[10] This society was for him, among other things, the opposite of the private ownership, greed, and aggressiveness of modern capitalism and imperialism, which he vaguely but increasingly saw as a major cause of the problems of the modern world. In this ancient society, he writes in "The Pompeii of Chinese Intellectual History," the state was born as a result of "people's contracts," and political institutions were "democratic" by nature.[11] The guiding "political ideology" at the time was one that was "people oriented" and had "a standard of universal love and universal benefit." There was no hereditary rule, and leaders were selected by the people on the basis of their merit and ability.[12] The ancient society also featured a "naive objective idealism" ("Naive, Objectiver Idealismus") and a "worldview" that was "active," "evolutionary," and "metaphysical."[13] In that society, there was "an idealism that was egalitarian and against differences." Under the guidance of such idealism, "all individuals were naturally equal to each other and all the land of the country naturally belonged to the whole of the people."[14] The "nine-square system [of land ownership] that started under Huang Di's rule," Guo notes, "was really the earliest practice of communism" in China.[15] In his November 1922 "The Two Princes of Guzhu," Guo also describes people in the ancient society as "free" and "pure," enjoying a world without private property and the boundaries of states. That society had little government except for a few "virtuous" leaders who had been "elected" as public servants by "the majority of the people."[16]

For Guo, the ancient ideal society was what Confucius referred to as the world of the Great Harmony (*datong*), whose existence and collapse Confucius[17] describes in the following, found in the Li Yun chapter of the *Li Ji* (*Book of Rites*):

> When the Grand course was pursued, a public and common spirit ruled all under the sky; they chose men of talents, virtue, and ability; their words were sincere, and what they cultivated was harmony. Thus men did not love their parents only, nor treat as children only their own sons. A competent provision was secured for the aged till their death, employment for the able-bodied, and the means of grow-ing up to the young. They showed kindness and compassion to widows, orphans, childless men, and those who were disabled by disease, so that they were all suf-ficiently maintained. Males had their proper work, and females had their homes. [They accumulated] articles [of value], disliking that they should be thrown away upon the ground, but not wishing to keep them for their own gratification. [They labored] with their strength, disliking that it should not be exerted, but not exert-ing it [only] with a view to their own advantage. In this way [selfish] schemings were repressed and found no development. Robbers, filchers, and rebellious trai-tors did not show themselves, and hence the outer doors remained open, and were not shut. This was [the period of] what we call the Great Harmony.*
>
> Now that the Grand course has fallen into disuse and obscurity, the kingdom is a family inheritance. Everyone loves [above all others] his own parents and cherishes [as] children [only] his own sons. People accumulate articles and exert their strength for their own advantage. Great men imagine it is the rule that their states should descend in their own families. Their object is to make the walls of their cities and suburbs strong and their ditches and moats secure. The rules of propriety and of what is right are regarded as the threads by which they seek to maintain in its correctness the relation between ruler and minister; in its generous regard that between father and son; in its harmony that between elder brother and younger; and in a community of sentiment that between husband and wife; and in accordance with them they frame buildings and measures; lay out the fields and hamlets [for the dwellings of the husbandmen]; adjudge the superiority to men of valor and knowledge; and regulate their achievements with a view to their own advantage. Thus it is that [selfish] schemes and enterprises are constantly taking their rise, and recourse is had to arms; and thus it was [also] that Yu, Tang, Wen and Wu, King Cheng, and [the] duke of Zhou obtained their distinction.[18]

Confucius's description here, Guo comments, "best illustrates the transition from the system of public ownership to that of private ownership in China's history" at the beginning of the Three Dynasties. He especially notes that Confucius was actually pointing out that "the system of private ownership was the cause of all conflicts."[19] Guo notes that what Confucius wrote, as a document in history, was "most valuable" and never "to be obliterated."[20] Based on what Confucius said here and in some other Chinese classics, Guo develops a theory that China, at the beginning of the Xia Dynasty, went through a "profound transition" from the ancient ideal society to the country's "first dark age"—the Three Dynasties. In that transition, the "metaphysical" and "energetic" worldview of the ancient society changed into "stagnant," "theological," and "religious" thinking; the "public ownership" and "democracy" in the ancient society changed into "private ownership" and "theocracy"; and the ancient spirit that featured "liberty" and "original creation" was lost under the tyranny of "political and religious autocracy."[21]

It is important to note that Guo's longing for a society that would be modelled after the ancient Great Harmony demonstrated his wish not only for an egalitarian world of public ownership, democracy, and liberty but also for a utopia (of course, Guo did not see it as a utopia) of rural, ancient, and natural harmony and simplicity, an ideal that revealed his profound urge to escape from the urban, industrial, commercial, and materialist mess of modern life.

Guo, it must be pointed out, was not without occasional interest in industrial and urban modernity. In a poem in June 1920, for instance, he writes:

Panorama from Fudetate Yama

Pulse of the great city,
surge of life,
beating, panting, roaring,
spurting, flying, leaping,
the whole sky covered with a pall of smoke:
my heart is ready to leap from my mouth.
Hills, roofs, surge on,
wave after wave they well up before me.
Symphony of myriad sounds,
marriage of man and Nature.
The curve of the bay might be Cupid's bow,
man's life his arrow, shot over the sea.
Dark and misty coastline, steamers at anchor,
steamers in motion, steamers unnumbered,
funnel upon funnel bearing its black peony.
Ah! Emblem of the Twentieth Century!
Stern mother of modern civilization![22]

In "Coal, Iron, and Japan," he also notes that "human beings are part of nature and the civilized creation of human beings is part of the overall creation by nature." In his eyes, therefore, "not only are mountains, rivers, flowers, and birds beauties of nature, but chimneys and railway tracks [as creations of human beings] are also decorations for the natural world." It is wrong, he writes, for some people to argue that modern industrialization has ruined the scenery of nature.[23]

His scattered praises for the modern material development of industrialization and urbanization, however, were often overshadowed by his consistent love for pastoral, ancient, and even primitive innocence and simplicity, which can be traced to his influence by the Confucian rural mentality, Taoism's teaching of a return to nature and its social ideal of primitivism, and Goethe's Romanticist celebration of pastoral and primitive life.[24] In the poems that he wrote on his tour from Shanghai to West Lake in April 1921, for instance, one can see his longing to escape from the busy and noisy life of the modern city and find peace in the simple and innocent country life of working peasants:

Notes on a Tour to the Western Lake

...

I am a son of "nature,"
I want to fly into my mother's arms!

...

Shanghai, you burning jail!
I am again leaving and abandoning you.

...

By the foot of the Leifeng Pagoda
there is an old man hoeing the fields,
he has taken off his cotton-padded coat
and hung it on a branch of a young mulberry.
He has stopped hoeing,
and raised his eyes to look at me.
Ah, his kind and amiable eyes,
his healthy yellow face,
his graying beard,
his veined and gold-colored hands.
I want to kneel down in front of him,
and call him: "my father!"
and lick all the yellow mud off his feet.[25]

Guo's admiration for pastoral life and peasants also can be seen in his "Coal, Iron, and Japan." In that article, while making some argument, he quotes Goethe in the following passage from *Faust*, whose high opinion of farming life he obviously shared:

... A recipe
that takes no money, magic, or physician:
Go out at once into the country
and set to hoeing and to digging;
confine yourself—and your thoughts too—

within the narrowest spheres;
subsist on food that's plain and simple,
live with your cattle as their peer, and don't disdain
to fertilize in person fields that you will reap.
Take my word for it, there's no better way
to remain young until you're eighty.[26]

In the same article, Guo also quotes the following section from *The Cotter's Saturday Night* by Robert Burns (1759–1796), whom he praises as "the most sincere poet in the world" and "Britain's Tao Yuanming," whose "description of peasants' life" very much touches his heart:

At length his lonely cot appears in view,
Beneath the shelter of an aged tree;
Th'expectant wee things, toddlin'stacher
through,
To meet their dad, wi'flichterin noise and
glee,
His wee bit ingle, blinking bonnily,
His elean hearthstane, his thrifte witie's
smile,
This lisping infant prattling on his knee,
Does a' his weary kiaugh and care beguile,
And makes him puite forget his labor and
toil.[27]

In his poem *The Lessons of the Cannons*, Guo also notes that he strongly agrees with Tolstoy's "advocacy of simple and plain life" and Tolstoy's belief that "it would be ideal if all people are like peasants."[28] He also had noted that he was "rather deeply attracted" to Zhuang Zi's "simple and plain life" in ancient rural times.[29] The extreme of his worship of peasants and their working life, then, is seen in the poem he published on *Shi Shi Xin Bao's Xue Deng* on September 7, 1920, *A Fragrant Noon*:

Fragrance!
Does it come from the pine trees with the wind?
Is it the scent of the sea?
Or is it from the silver light of the white sand?
Ah, where does this fragrance of muck come from?
Geluo! Geluo,
Geluo! Geluo.
A muck cart,
is coming through the pine forest.

A girl is pushing the cart from behind,
her old father is pulling the cart in front.
Geluo! Geluo,
Geluo! Geluo.

Fragrance?
The muck is fragrant!
The sweat and blood [of the girl and old man] is fragrant,
the golden mud on the old man's feet is fragrant!
The girl's rosy face is fragrant![30]

Guo's admiration for the simplicity and innocence of primitive life is, for example, expressed in the preface to his translation of *The Sorrows of Young Werther*, in which he specifically notices that he has found himself in agreement with Goethe's admiration for the simple and pure life of primitive people and for the life of peasants. "The life of primitive people," he writes, "was the simplest and purist and it was the most harmonious with nature." People like Goethe who "worshiped and praised nature," therefore, were "bound to admire the primitive life." He notices that Goethe also greatly admired the simple, self-sufficient, and rewarding life of farmers. Only people like farmers and those of primitive times, he comments, "had the utmost integrity, made the most reverent efforts, and experienced the most passionate love," and only they "could completely go all out in doing everything." They are "models" of the philosophy of concentrating on "the instant" and of "the life of the complete self."[31]

His passion for the primitive age also is found in the poem he published in November 1919, *Dawn*, which describes the joy in a "restored" "paradise." In that poem he carefully sets the scene of his paradise in "the forest of remote antiquity" of an "isolated island," clearly indicating his admiration for some primitive and innocent life that was removed from modern civilizations. "Forest of remote antiquity! Forest of remote antiquity!" he writes in the poem, "We want to make our home in your arms. We want to make our home in your arms."[32]

His desire to escape from modern sophistication and his admiration for simple and plain life also were related to his love for nature and his desire to live a life close to nature, which can be seen in a poem that he wrote in December 1919:

O Earth, My Mother

. . .

O earth, my mother,
through past, present, future
you are food, apparel, shelter for me;
how can I repay the benefits you have bestowed upon me?

O earth, my mother,
henceforth I shall seclude myself less indoors;

in the midst of this opening up of waste lands
I would fulfill my filial duty to you.

. . .

O earth, my mother,
I do not wish to fly in the air,
nor ride in carts, on horseback, wear socks or put on shoes,
I only wish to go barefoot, ever closer to you.[33]

In the preface to his translation of *The Sorrows of Young Werther*, Guo also expresses his agreement with Goethe's "praise of nature." Goethe, he writes, considered nature an "expression of God" and "took nature as a loving mother, a friend, a lover, and a teacher." Goethe "loved and worshiped nature and nature gave him endless love, comfort, inspiration, and nourishment. As a result, he was against techniques, against established ethics, against class systems, against existing religions, and against all learning."[34]

The Cosmopolitan World and the Individual and the Cosmopolitan World and the Nation

It is necessary to pay some attention here to Guo's May Fourth thought on the relationship between the cosmopolitan world and the individual and that between the cosmopolitan world and the nation.

THE INDIVIDUAL AND THE COSMOPOLITAN WORLD

Guo's May Fourth thinking on the relationship between the whole human race (the cosmopolitan world) and the individual can be approached from two angles. First, from a cosmopolitanist angle, Guo held what may be called a "personalistic cosmopolitanism," which strove for a collective, worldwide harmony but at the same time allowed the fullest development of individuals. Second, from the angle of the individual, Guo held what may be called a "cosmopolitanist personalism." This personalism emphasized the development of the self, but its ultimate purpose was to benefit the whole mankind. Whichever way one looks, the individual in his system always had the Confucian cosmopolitanist perspective of being an integral part of the human race. In "Coal, Iron, and Japan," for instance, Guo notes that the purpose of developing people's "individual gifts" and "expanding the energy of the individual" is to promote "the life of evolution of the whole of mankind."[35] In his September 1920 *Wild Cherry Blossoms*, he further expresses willingness to sacrifice the self for the collective of mankind by making Nie Ying, one of his two heroic characters in the poetic drama, say the following: "Right now all our sisters and brothers under heaven are suffering bitterly in their lives. It will be our ultimate happiness if we can save them from their sufferings with the sacrifice of our own individual lives."[36]

Such May Fourth cosmopolitanist thinking by Guo was related to his influence by pantheism, which identifies all things in the cosmos on a divine basis. Roughly speaking, pantheism affected Guo's thinking on the relationship between the individual and the universe in two ways. First, by identifying the individual with things beyond and larger than his self, pantheism prepares one for a transcendence of the self. As Guo puts it, according to pantheism, the "expansion of the self" is just an "active way" to reach the ultimate goal of being "selfless." Once one becomes "selfless," he "will transcend all time, space, life, and death" and "be integrated with God," whose expression is all that is in the universe.[37] Such pantheistic thinking is in a way consistent with his willingness to sacrifice his self for a cosmopolitanist cause, as expressed in *Wild Cherry Blossoms*. Second, pantheism in a sense relates the individual directly to the ultimate collective of mankind and the universe and to a certain extent devalues and even bypasses lesser collectives, such as society, in between the individual and the universe. As a result, with his direct identification with and transcendence to the ultimate collective, the individual is relatively emancipated and feels less intimidated in his relation with the lesser collectives. This pantheistic promotion and assertion of the individual can be seen in Guo's poem *Heavenly Dog*, which literally equates him, the "heavenly dog," to the "total of all the energy in the universe."[38] Identifying himself in such a pantheistic fashion with the ultimate being and existence, he should feel empowered at the time when he confronts the lesser collective of *lijiao* society on the issue of his arranged marriage.

Interestingly, the cosmopolitanist/pantheistic transcendence of the self and pantheistic/cosmopolitanist assertion of the self took place simultaneously in Guo's case: his willingness to sacrifice his self for the cause of the ultimate collective of the cosmopolitan world was expressed in *Wild Cherry Blossoms* in late 1920, a time when he was at the peak of asserting his self against the Confucian *lijiao* society.

THE COSMOPOLITAN WORLD AND THE NATION

Maintaining his *datong* ideal meant that Guo always carried a cosmopolitanist perspective to his concerns for his nation. This can be seen, for instance, in the cosmopolitanist approach with which he makes his argument in "Coal, Iron, and Japan" about China's cutting its supply of coal and iron to the Japanese. Despite his patriotic and sometimes ethnic resentment against the Japanese, he writes, "If Japan purchases our coal and iron for industrial development and for the benefit of mankind, then in broad perspective it could be our obligation as part of mankind to forever supply Japan with those materials."[39] After all, China should use its rich coal and iron resources to "greatly contribute to mankind and world civilization."[40] What was wrong with the Japanese was that instead of using China's coal and iron to benefit the "whole human race," they were using those materials to "build warships and make weapons to satisfy their militarist ambitions" and to bully the Chinese and jeopardize peace in East Asia. It was, therefore, for the broad purpose of safeguarding "long-lasting peace in East Asia" and "contributing to the happiness of the whole of mankind," as well as for protecting China's national interest, that China should make good use of its own natural resources and cut the supply of coal and iron to militarist Japan.[41]

Guo's May Fourth cosmopolitanist transcendence of nationalist concerns was probably best seen in his 1923 "Nations and Transcending Nations," which amounts to a cosmopolitanist criticism of problems caused by nationalism. In that article, he describes nations as "man-made institutions" and notes that such institutions have gradually become "the prisons of mankind" in the process of historical development. He profoundly regrets that nations fight each other for nationalist interests. To support his argument, he quotes *La Clarte*, by French novelist Henri Barbusse (1873–1935), whose reflection on the disastrous fighting among Western nations during World War I had obviously influenced him. While criticizing selfish nationalism and praising cosmopolitanism, however, Guo as a Confucianist did manage to leave a legitimate space for the nation. According to traditional Chinese thinking, he writes toward the end of the article, nations should not be "abandoned," even though people's ultimate goal is to achieve a cosmopolitanist world. With the Confucian ideal of managing the state and harmonizing the world, which he strongly promotes, nation building is a necessary stage toward the realization of the cosmopolitanist goal.[42]

The Cosmopolitanist Ideal and a "Mentality of Extremes"

In Guo's May Fourth longing for the ideal of a perfect, cosmopolitanist Great Harmony one can see what Chang Hao calls a "mentality of extremes." As Chang puts it, because of the "political and cultural crises" in China in the 1920s and 1930s, there existed among some Chinese a mentality of seeing things in terms of two extremes: on the one hand, there was the extreme of the "darkness" and "death" of the reality of the time; on the other hand, there was the extreme of an "eagerly expected" future, whose "light" and "rebirth" would contrast sharply with the dark reality.[43] Such mentality often was expressed in Guo's May Fourth writings. In his letter to a friend in July 1920, for instance, Guo writes: "I have suffered a lot and I have witnessed too much darkness. What I need now is salvation and light."[44] In his poetic drama *Rebirth of the Goddesses*, he repeatedly lets his goddesses sing the following:

> I will go forth and create new light,
>
> . . .
>
> I will go forth and create a new sun
>
> . . .
>
> We will create a new sun,
>
> . . .
>
> Let our newly created sun issue forth,
> then will it shine through all the inner world and the outer.
>
> . . .
>
> We desire to embrace all things.
> Let us sing a song of welcome to the newly created sun.
>
> . . .
>
> Sun, although you are still far away,
> sun, although you are still far away,

now the morning bell can be heard pealing in the sea:
ding-dong, ding-dong, ding-dong!

Ten thousand golden arrows shoot at the Wolf of Heaven;
the Wolf of Heaven grieves in the dark.
Now the funeral knell can be heard in the sea:
ding-dong, ding-dong, ding-dong!

We wish to quaff a stoup of wine.
Drink to the everlasting life of our new sun.[45]

Further, at the end of the drama, he lets a "stage manager" appear and make the following speech to the audience:

Ladies and gentlemen, you have become tired of living in the fetid gloom of this dark world. You surely thirst for light. Your poet, having dramatized so far, writes no more. He has, in fact, fled beyond the sea to create new light and heat. Ladies and gentlemen, do you await the appearance of a new sun? You are bid to create it for yourselves. We will meet again under the new sun.[46]

This longing for the "new sun," as well as light-versus-darkness mentality, one may argue, was one of the reasons Guo would eventually be attracted to the Marxist, perfectionist ideal of cosmopolitanist Communism, which he was to consider the modern scientific version of the traditional Confucian dream of *datong*.

The Means to Achieve the Ideal: Leftist Radicalism to Save the World?

Guo, during the May Fourth period, was increasingly interested in Leftist radicalism and in the use of revolution, force, and violence as the means to quickly achieve his goal of saving the world, which was partly a result of the frustration and impatience that he felt over the contrast between the extremes of the dark reality and the perfect future for which he was hoping. This interest in radicalism, though not yet consistent, was to eventually lead to his commitment in the mid-1920s to Marxist/ Leninist revolution as the means to reach his cosmopolitanist ideal.

Guo's May Fourth radical tendency can be seen, for instance, in *Ode to the Bandits*, in which he enthusiastically salutes various "bandits" of a wide range of revolutions.[47] In *I Am an Idolater*, he also notes that he worships "blood," "bombs," and "destruction."[48] In *Wild Cherry Blossoms*, then, he lets the heroine in the poetic drama sing the following to her brother:

I expect that your fresh red blood
will blossom into flowers of liberty
all over China![49]

In his 1920 poem *A White Sheep amongst Wolves* he also expresses the idea that "bombs,""rifle[s],"and"swords" should be used against imperialist powers in the world.[50] Then, in his *My Prose Poem*, also published in 1920, he writes the following:

The Wails of the Earth

In the past few nights I kept hearing a loud crying from the earth:

"I am in pain! I am in pain! I am being trampled by the whole bunch of you unambitious villains and thieves and I can not bear it any more. I do not believe that there won't be another Chen She and Wu Guang among us [to stand up and rebel against you]."[51]

Perhaps his celebration of revolution is best seen in the poem that he wrote in August 1921 as a preface for his friend Zhu Qianzhi's (朱謙之) (1899–1972) book *The Philosophy of Revolution*:

A Wild Song for Revolution in the Universe

. . .

A great hint—the Yellow River! The Yangzi River!
I have traveled across the bloody surge of the Yellow Sea,
the blood that you have poured out from your bodies,
has colored the water of that sea red!
The inhabitants of the Yellow and Yangzi Rivers:
your eyes have been blinded by that overwhelming pressure?
You don't even get such a visible, bold, and great hint?

. . .

Quick! Add a bit more blood into those rivers of blood!
Quick! Add a bit more blood into that sea of blood!
Let the bloody surge of the Yellow River
color all the seawater red in the whole world!
It is the spirit of revolution that is the existence of the whole universe!

The universe is nothing but a movement!
The universe is nothing but a mind-heart!
The mind-heart is a bomb!
The explosive in that bomb is a true feeling!
That true feeling is the spirit of revolution!
It just takes us a throw [of the bomb]!
and this huge universe
will burst into clouds of fresh red fire!
Throw! Throw! Throw!
Destroy these sand-based buildings of ours![52]

Guo's interest in revolution and violence, it should be noted, can be traced to his early experiences in Sichuan. As a youngster he was attracted to the activities and thinking of various revolutionaries. He was especially overjoyed and impressed when the 1911 revolution took place which, among other things, was a historic example of using violence for radical changes in modern China. In addition, his involvement in the activities of his hometown militia and his witnessing the use of force in Sichuan during the days of the revolution all seemed to have exposed him to the power and effectiveness of using violence as a means to get things done.

The schools of Leftist radicalism to which Guo was attracted during the May Fourth period included radical anarchism, at least for a while. His *Wild Cherry Blossoms*, as he himself later mentioned, had a "strong" anarchist touch.[53] In the preface to his November 1922 drama "The Two Princes of Guzhu," he also demonstrates certain interest in and knowledge of the anarchist thinking of Prince Pëtr Alekseevich Kropotkin (1842–1921) and Mikhail Aleksandrovich Bakunin (1814–1876). He notes that the anarchist thinking of the ancient Chinese heroes that he praises in the drama was the same as that of Kropotkin and Bakunin.[54] His friendship with Zhu Qianzhi, an anarchist and a nihilist during the May Fourth period, is also worth mentioning. His acquaintance with Zhu began in Shanghai in 1921 when he was working for the Tai Dong Book Company, which was publishing Zhu's *The Philosophy of Revolution*. Guo's friendship with Zhu was such that Zhu greatly admired him, and Guo wrote the preface to Zhu's book. In fact, when waiting for Tai Dong to publish his book, Zhu decided to live with Guo on the company's premises.[55]

The radical schools that attracted Guo the most were Marxism and Leninism. By late 1919 he had already included Lenin as one of the "bandits of social revolutions" he admired.[56] In *The Lessons of the Cannons*, he also imagines that he has been awakened from a dream by Lenin's shouting:

> My fellow human beings!
> Let's fight for liberty!
> Let's fight for humanism!
> Let's fight for justice!
> The final victory will belong to us!
> The loftiest ideal lies only in peasants and labors!
> My fellow human beings![57]

In "Coal, Iron, and Japan," he again shows interest in "socialism" and openly criticizes capitalism and imperialism as part of his reflection on the disaster caused by the ruthless fighting between capitalist and imperialist powers during the First World War.[58] In his preface poem to *The Goddesses*, then, there appears one of his most overtly Marxist uses of terminologies in the May Fourth period:

> I am a proletarian:
> because, apart from myself,

I have no private properties at all.
The Goddesses is my own product,
it may then be said to be my private property,
but here I am making it public,
because I want to be a Communist.[59]

Further, in his November 1922 "A Dialogue between the Yellow River and the Yangzi River," he expresses great admiration for Lenin's Communist revolution. Among other things, he writes that China should follow Russia's example to have a revolution and practice "proletarian dictatorship." With such a revolution, China and Soviet Russia would be the twin "new stars of the twentieth century" that would carry out the mission of "liberating mankind" and bringing "world peace."[60] In "On Tagore's Visit to China" in October 1923, he also writes that he "believes" that "the theory of historical materialism was the only solution to the problems of the world."[61] He seriously "grieved" when Lenin died.[62] In a poem in memory of Lenin, written on January 25, 1924, he compares the death of Lenin to the loss of a sun. As a sun, he notes, Lenin had benefited "the poor people who are without clothes and without jobs." At the end of the poem, he calls upon his comrades to follow Lenin's example and be themselves "suns" that would "drive away darkness and eliminate evils."[63] Despite his influence by Marxism and Leninism, however, Guo before the mid-1920s did not have enough interest in or knowledge of Marxism to be considered a Communist. As he himself later described it, even though he had expressed the willingness to be a proletarian and a Communist, even though at the time he did consider Marx and Lenin "great figures," he really did not understand "the concepts" of "the proletariat" and "Communism," and he knew little about the "detailed contents of Marxism and Leninism."[64] In fact, when in late June 1921 a Chinese student who studied with Kawakami Hajime tried to persuade Guo to educate himself on Marxism by reading Kawakami's works, Guo showed little interest. The student also tried, but failed, to make Guo understand such Marxist concepts as "the law of historical materialism," "the inevitability of the collapse of capitalism," and "the dictatorship of the proletariat." As Guo later wrote, he "did not have a clue" what the student was talking about.[65] An interesting footnote here is that a few days later, in early July 1921, when a group of Chinese intellectuals was founding China's Communist Party in Shanghai, Guo was with his literary friends in Japan forming the Creation Society and planning the publication of a "purely literary journal."[66]

Not yet committed to Marxist/Leninist radicalism, Guo during the May Fourth period also was experimenting with gradualist approaches in solving social and political problems. As mentioned previously, he sometimes demonstrated interest in the Western "bourgeois" concept of democracy, which was consistent with May Fourth China's enthusiasm for "Mr. Democracy" and Taisho Japan's limited democratic experience.[67] In his poem *The Lessons of the Cannons*, he also speaks highly of Tolstoy's "love" for Mo Zi's (墨子) concepts of "universal love" (*jian ai* 兼愛) and "nonconfrontation" (*fei zheng* 非爭). He notes in the poem that he also agrees very much with Tolstoy's concept of "nonresistance" (*wu kang* 無 抗), a concept that is significantly similar to Gandhi's (1869–1948) concept of nonviolence.[68]

THE MID-1920s: FINDING A MODERN "SCIENTIFIC" ECHO OF *DATONG* IN MARXISM AND COMMITTING TO REVOLUTION

When Guo in the mid-1920s shifted from his May Fourth focus on individualist rebellion against *lijiao* to a focus on collective causes, he found himself facing a world plagued with the materialist evils of capitalism and imperialism. It was under capitalism, as he was increasingly convinced, that people's material desires flooded, resulting in endless troubles and disastrous wars in the modern world. For him, the most telling example to show that the world had been experiencing a crisis at the hands of capitalism was the disaster of the imperialist war of World War I. To save the whole of mankind from its sufferings and crisis, as he came to believe, capitalism and imperialism had to be exterminated and, to this end, the radically anti-capitalist and anti-imperialist theories of Marxism and Leninism strongly appealed to him.

Attracted to the Marxist Cosmopolitanist Ideal

IDENTIFYING THE MARXIST IDEAL WITH *DATONG*

One of the major attractions Guo found in Marxism was the Marxist cosmopolitanist ideal, which stood for him as the sharpest contrast to the darkness and chaos of capitalist society and the ultimate correction of the modern world's problem of capitalism and imperialism.

In his letter to Cheng Fangwu in August 1924, Guo describes with great longing and admiration his newly found Marxist Communist ideal. He tells his friend that in the cosmopolitanist society of Marxist Communism "there will no longer be any classes," and material wealth will be "evenly distributed." People will be "liberated from the trammels of material life" and "will have no more worries and sufferings in their life other than those caused by natural and physical factors." "Each" in that society "will work according to his ability, and each will take what he needs." "All people will be able to develop themselves according to their talents, all people will be able to devote themselves to truth so that they will make contributions [to society], and all people will be extricated."[69]

Most excitingly for Guo, the modern Communist paradise that Marx had promised seemed identical to the traditional Confucian ideal of *datong* (Great Harmony). In his November 1925 "Marx Enters Confucius's Temple," for instance, he writes that in Marx's society the principle of "from each according his ability and to each according his needs" would be practiced. In this society, all will "freely and equally develop their abilities," "all will work hard and not be concerned about their remuneration," and "all will be secured in their [material] life and free from fears of hunger and cold."[70] This cosmopolitanist and egalitarian ideal of Marxism, Guo states, is similar to Confucius's ideal world of *datong*, in which "a public and common spirit ruled all under the sky"; "men of talents, virtue, and ability" would be chosen, the "able-bodied" (males) would have "proper work" and labor "with their strength," and all people, including "the aged," "the young," "widows," "orphans," "childless men," and "those who were disabled by disease," would be well taken care of.[71] In his "The Creation of a New State," Guo also uses the Confucian phrase "Great Harmony" to describe the Marxist cosmopolitanist ideal of Communism, which promises "the material and spiritual freedom and emancipation of all mankind."[72]

Guo's identifying the Marxist cosmopolitanist ideal with the Confucian cosmopolitanist dream of *datong* shows that his Confucian cosmopolitanist idealism, which had existed long before his acceptance of Marxism, was an important reference in his comprehending and accepting the Marxist ideal. One may argue that to a great degree it was Guo's May Fourth (and earlier) Confucian cosmopolitanist idealism that helped lead to his attraction to the Marxist Communist cosmopolitanism. A point can be made that it was in Marxism that he had finally found a modern scientific way to realize the dream of Confucius, who as he now suggested was only a premodern "utopian socialist."[73] Relating *datong* to the Marxist ideal, of course, also had brought his beloved Confucius farther into modern relevance.

THE COSMOPOLITANIST IDEAL AND THE INDIVIDUAL

As a Communist, Guo saw no conflict between his ideal of individual freedom and the Communist collective goal of emancipating the whole of mankind. For him, the freed individual in Communist society will be in complete harmony with the collective interests of that society. In fact, the individual's freedom will be interdependent with the well-being of the society, since not only is the individual's "free development" the "condition" of the "free development" of all members of the Communist society but, more importantly, it also relies on the realization and functioning of that society.

While it is hard to tell how much pantheistic thinking Guo had carried over from his May Fourth years into his Marxist years after 1924, it is at least noticeable that his now Marxist readiness to devote the individual to the Communist cosmopolitanist cause was not inconsistent with his May Fourth pantheistic concept of the transcendence of the self. By the same token, his longing for the Marxist ideal of development and freedom of the individual in the Communist society also recalls his May Fourth pantheistic assertion and promotion of the self. In fact, one can argue that on both the subject of cosmopolitanist selflessness and the issue of cosmopolitanist assertion of the self, the pantheistic concept that he held during his May Fourth years might have helped lead to his interest in atheistic Marxism. After all, at least as he saw it, "pantheism is an atheism," for the pantheistic belief in the divinity of everything actually negates the divine authority of any particular being over others.[74] The interesting thing here is that, just as his May Fourth pantheism empowered him with a cosmopolitanist selflessness as well as an individualist justification against the *lijiao* society, Marxism now provided him with a theoretical basis to transcend himself for a cosmopolitanist cause as well as a justification to tackle any evil collectives or society.

THE COSMOPOLITANIST IDEAL AND THE NATION

With his conversion to Marxism in 1924, Guo was confronted with a new challenge to balance his concerns for his nation and the Marxist ideal of a world without national boundaries.[75] Similar to his 1923 argument, that the tension between nationalism and cosmopolitanism could be solved with the Confucian model of managing the state and harmonizing the world, he now saw that tension solved with the Leninist concept of starting a Communist revolution first in individual nations and then eventually merging the individual Communist nations into a cosmopolitan Communist world in which old national boundaries would no longer be needed. In the process of making his commitment to China's revolution, however, Guo now emphasized the importance of individual nationalist revolution as a vital transitional step toward the ultimate goal of Communist cosmopolitanism. In late 1925 and early 1926, he published several articles debating against the Nationalist Group (*guojia zhuyi pai* 國家主義派), which argued that Communism is incompatible with nationalism. The essence of his argument is that the early stages of Communist revolution are carried out in individual proletarian nation-states and have to be achieved and consolidated by developing each of these nation-states. In this sense, he claimed, Communist revolution is compatible with nationalism. In "A Poor Man's Poor Talk," for instance, he writes that the Soviets, who were first strengthening their country with "state capitalism" in order to later achieve the Communist ideal, demonstrated that Communism is in no tension with nationalism.[76] In "Public Ownership of Property and Joint Control of China by Foreign Powers," he argues that Leninist "state capitalism" is not only the "form" that China as an underdeveloped nation has to take in its Communist revolution, but it is also the only way to save it as an underdeveloped nation, as "state capitalism" would nationalize its capital and therefore maximize its competitiveness against imperialist powers'"economic invasion." Sharing the same method of "state capitalism," therefore, Communism and nationalism go hand in hand for China.[77] In "The Creation of a New State," he further notes that Marxist Communism is not against all nation-states. Marx, he argues, acknowledged the historical necessity and importance of the existence of proletarian "new states" before the ideal cosmopolitan society of Communism is eventually achieved. What Marxism strives for is the destruction of the old nation-states of private ownership that exploit and oppress the masses and are therefore not really their true nations to begin with and the establishment of new proletarian nation-states for the masses in order to eventually reach the cosmopolitan stage of the Communist revolution. To save China as a nation, and especially to save its masses in the 1920s, the only way to proceed is to carry out a Communist revolution, practice "state capitalism," and make the country into a new proletarian state.[78]

Guo's argument here had in a sense put China's nationalist emancipation into the cosmopolitanist perspective of the Communist revolution. In so doing, he had assigned broader meaning and greater significance to China's nationalist cause and therefore made it more historically relevant and necessary. Compatibility between nationalism and Communism, however, was overall not that easy for him to prove. There is, after all, the Marxist insistence that all nation-states will disappear in the ideal Communist world. For the convenience of argument, therefore, Guo, in his writings against the Nationalist Group, tended to concentrate on the compatibility between nationalist movements and early stages of Communist revolution and seldom elaborated on the Marxist cosmopolitanist goal unless he was cornered by his opponents.[79] Interestingly, back in 1923, he was having an easier time trying to balance nationalism and cosmopolitanism with the Confucian model of managing the state and harmonizing the world, because at least it is not clarified in Confucian works that once the world is harmonized the state will no longer exist.

Committing to Marxist/Leninist Revolution as the Means to Achieve the Cosmopolitanist Ideal

What attracted Guo to Marxism/Leninism was not only its cosmopolitanist ideal but also its (specifically Leninist) promise of reaching that ideal with the powerful and effective means of a Soviet-type Communist revolution. As a result of the desperation that he had increasingly felt in coping with the various crises in his life, his nation, and the world, and also under further Marxist/Leninist influence, by the mid-1920s Guo's May Fourth interest in Leftist radicalism had developed into a commitment to Marxist/Leninist revolution as the means to achieve his cosmopolitanist ideal. In "Revolution and Literature," for instance, he celebrates the Communist revolution as the latest of many revolutions in human history, which he now consistently views as the universal means to achieve "social progress." There have always been revolutions, ever since the beginning of private property in human society, he writes. The purpose of these revolutions is to destroy by force the monopoly of wealth by a few and redistribute the wealth to the masses. These revolutions are always good because they pursue "the ultimate happiness of the vast majority of people" and are thus in the interest of mankind.[80] In his time of history, Guo is convinced, it is Communist revolution that will serve as the only effective means to fight against the capitalist form of private property and reach the goal of saving the world from modern capitalist evils. In "Appendicitis and Capitalism," he also discusses the necessity of having a Communist revolution against "capitalists," the few that are monopolizing wealth and hindering social progress. Making use of his medical background, he compares capitalists to a person's "appendix." Just as an appendix can cause "appendicitis" for the person, capitalists, who hardly make any contributions to society, can cause economic crises with their selfish competition with each other and thus result in the unemployment and suffering of workers. As surgery is the effective and ultimate cure of appendicitis, the best way to fight the capitalist disease of society lies in having a Communist revolution and radically eliminating capitalism as the cause of the disease.[81] In "The Timing of Social Revolution," he also argues that nonconfrontational approaches to labor-capital relationships will only "prolong" the "pains" of the proletarians.[82] In order to achieve a classless and "thoroughly free" world, he writes in "The Awakening of Writers and Artists," people first have to fight with their "blood" and "energy" in class struggle.[83] In his April 1926 "From Economic Struggle to Political Struggle," he also notes: "To save mankind from their pain, we have to have thorough revolution, take the power from the dominant classes, and completely overthrow all the oppressing classes."[84]

Guo's belief in the radical and confrontational means of Communist revolution was in striking contrast to his ultimate ideal of a harmonious Confucian/Communist society. Extremes meet, and the best medicine often tastes bitter—these old Chinese concepts were reinforced for him by the modern thinking of Lenin and Marx. In his attitude toward "radical Communist revolution," it needs to be mentioned, Guo differed substantially from Kawakami Hajime. While Kawakami paid serious attention to Marx's comment that Communism might be achieved through peaceful means in advanced countries such as the United States and Britain, Guo focused on what he saw as Marx's "consistent" advocacy of violent (that is, "bloody") Communist revolution. In fact, Guo criticized the fact that Kawakami had reservations about radical Communist revolution and noted that Kawakami's reservation was because of his Japanese background. Unlike Kawakami, who had the privilege of being born into a country that benefited from the existence of capitalism and modern imperialism, Guo, in coping with the overwhelming darkness of China's society, felt the urgent need to save his country and the whole world through the radical and effective means of revolution, and he had little interest in leisurely discussing the possibility of a peaceful transition to Communism.[85]

CHAPTER 4

Toward a Solution to
Modern China's Intellectual Crisis

Guo turned to Marxism and Leninism in the mid-1920s also for the purpose of solving his country's intellectual crisis at that time. Ever since the Opium War (1839–1842), China had increasingly experienced new intellectual changes that eventually developed into a crisis that climaxed during the May Fourth period. At the core of this intellectual crisis was the tension between China's traditional ideological and value system and the modern Western thinking that had invaded the country since the war. Under Western impact, the Chinese found that they had to reevaluate their traditional ideological and value system that increasingly, to many, seemed inadequate and unfit to meet the need of guiding them and their nation to survive and succeed in the modern world. Growing up in China at the turn of the twentieth century, Guo's life and thinking were profoundly affected by this intellectual crisis. Among other things, his personal crisis over the arranged marriage was a direct result of the collision between the modern Western concepts of individual freedom and romantic love and traditional Confucian social norms of *lijiao*. It is, of course, too simplistic to view his personal crisis as a black-and-white case of the modern West versus Chinese tradition, for eventually he did manage to find some encouragement for his rebellion in the tradition, (and not all the Western thinking that he encountered fully approved of his rebellion). What it all boiled down to, however, was his longtime seesaw between Western individualism and Confucian *lijiao* ethics: while confronting each other head on, neither of the two sides, Western individualism or *lijiao*, was strong enough to completely dominate his thinking and thus decisively direct him on what he should do. Specifically, Western individualist influence, while enough to have encouraged him to take the step of living with Tomiko, was for a long time still too weak to help him fully justify his actions. On the other hand, the traditional ethics with which he had been brought up, while not enough to stop him from taking the rebellious step, were for a long time still strong enough to make him feel guilty and suffer mentally for his offense against *lijiao*.

To solve his personal crisis, obviously Guo needed to solve the intellectual problem for himself: he needed to figure out exactly what to follow, Chinese or/and Western thoughts and values, as moral guidance on the issue of his arranged marriage. He needed to solve the intellectual problem also because he needed to decide what to rely on as his ideological guidance and resources for achieving his personal goal of spiritual/moral transcendence as well as his collective goals of saving China and the world. As he matured intellectually and became an influential writer, this personal search for ideological guidance increasingly turned into a conscious pursuit of the goal of providing (as an intellectual and a public figure) his solution to his country's intellectual crisis of that time. In contrast to many of his fellow May Fourthians' antitraditional and pro-Western rhetoric, Guo's pursuit always featured a determination to solve China's intellectual crisis by combining the best of Chinese tradition and Western modernity. It was this pursuit and determination that helped result in Guo's May Fourth thinking, which was a combination of modern Western Goetheanism, science, and Chinese Confucian and Taoist tradition. It also was this pursuit and determination that further helped lead to the transition from his May Fourth thinking to his combining Confucianism with Marxism/Leninism in the mid-1920s as his new version of the best of the two worlds.

A MAY FOURTH SOLUTION TO THE INTELLECTUAL CRISIS

Defending the Best of Chinese Tradition

In contrast to many of his fellow May Fourthians' seemingly comprehensive attacks on Chinese tradition, Guo, during the May Fourth period, insisted that the solution to China's intellectual crisis lay in abandoning the worst of both traditional China and the modern West and combining the best of both worlds. For Guo, the worst to abandon included the Confucian ethics and norms of lijiao in China and the capitalist/imperialist evils of the West. The best for him to keep from both worlds, then, consisted of Confucianism (minus lijiao), Taoism, modern Western science, and Goetheanism.

In "The Traditional Spirit of Chinese Culture," written originally for the 1923 New Year's special issue of Japan's Asahi Shimbun (Osaka), Guo praises Confucianism, Taoism, and the "liberal thinking and natural philosophy" of China's golden age before the Three Dynasties, which he saw as the basis of Taoist and Confucian developments:[1]

> From Lao Zi, Confucius, and the ancient thinking before them we can hear two messages:
>
> First, see everything as the expression of active reality!
>
> Second, start all causes by striving to perfect one's self!
>
> This is the spirit of our tradition. It teaches us that one, with the belief that all is god, should infinitely purify and enrich himself till he becomes as great and

benevolent as God and strive for the realization of an ideal future when all fellow human beings in the world will live with each other in one cosmopolitan country. It is this dualistic spirit of our Chinese tradition that will serve as the basis for our revival in the future.[2]

To counter many of his May Fourth contemporaries' public attacks on Confucianism, Guo went to great lengths to openly and enthusiastically defend Confucius. The thinking of the Confucius that he defended, of course, no longer included the ethics of *lijiao*. In "The Traditional Spirit of Chinese Culture" he states:

> Nowadays most people see Confucius as an advocator of loyalty and filial piety. Some respect him, others curse him. There are also people who further go to the extreme of often criticizing Confucius as one who gained fame by deceiving the public and they blame Confucius for all the degeneration of the Chinese nation. There are indeed many new people in our China today who hold such outrageous views. You who wrong Confucius: you after all have to be saved from your stupidity and ignorance!
>
> I announce here that we worship Confucius. There are some people who say that we are against our times. We don't care. We still worship Confucius.... The Confucius that we see was an ever-vigorous giant with great talent and perfect character, like those of Kant and Goethe. He had developed his own individuality to extreme [perfection]—in depth and scope. He was proficient in mathematics, rich with naturalist knowledge, and multi-talented in entertainment and arts.... He was perfect both physically and spiritually.[3]

Guo promoted Taoism as a revolution against the dark age of the Three Dynasties. In "The Traditional Spirit of Chinese Culture," for instance, he praises Lao Zi and Zhuang Zi for being "extremely against the religious thinking of the Three Dynasties."[4] Lao Zi, specifically, was a "revolutionary thinker" who had "completely destroyed the superstitious thinking of the Three Dynasties."[5] In reacting to the dark age, the Taoist thinkers developed a "metaphysics" and an ideological/value system that was active in spirit and liberating for individuals.[6]

Guo saw Taoism as being "not fundamentally different" from the "active" and "enterprising" spirit of Confucianism. Contrary to what people often believe, he writes in "On Chinese and German Cultures," the Taoist concept of *wuwei* is not similar to the Buddhist negation of life in this world. Buddhism, he criticizes, seeks a "deadly static" state. In contrast, Taoism seeks a "lively static" state. Taoism, he notes, carries a "positive spirit" and teaches people to "learn from nature" and "rid themselves of all desires" so that their spirit will be "clear" and their "creative instinct" will be brought into full play.[7]

Consistent with his May Fourth individualist thinking, Guo also praised Taoism for encouraging people's individual development. In "On Chinese and German Cultures," he writes that Lao Zi, like Friedrich Wilhelm Nietzsche (1844–1900), based his thinking on "the individual" and "strove for positive development." Further, Lao Zi was against "religious thinking" and the "established ethics" that suppressed "individuality."[8]

Combining the Best of China with Modern Western Science and Goetheanism

IN NEED OF MODERN WESTERN SCIENCE

Despite all of his enthusiasm for Confucianism and Taoism, however, Guo gradually came to face the fact that both lacked the element of scientific thinking. In his 1921 outlines of "The Pompeii of Chinese Intellectual History," for instance, he puts Confucius's thought in the category "metaphysical" thinking, different from the category "scientific thinking."[9] In his early 1923 "The Traditional Spirit of Chinese Culture," he also stops calling Confucius a "scientist" as he did in 1920 in *San Ye Ji*, even though he still admires Confucius for being good at mathematics and having naturalist knowledge.[10] In his May 1923 "On Chinese and German Cultures," then, he begins to admit that Confucianism and Taoism "regrettably" lacked "pure reason" and did not have sufficient development in the "objective study of natural phenomena" or in the study of "pure sciences."[11] In his "The Character and Thinking of Hui Shi (惠施)," written in December 1923, he again defines Confucianism and Taoism as being different than scientific thinking and notes that they had "largely neglected" the study of "the physical world."[12] In that same article, he also regrets that Zhuang Zi's thinking lacked "logic."[13]

Guo did notice though that traditional China was not without the incipient development of scientific elements. In his January 24, 1921 letter to a friend, for instance, he expresses the opinion that during the Spring and Autumn period (770–476 B.C.) and the Warring States period (475–221 B.C.) China had already seen the beginning of "scientific thinking." This was seen in the thoughts of Zou Yan (鄒衍) (circa 305–240 B.C.) and Gongsun Long (公孫龍) (circa 325–250 B.C.) and the "materialist thinking" and "analytical and inductive methods of study" of Hui Shi (circa 370–310 B.C.), which were "rather similar" to the "spirits" of European thinkers René Descartes (1596–1650), Francis Bacon (1561–1626), and Gottfried Wilhelm von Leibniz (1646–1716). The beginning of "scientific" thinking in China, however, was killed by the "fire" (book burning) of the Qin Dynasty.[14] In "On Chinese and German Cultures," he further notes that Chinese culture "started with observation of nature," and that before or during the Zhou period, China already had "systematic" knowledge of the stars.[15] Elaborating on his earlier view, Guo notes that during the latter part of the Spring and Autumn period and the Warring States period there was substantial scientific development in China. He notes that Mo Zi's thought had the beginnings of "logic" and "physics." Zou Yan's "inductive method" and Hui Shi's thinking, he continues, also "looked scientific."[16] Then, in "The Character and Thinking of Hui Shi," Guo notices that "most of the scholars" during the late Spring and Autumn period and the Warring States period were "ninety percent natural scientists, as they had gradually shifted their attention to the physical world as their research objects, and they had gradually learned to use observation, empiricism, and logic as their research methods."[17] Among those scholars, he points to Hui Shi as a "major" and an "outstanding" figure.[18] In his detailed analysis of Hui Shi's thinking, based largely on what Zhuang Zi and Xun Zi (荀子) (circa 313–238 B.C.) said about Hui Shi, he notes that Hui Shi as a "scientific thinker" had put forward an "atomic theory" and a concept that the earth is round.[19] To his great regret, however, Hui Shi's thinking was largely lost with his books, which were possibly burned during the Qin Dynasty.[20] Neither did the "scientific" thinking of other scholars of Hui Shi's time later enjoy substantial development which, according to Guo, was partially a result of the negative influence of Buddhism on China and the fact that later Chinese had "misunderstood" the spirit of Chinese tradition.[21]

As Confucianism and Taoism lacked scientific elements and as the incipient "scientific" thinking of Hui Shi and his contemporaries was arrested, China failed to develop sciences and scientific thinking. This shortcoming of China's, as Guo believed, had to be remedied by learning from modern Western scientific civilization.

Consistent with May Fourth China's embracing of "Mr. Science" and Taisho Japan's solid atmosphere of scientific learning, Guo had a strong faith in science and an enthusiasm for modern Western scientific civilization.[22] In his 1921 "Coal, Iron, and Japan," for instance, he strongly argues against the view that the disaster of the First World War symbolized the "bankruptcy of scientific civilization" in the West. There was nothing wrong with "scientific civilization" itself, he writes. What was wrong was "scientific civilization under the capitalist system."[23]

Guo's faith in modern Western science, however, was not blind. For one thing, his enthusiasm for Western science was not carried to the extreme of scientism, which believes that science alone can fully describe and explain everything in the universe. In "On Chinese and German Cultures," for instance, he clearly states that he considers science as just a part, however important that part is, of what fully "enriches" people's life. To make life meaningful, "complete," and "perfect," he needs not only science but also the "spirit" of Chinese tradition as "guidance for life."[24] In other words, good as it was, modern Western science did not provide Guo with the moral/spiritual guidance that the best of China offered. This being the case, not only did he need modern Western science to make up for what Chinese tradition lacked, he also needed the best of Chinese tradition to cover for what modern Western science failed to provide, hence his urge to integrate the two. In "On Chinese and German Cultures," he writes, "the traditional spirit of our country provides us with guidance for our life. [In the meantime], the [Western] scientific spirit that has developed from [ancient] Greek civilization is also a nutriment that we young people should deeply absorb." To save China, "we should both revive the traditional spirit of our culture and absorb the sweet milk of the pure sciences of the West."[25]

CELEBRATION OF GOETHEANISM: A MODIFICATION OF GUO'S FAITH IN SCIENCE

The Goethean celebration of romantic love and individual freedom was what saved Guo in his desperate struggle against the Confucian family and *lijiao*. For a few years during the May Fourth period, Guo also came to appreciate Goethe's pantheism, his longing for the simplicity of farming and primitive life, his proactive mentality, and his Romanticist emphasis on emotion and intuition.[26] With his dedication and contribution to natural sciences, Goethe sometimes also personified for Guo the "spirit" of modern Western science. In *San Ye Ji*, for instance, Guo praises Goethe's scientific achievements as a major example of his overall genius.[27] In his 1922 article "Goethe's Contribution to Natural Sciences," Guo also worships Goethe as a "pioneer in scientific research" who "greatly contributed to natural sciences." He "reveres" Goethe for his talent and accomplishments in the study of natural sciences as well as in literature and the arts.[28]

Despite his worshiping Goethe as a scientific figure, however, Guo saw his May Fourth faith in modern Western science substantially modified by Goethean Romanticism, whose celebration of emotion and intuition is at least different from science's emphasis on reason and logic. In the preface to his translation of *The Sorrows of Young Werther*, Guo specifically states that he is attracted to Goethe's "emotionalism." He praises the fact that Goethe did not "analyze" the various things in the universe with "reason" but instead relied on his emotion to "comprehend and create." With his heart and emotion, Goethe could create "paradise" "anywhere around him."[29]

Guo's Goethean Romanticism led him to argue strongly that science could not govern literature and arts, which for him were to a great extent products of emotion and intuition. In his 1923 essay "Nature and Arts," he writes that "literature and arts" should stay beyond the coverage of science. He criticizes that literature and the arts have become "slaves of science" in the modern era. The twentieth century, he states, should be the time to "liberate" literature and the arts from science.[30]

Guo himself was keenly aware of the dichotomy between his Goethean emotionalism and his overall faith in science and reason.[31] In a letter he wrote to Zong Baihua on February 16, 1920, for instance, he talks about a "contradiction" in the minds of "young people" like him: "On the one hand, we want to seek truth and develop our reason; on the other hand, we want to follow our dreams and find it hard to abandon our intuition. This is not simply a hereditary mentality of us Chinese. It is truly something that all people have as a common human nature. I believe that we should neither be lopsided nor make sweeping generalizations on this issue. In my opinion, on the one hand, we should make every effort to develop our reason wherever reason should be developed; on the other hand, we should fully use our intuition wherever intuition should be used."[32]

Guo's effort to make sense of the "contradiction" in his thinking also was seen in his letter to Zong dated January 18, 1920. In a not very clear manner, he tries in that letter to compare the poet's intuition to the philosopher's reason and tries to find a balanced relationship between intuition and reason by integrating them in the philosophy of pantheism, which he believes should be the ideal "worldview of the poet." He writes:

The poet is similar to the philosopher in that they both consider the whole of the universe as their object and both take it as their bounden duty to see and examine penetratingly the essence of all the myriad things. The difference between the poet and philosopher, however, is that the poet only has pure intuition as his efficient tool whereas the philosopher has accurate reasoning as an additional efficient tool. The poet is a favorite son of feelings while the philosopher is a nominal son of reason. The poet is an embodiment of "beauty" while the philosopher is an example of "truth." . . . I believe that pantheism in philosophy is really a lovely child who is fathered by reason and mothered by feelings. If a philosopher is not satisfied with the lifeless worldview provided by those upholsterer[s], he will naturally lean toward pantheism and consider the whole universe as a lively and active organism. Every human being has reason. Every human being has his own worldview and his own outlook on life. Even though the poet is a favorite son of feelings, he also has his reason and his worldview and outlook on life. It is thus natural that, as you said to me, "the ideal worldview for the poet should be pantheism."[33]

A May Fourth Synthesis of the Best of the East and West as a Solution to the Intellectual Crisis

Guo's May Fourth synthesis of the best of the two worlds, which centered on major features of Confucianism (minus *lijiao*), Taoist thinking, modern Western science, and Goetheanism, was his solution to China's intellectual crisis.[34] It also functioned as his ideological and moral guidance in trying to solve his personal crisis and the situational crises of China and the world.

In some respects, the two sides of Guo's Chinese/Western synthesis made up for each other's shortcomings. First of all, the Western Goethean individualism in his synthesis compensated for the lack of individual freedom in the Confucian system. Western science also compensated for the lack of science in Confucianism and Taoism. On the other hand, the elaborate Neo-Confucian teaching on people's inner transcendence through moral self-cultivation was something that could not be found in Western Goetheanism or Western science. In this regard, Confucian moralism made up for what he saw as a lack in the modern West. Further, the Confucian utopianism and egalitarianism in his synthesis, increasingly reinforced by modern Leftist thoughts, also in a sense compensated for the lack of an elaborate social ideal in Goetheanism.

While making up for each other's shortcomings, the two sides of his synthesis could also compare with each other in certain aspects and to different degrees. Despite their significant differences, for instance, Western individualism and Confucian personalism are not necessarily poles apart from each other. The Goethean Romanticist celebration of individual freedom also can remind one of the Taoist teaching to free oneself from the rules and norms of established mundane and material society. Further, though different than Western Goethean pantheism, Chinese (Neo-) Confucianism is not without pantheistic connotations. The Goethean preference for pastoral and primitive life also recalls Confucian ruralism and the Taoist pursuit of nature and primitivism.[35] Finally, Wang Yangming's Neo-Confucian attention to action also can compare to Goethe's celebration of action.[36]

Guo's May Fourth synthesis, however, was not without major weaknesses. For one thing, the lack of a clearly defined means to achieve the goals of saving China and the world made his synthesis ineffective in coping with China's and the world's situational crises. Given the seeming urgency of saving the country and the world at the time, it sounded like vague, empty talk when he focused on advocating Western science, reviving Chinese tradition, and realizing Great Harmony through literature and the arts. Further, as an effort to combine the best of the West and East, Guo's synthesis did not seem to fully include the best of the scientific modern West. Specifically, it lacked a system of social science. At least as early as 1922, he was already aware that Western science consisted of not only natural but also social science.[37] He would later recall that he had been "longing" for social science.[38] To a certain extent, this longing for the guidance of social science on social and political matters was a result of the fact that his synthesis had little more than Confucian utopianism and egalitarianism for social ideals. Though beautiful, these Confucian ideals lacked the modern appeal of being scientifically conceptualized and elaborated and therefore did not look convincingly feasible in the modern world.

THE MID-1920s: SOLVING CHINA'S INTELLECTUAL CRISIS THROUGH THE COMBINATION OF CONFUCIANISM AND MARXISM/LENINISM

Redefining the Best of the East and West

Guo's drive to solve modern China's intellectual crisis was greatly stimulated by debates among Chinese intellectuals over Eastern and Western civilizations and over science and metaphysics, which started around 1923, partly as a reflection on the disaster of the First World War. Guo was actively involved in these debates, with some of his major articles, including "On Chinese and German Cultures" and "Wang Yangming: A Great Spiritualist," written at least partially to participate in the debates.[39] Throughout the debates, his point of view was always very clear: he continued to believe that China's intellectual crisis could only be solved by combining the best of both Chinese tradition and modern Western "scientific" civilization. It was in the middle of these debates that he came to increasingly realize the weakness and inadequacy of his May Fourth ideological/moral synthesis and began to shift his focus to a combination of Confucianism and Marxism/Leninism as his new version of the best of the East and West. In other words, his search for a better synthesis of the best of the two worlds as a solution to China's intellectual crisis and as ideological/moral guidance to solve his personal crisis and China's and the world's situational crises was a major reason he turned to Communism in the mid-1920s.

By the mid-1920s Goetheanism had ceased appealing to Guo as a symbol of the modern West. Goethean Romanticism and individualism had by then accomplished the task of emancipating him from *lijiao* suppression and had turned out to be at least irrelevant in guiding him to cope with the financial crisis in his personal life and with what in his eyes came to be the increasingly urgent crises in China's and the world's situations. As he later recalled, around late 1923 and early 1924, the time when he was going through the worst moment of his personal crisis, Marx and Lenin had already replaced Goethe (and Spinoza) as "the focal point" of his "consciousness." Even though he still did not "clearly" understand the thinking of Marx and Lenin at the time, he did want to "grasp the content" of that thinking.[40] By about late 1923, Taoism also had lost its attraction for Guo as part of the best of Chinese tradition. In his August 1923 *Han Gu Guan*, for instance, he repeatedly criticizes Lao Zi as a "selfish, base person." While "talking volubly about nature," Lao Zi approached "everything" from a "selfish" perspective.[41] He points out in the novel that there is a major contradiction between Lao Zi's concept "*dao*" (道 way), which refers to a "completely purposeless and active entity," and his concept "*de*" (德 ethics), which is "full of" selfish "purposes" and is like a "lifeless stone coffin."[42] Lao Zi, he notes, was a "hypocrite," and Lao Zi's *Dao De Jing* is a "hypocritical classic."[43] Then, in his June 1924 "Wang Yangming: A Great Spiritualist," he writes that China's traditional thinking has "two major schools": Confucianism and Taoism. Even though Taoism and Confucianism are both this-worldly, "the practical ethics of Taoism are selfish and self-benefiting." If practiced to its "extreme," Taoism could result in the same evils and disasters perpetrated by the "Western capitalist system." As Taoism has such serious flaws, he concludes, the "only" good part now "left" within the Chinese tradition is Confucianism.[44]

After learning about Marxism/Leninism through his translation of Kawakami's book, Guo announced in June 1924 that he "believed in both the religion of Confucianism (*kongjiao* 孔教) ... and socialism [Marxism/Leninism]."[45] From then on, he made elaborate efforts to promote the combination of Confucianism and Marxism/Leninism as his new version of the best of the East and West. In "Wang Yangming: A Great Spiritualist," he writes:

> My view is that, for our individual cultivation, we should follow Confucian spirit and strive for the expansion of our selves in order to reach the sacred status of being perfect; for social progress and reform, then, we should follow the guidance of socialism, make great efforts to absorb what scientific civilization offers, increase material productive forces, achieve even distribution of material products, and enable everyone to comprehensively develop his spirit.[46]

The connotation here is that Confucianism is better than Marxism/Leninism, in that it has a transcendental perspective and provides people with moral guidance for their self-cultivation. Marxism/Leninism, on the other hand, is better than Confucianism in guiding socioeconomic progress and reforms. Confucianism and

Marxism/Leninism, therefore, should be combined as the best of the East and West so that Confucian transcendentalism could make up for the lack of transcendental thinking in Marxism/Leninism. In turn, Marxist/Leninist social science would compensate for the Confucian inadequacy in meeting the needs of modern socioeconomic development.[47]

While suggesting the differences between Confucianism and Marxism/Leninism, Guo also made efforts to identify the two with each other in a variety of ways. As discussed earlier, in "Wang Yangming: A Great Spiritualist," Guo states that Wang Yangming's Neo-Confucian concept of "getting rid of human [selfish] desires" is similar to the antiprivate ownership theory of Marxism/Leninism.[48] In the article he also identifies what Soviet Russia practiced after the 1917 revolution with Confucius's "kingly way" (wangdao 王道). Further, with his Confucian emphasis on individual moral cultivation, Guo points out that the "noble and pure characters" of Marx and Lenin could be compared to those of Confucius and Wang Yangming.[49]

Another writing in which Guo identifies Confucianism with Marxism is his "Marx Enters Confucius's Temple." In that essay, he compares Confucius's thought with that of Marx on several issues. First, he considers Marxism and Confucianism comparable on the issue of this-worldliness. In contrast to "many religious or metaphysical thinkers," he writes, Marx "stood" in this world, "talked" the "language" of this world, and never viewed life as being "empty" or "sinful." In this regard, Marx's "thorough affirmation of [human] life in this world' is "completely identical" to Confucius's "emphasis" on "life."[50] Guo then goes on to compare Marx's ideal of an egalitarian and a cosmopolitan Communist society to Confucius's ideal of Great Harmony. Marx was not a "material" person without idealism. With his ideal of Communist society, in which all would "freely and equally develop their abilities" and the principle "from each according his ability and to each according his needs" would be practiced, Marx was actually a "most idealistic idealist." This idealism was similar to Confucius's ideal of Great Harmony, in which "a public and common spirit ruled all under the sky," "men of talents, virtue, and ability" would be chosen, the "able-bodied" (males) would have "proper work" and labor "with their strength," and all people, including "the aged," "the young," "widows," "orphans," "childless men," and "those who were disabled by disease" would be well taken care of.[51] In trying to identify Confucius with Marx, Guo does run into difficulty comparing the two on their attitudes toward material development. He is keenly aware, for instance, that while Confucius said that "the head of a state or a noble family worries not about under-population but about uneven distribution, not about poverty but about instability," Marx "worried about" "under-population" and "poverty" as well as "uneven distribution" and "instability."[52] To cover this difference between Confucius and Marx, he quotes Confucius's other sayings such as "make the people rich" when the population is "flourishing" and when people become rich "train them" and "give them enough food, give them enough arms, and the common people will have trust in you." These other sayings of Confucius, Guo manages to conclude, are enough to prove that Confucius after all did not lack interest in material matters and in that regard was "identical" to Marx. To make his point, Guo also vaguely tries to get around Confucius's moralistic dislike for profit making in trade ("merchants"), suggesting that at least Confucius's disciple Zigong (子貢) (520–? B.C.) engaged in commercial activities. Guo in the essay also defends the Confucian emphasis on frugality (instead of expansion of material production), a virtue that he still sees necessary in modern times. When many people are still underfed, he argues, a few should not be allowed to indulge in extravagance.[53]

As a response to the criticism of a certain Tao Qiqing (陶其情), in December 1925 Guo wrote an open letter to confirm and elaborate the view that he had expressed in "Marx Enters Confucius's Temple." In that letter, he claims again that "Marx's theory is not contradictory with Confucius's thinking."[54] Confucius, whom Guo "worships," was "commendable" for having already developed a concept of "Communism" "over two thousand years ago."[55] He notes that Confucius's "kingly way" (wangdao) was opposed to "private ownership."[56] According to Confucianism, he writes, rulers should have moral qualities and should "abdicate" in political succession. Such a Confucian concept of rule by "men of virtues," Guo argues, was different from the concept of theocratic rulership and was not "fundamentally" different from the Marxist concept of government by "proletarians."[57] Confucius's "nationalism," he also notes, was not contradictory to Marxism, because Marx recognized the importance of having "proletarian countries" before the cosmopolitan Communist ideal is achieved.[58] Marxism and Confucianism, Guo also says in the letter, did not diverge greatly on the issue of family. Marxist Communism is not against "filial piety" or "family," two key elements that were emphasized by Confucius.[59] Marxism, he argues, "does not teach people not to have families." Nor was Confucius's emphasis on family "contradictory" to the Marxist concept of Communism because if "every family" lives well and is "in good shape" in a society, then that society is a Communist one.[60]

The Formation of a Confucian/Marxist/Leninist Communist Synthesis

The new East/West synthesis that Guo came to promote in the mid-1920s centered on the Marxist concept of achieving the emancipation of the individual through collective revolution, the Confucian drive for moral/spiritual inner transcendence through self-cultivation, and a determination to reach a cosmopolitan Communist/datong ideal (and in the process reach the goal of liberating China as a nation) through the radical means of Marxist/Leninist revolution.[61]

While it functioned the same way as his May Fourth synthesis on the Confucian moral self-cultivation of the individual, Guo's new Confucian/Marxist/Leninist system in several ways satisfied his needs better than the previous May Fourth synthesis. First, at the personal level, his new system forcefully promised to destroy once and for all the capitalist society that had caused his personal crisis and deprived him of his individual development and freedom, a society about which his May Fourth synthesis had been unable to do anything. It is true that he as an individual might never see or benefit from the ideal society that Marx promised. In fact, he was putting his own life at risk by joining the Communist revolution, let alone sacrificing his immediate individual interests. However, since he could neither freely develop himself in the old society, nor was he willing to compromise to adapt himself to that society, it seemed natural for him to work for the destruction of the old society and devote himself to the ideal of the future. The dedication to the future, in a sense, enabled him to transcend his current personal crisis. Second, at the national and world levels, his new system offered what seemed a most effective means, partly already proven in Soviet Russia, to save the world and China from their situational crises, which his May Fourth synthesis had been practically inadequate in tackling. Third, at the intellectual level, his new system better represented for him the best of the scientific civilization of the modern West, because Marxism now thoroughly covered for him the lack of social science in his previous May Fourth synthesis.[62]

Guo's new system, however, was not without serious inner tension, which centered on his ambivalence toward the economic/historical determinism of the Marxist concept of historical materialism.

Guo was, to begin with, attracted to historical materialism as a key part of the "social science" of Marxism and as a "light of reason," which was consistent with his May Fourth interest in modern Western science and reason.[63] After all, one of the factors that led to his reading and translating Kawakami's book was his "longing" for the "social science" and "scientific socialism" of historical materialism and the Marxist theory in general.[64] With scientific reasoning and "solid and accurate evidence," the Marxist thinking proved to him that the "ideal" and "perfect" Communist society was not a "utopian," "unreal" dream but could "really be achieved" "step-by-step" on the earth.[65]

Despite his interest in the social science of Marxism, however, Guo often found himself in profound disagreement with the deterministic thinking that Kawakami conveyed in his introduction of Marxist historical materialism. What troubled him was the Marxist notion that Communist revolution would come only when material production reached a high level, suggesting that underdeveloped nations such as China would have to wait for their economies to mature in order to achieve Communism.

Kawakami, it should be mentioned, was himself not a strict follower of the rules of historical materialism. As Gail Lee Bernstein points out, Kawakami made efforts to try to strike a balance between Marxist historical determinism and what he saw as Marx's activism.[66] On the one hand, he stuck to historical materialism and stated that before a certain level of the development of material "productive forces" was achieved, people's attempts at "social revolution" could cause "retrogression" of the "productive forces" and would ultimately fail.[67] On the other hand, he believed that there was a certain amount of room left in Marxism for human will to play its role in history, and while holding a wait-and-see attitude toward the Soviet revolution, as shown in *Social Organization and Social*

Revolution, he demonstrated interest in the Leninist attempt to carry out a Communist revolution in the underdeveloped nation of Russia. Kawakami agreed to the Leninist logic that against the law of historical materialism human revolutionary acts should and could legitimately get started under the condition of Russia's backward economy. A Communist revolution, he writes along a Leninist line, consists of three stages of development: the period of "spiritual preparation," the period of "political struggle," and the period of "economic construction." In other words, it was acceptable for him to have a Communist revolution prepared and started "politically" first and to put off the high-level economic development required by historical materialism to some time in the future.[68]

Like Kawakami, whose *Social Organization and Social Revolution* was basically Guo's sole source of information on Marxism/Leninism, Guo tried to justify his reservation about Marxist historical materialism by arguing that Marx himself also promoted revolutionary activities. There was really no contradiction, Guo argues, between Marx's historical materialism and his activism.[69] Historical materialism, Guo writes, was the result that Marx achieved through his study of the development of human society with an approach of "pure, natural science." When conducting this study, in order to be "most convenient" and "free of various complications," Marx "temporarily left out the factor of human subjectivity" and analyzed human society as an "objective natural being." It was through this study that Marx came to conclude "unemotionally" that regardless of human will, "advanced social systems" were bound to replace old social systems, but that such historical progress would not take place until the old systems had developed to their limits and become "shackles" on "productive forces."[70] Once the "scientific" conclusion was reached, Guo argues awkwardly, the human factor somehow came back into the picture for Marx, leading him to become an "enthusiastic" propagandist who wrote (or co-wrote) the following to promote revolutionary activism in historical development:

> The Communists everywhere support every revolutionary movement against the existing social and political order of things.
>
> In all these movements they bring to the front, as the leading question in each case, the property question, no matter what its degree of development at the time.
>
> . . . Let the ruling classes tremble at a Communist revolution. . . .[71]
>
> There is only one means by which the murderous death agonies of the old society and the bloody birth throes of the new society can be *shortened,* simplified and concentrated, and *that* is by *revolutionary terror.*[72]

This activism of Marx, Guo says, does not conflict with historical materialism—it simply exists "dualistically" (*eryuan* 二元) with historical materialism within Marx's ideological system.[73] It was this dualism that led Marx to state (in his preface to the first German edition of *Capital*) that, on the one hand, "even when a society has got upon the right track for the discovery of the natural laws of its movement . . . it can neither clear by bold leaps, nor remove by legal enactments, the obstacles offered by the successive phases of its normal development; but, on the other hand, the society "can shorten and lessen the birth-pangs."[74]

The dualism that Guo found in Marx to a great extent assured Guo that he could push for revolutionary actions and still stay within the boundary of the social science of Marxism. Feeling justified and legitimized, he freely elaborated on his perceived Marxist activism. Instead of waiting passively for history to take its course, he writes, people, who are not "dead things in nature," should take actions to help bring about as soon as possible the death of the "old society" and the birth of the "new society." He uses a medical analogy to make his point. If people have distoma in their lungs and know that the pathogen without treatment will die in twenty years, he asks, then should people wait for those twenty years to let the pathogen harm them before it dies in its natural course? The answer is very simple: people should, for their own health, take action and use medical treatment to kill the pathogen "as soon as possible."[75]

Despite Kawakami's deviation from historical materialism, Guo with his impatience with history even found Kawakami to be too much of a historical determinist.[76] In July 1924, right after translating Kawakami's book, in a letter to a friend Guo seriously challenges Kawakami's view that premature "social revolutions" could hinder economic development and would ultimately fail. He notes that Kawakami did not have sufficient evidence to support his view and had actually jumped to his conclusion. The evidence that Kawakami provided in the book, Guo points out, could actually work against Kawakami's own view and prove that instead of causing "retrogression" of "productive forces," "social revolution" that took place under premature material conditions could actually help increase "productive forces." Further, he writes in the letter, it is not necessarily the maturity of material conditions but rather the "policies and tactics" of the revolutionaries that determine whether or not a "social revolution" will succeed. In his opinion, as an economically backward country China should not wait, as Kawakami suggested, for "productive forces" to further develop before it could have a Communist revolution. Since the country, like all other nations, is most definitely heading toward Communism, it should take "the shortest route," in other words, learn from Soviet Russia and have a Leninist revolution, in order to develop a Communist society as soon as possible. (Not surprisingly, Guo embraced the Soviet revolution more enthusiastically than Kawakami did.)[77] Then, in his 1926 "The Timing of Social Revolution," he further argues that Kawakami "misinterpreted" Marxism by insisting that Communist revolution would not take place until a capitalist system was "on the verge of collapse." As far as Guo is concerned, it is not "risky" nor is it necessarily "infeasible" to have a Communist revolution before the dying phase of capitalism. Besides, he wonders, who is to tell when exactly a capitalist system is going to reach that moment of being "on the verge of collapse"? If nobody can tell, then what is the point of waiting? Why not start the revolution now, so that "the proletarians" will be liberated sooner from their sufferings? After all, is it not "worthy of our human efforts" to, in Marx's words, "shorten and lessen the birth-pangs" of the new society?[78]

Guo's deviation from historical materialism was clearly a result of, among other things, his influence by the Leninist revision of Marxism. Inspired by the success of the 1917 Soviet revolution in Russia, he was convinced that a Communist revolution should and could be carried out in a materially underdeveloped country such as China. To have such a Communist revolution in China did not mean to ignore the importance of material development as required by historical materialism, he argued. It only meant that the development of material production would be taken care of *after* instead of before the Communist radical change of political and socio-economic institutions. To reach the ultimate goal of Communism, he stated, a high level of material development was still expected under the Communists after the success of their revolution.[79]

The very fact that Guo advocated the postponement of material development, however, revealed the low priority of such development for him. While claiming that he now believed in the Marxist concept that "matter mothers spirit" and that "new spiritual civilization" results from "high-level material development" and the "equal distribution" of material products, he was still very much a Confucianist who had relatively little enthusiasm for material matters.[80] His continuous Confucian lack of material concerns and his consequent indifference toward Marx's emphasis on material development were perhaps best seen in his October 1924 autobiographical novel *Hard Journey*, which was written in Japan several months after his announced conversion to Marxism. In that novel, he reflects on his stay in an "isolated" rural area in Japan where life is simple and easy. Living in the countryside, where everything is "so leisurely and carefree," he writes, people feel no "excessive desires" and therefore do not have much demand for "material" products. Observing such a comfortable rural life, he cannot help but "doubt" Marx's idea that the ideal Communist society will not be achieved until "material productive forces develop to the fullest." If people live simple country lives, he says, they will not need "the fullest development of material production." If his "minimum" material life can be guaranteed, Guo adds, he himself will have no problem practicing the Communist principle of working according to one's ability and contributing to society.[81]

Guo's taking comfort here in the simple country life recalls vividly his May Fourth passion for the simplicity and innocence of rural and primitive life and his only halfhearted interest in industrialization, urbanization, and modernization.[82] More importantly, it was consistent with his strong Confucian resentment toward human desires for material gains. This resentment, clearly carried over from his May Fourth thinking, was one of the factors that had led to his interest in the Marxist criticism of capitalism, which for him was the quintessential evil of material cravings, "profit-making," and private possession.[83] Ironically, his Confucian antimaterialist attitude, while attracting him to the Marxist anticapitalist conclusion, profoundly conflicted with historical materialism, the "social scientific" thinking that Marx developed to reach his conclusion.

Guo's ambivalence toward the economic/historical determinism of historical materialism also was shown in his ambivalence toward Marx's approach to analyze society and history on the basis of socioeconomic classes. On the one hand, he to a certain degree accepted the Marxist approach. In "The Awakening of Writers and Artists," for instance, he suggests that the division between socioeconomic classes cuts across national boundaries in deciding people's political positions. He writes that for the majority of Chinese people, China's "capitalists," such as the "big merchants" and "big compradors" in Shanghai, are just as evil as foreign capitalists/imperialists: their interests are "completely the same," and they are both enemies of China's (nationalist/Communist) revolution. With the existence of "capitalists" in China, there will be no such thing as an "all-people revolution" in the country.[84]

On the other hand, Guo was not at all rigid in sticking to the Marxist emphasis on people's socioeconomic statuses. Consistent with his May Fourth idealist tendency, which considered ideas more important than material matters, he believed that people's subjective factors could overshadow their socioeconomic backgrounds in determining their political attitudes.[85] In "The Awakening of Writers and Artists," for instance, he writes that young people from "capitalist" or "petty capitalist" families can reach beyond the limitation of their classes if they are "awakened" after "seeing the dark side of society."[86] In "The Creation of a New State," Guo also suggests that the subjective factor of nationalism can, after all, cut across the boundary of classes and turn Chinese capitalists into nationalist/Communist revolutionaries. If, he writes, "the haves" (capitalists) in China become "awakened" to the fact that they cannot well develop their businesses under the "economic oppression" of foreign powers, that their businesses will "eventually" be "swallowed" by foreign imperialists, and that their own "descendants" will enjoy "endless happiness" in the future Communist society, and, further, if they love China more than they love their wealth, then they can join the "proletariat" in the Communist revolution and can even become "the core of the proletariat." If "the haves" are so "awakened," there after all can be an "all-people revolution" in China.[87]

What needs elaborating here is Guo's view of the "proletariat." In "Going to Yixing," written after his announced conversion to Marxism, he seriously challenges the Marxist concept that a strong socioeconomic class of industrial "proletarians," whose birth and maturity came with the development of productive forces in the capitalist system, is an important precondition for Communist revolution. He counters some people's argument that China still does not have a strong "proletarian class" for its "socialist political revolution." China, he writes, does not necessarily need a strong socioeconomic class of proletarians for the revolution. "It does not make sense," he argues, "to say that only proletarian workers can carry out the task of the revolution. Marx and Engels, for instance, were not themselves workers." What China needs is not necessarily industrial workers but people who "spiritually" "agree to socialist revolution." If some "wise" capitalists "spiritually" "agree to socialist political revolution," then they too can "join the revolution," he elaborates along the line of his argument in "The Creation of a New State." What is needed, he emphasizes, is "spiritual agreement [to the revolution]." Marx's "proletarian dictatorship," he adds, "can be interpreted spiritually" and rephrased as "dictatorship by Communists."[88] On another occasion, Guo also stated that the Marxist concept of government by "proletarians" was not "fundamentally" differ-ent from the Confucian concept of rule by "men of virtues," revealing again his preoccupation with the "proletarians" as people of moral/spiritual quality rather than a socioeconomic class.[89]

Guo's concept of relying on moral/spiritual proletarians in China for Commu-nist revolution and his reservation in general about historical materialism not only recalled Confucian (especially Wang Yangming's Neo-Confucian) moral/spiritual emphasis but was also a result of what may be called a Confucian moral/spiritual activism. With its teaching that people constantly cultivate themselves individually and through collective activities in the process of reaching inner transcendence, this activism, in contrast to historical materialism's assigning rather passive roles to man in history, sees people with their moral/spiritual quest being very active partici-pants in the life and history-making of this world and in the overall moral/spiritual evolution of the universe.

Guo's refusal to surrender human subjectivity and action to the rigid law of historical materialism also recalled his May Fourth celebration and deification of man and his May Fourth emphasis on action. Furthermore, his profound diffi-culty with the scientific rule and reason of historical materialism also reminds us of the tension and dichotomy in his May Fourth thinking between reason and emotion/intuition.

Conclusion

Guo Moruo's conversion to Communism (or the formation of his Chinese version of Communism) in the mid-1920s was a result of his struggle to cope with the crisis in his personal life, China's national crisis, what he perceived to be a situational crisis of the whole world, and China's intellectual crisis at that time. These crises were more or less also felt by many of his fellow May Fourthians, driving some of them toward the same Communist cause.

From a global perspective, part of the crises that Guo and his fellow May Fourthians suffered resulted from the overall tensions and problems created by the modern capitalist system, which gave rise to Communist movements not only in China but also in some other parts of the world. The feeling of being suppressed and exploited as individuals, for instance, was shared not only by Guo and others in China's nascent capitalist society but also by many throughout the world in various forms of the capitalist system. The observation that the disaster of the First World War symbolized a fundamental crisis of the whole world under capitalism also was shared by some not only in China but also in the world.

There were, however, factors that made China's transition to Communism unique. When coping with problems of capitalism, for instance, the Chinese also had to struggle with the pressing issue of their national crisis, which boiled down to their being victimized by modern Western and Japanese imperialist powers. Further, the Chinese Communist movement also began in the context of China's intellectual crisis at that time, which centered on the issue of Chinese tradition versus Western modernity. These meant that the Chinese, with their disadvantaged position in the modern world, found themselves having to deal with several global issues at the same time: the problems of capitalism, the impact of modern imperialism (which some consider the extension of capitalism), and the issue of tradition versus modernity, hence we see the formation of a uniquely Chinese Communism.

From the perspective of Chinese history, the beginning of the Chinese Communist movement took place during the May Fourth period, which was a climax in China's struggle to cope with the impact of the modern West since the Opium

109

War of 1839 to 1842 and, more narrowly defined, the climax in what Chang Hao refers to as the Transitional Period of 1895 to the 1920s. As such, the Chinese Communist movement, while being the Chinese part of a worldwide Communist battle against capitalism, was also a continuation of what the May Fourth period had climaxed in modern Chinese history: a struggle against the impact of modern imperialism and an effort to find a solution to the issue of Chinese tradition versus Western modernity.

Specifically, on the issue of Chinese tradition versus Western modernity, the Chinese Communists, in their fight against capitalism and foreign imperialism, inherited much of the May Fourth's discontinuity and continuity with the tradition. On the one hand, for instance, there was a substantial link between the Communists and the May Fourth's break with the Confucian family and *lijiao* society, not only in the sense that the May Fourth individualist awakening (against the Confucian family and *lijiao*) helped lead some of them to be attracted to Marx's promise of individual emancipation, but also in the sense that they later popularized among the masses the May Fourth theme of rebelling against the Confucian family and *lijiao* society. On the other hand, the May Fourth's continuation with the *xiu, zhi,* and *ping* portions of the Confucian orientational model also found its way into the Chinese Communist cause, to the extent that it helped result in a Confucian moralist modification of Marxist historical materialism, and to the extent that the Confucian calling to manage the state and harmonize the world contributed to the Communists' drive to save China and the whole of mankind.

As far as Guo Moruo was concerned, while he had a break from his early commitment to the Communist cause between the end of the Northern Expedition and 1949, he ended up being a major figure in the Maoist revolution from the 1950s all the way to Mao's death in 1976. He held various high-level government positions under Mao Zedong, and with his fame as a leading modern Chinese intellectual, he became a symbol of intellectuals' participation in and loyalty to Mao's revolution. Such symbolism became especially noteworthy when more and more intellectuals were alienated and persecuted during Mao's increasingly radicalized revolution.

From time to time, of course, Guo himself also became a target of Mao's thought reforms. But he took it willingly and adjusted accordingly, so much so that many came to criticize him for being a shameless survivor without any principles in the ever-changing tide of the Maoist radical revolution. This may be true, except that one also can argue that one major reason Guo followed the revolution so closely was because he really believed in its cause. In other words, the seeming lack of principles in Guo's political career under Mao might have actually resulted from an ultimate principle of his own—the principle that he developed in the 1920s— one that was basically the same as the Maoist principle of Communist revolution.

Guo heavily paid for his principle and cause. One of his sons was persecuted to death during the Cultural Revolution, the ultimate Maoist revolution that he followed.[1] Some also regret that Guo, in devoting himself to the collective cause of Maoism, had profoundly and tragically lost himself as an individual and intellectual.

Guo himself, however, might not have felt that he had completely lost his self in the Communist revolution. From the point of view of his Confucian/Marxist Communism, the ultimate fulfillment of oneself (self-cultivation) is achieved only through participating in the collective cause of nation building (managing the state) and worldwide Communist revolution (harmonizing the world). And participating in this cause was exactly what Guo did in the Maoist revolution. In devoting himself to such a collective cause, which was larger than himself, lofty from his perspective, and promising at his time, he might have had a sense of self-fulfillment some time during the course of the revolution.

Tragically, one may say, Guo was not alone at all in following this path. Millions of Chinese, in answering Mao Zedong's call, followed in the 1960s and 1970s the example of Lei Feng (雷鋒) (1940–1962), a Liberation Army soldier who devoted himself to the Communist cause and eventually died young for the cause. What Lei Feng's case symbolized was a key concept of the Maoist revolution: to fulfill the meaning of one's individual life, one should devote his limited life to the limitless (eternal) cause of serving the people (把有限的生命投入到無限的為人民服務中去). It is not difficult, of course, to see the similarity between this Maoist mentality and Guo's early Confucian/Marxist concept of fulfilling oneself through the collective Communist cause.

Can one say, then, that Guo and his fellow Maoists lost themselves in a revolution that had completely failed? Not entirely so. While ultimately a disaster in many aspects, their revolution did strengthen China as a nation. Out of the Maoist era, the country had become a military power in the world. The nationalist goal of their revolution, therefore, was to some extent achieved.

When the Chinese Communist revolution was born, Guo's conversion to it substantially represented the revolution's path from the May Fourth movement. When the Maoist revolution died, Guo was a noticeable figure in and at its deathbed. Whatever the revolution turned out to be, Guo was significantly relevant in its history.

Notes

INTRODUCTION

1. After participating in the Northern Expedition, Guo distanced himself to some degree from practicing Communists in China. After 1949, however, he did come back to Communist practice and became a significantly influential participant in some of the revolutionary movements led by Mao Zedong.

2. Various scholars have studied Guo. Their works include David Roy's *Kuo Mo-jo: The Early Years*, Leo Ou-fan Lee's *The Romantic Generation of Modern Chinese Writers*, and Jaroslav Prusek's *The Lyrical and the Epic: Studies of Modern Chinese Literature*. This study significantly differs from their works, especially because of its elaborate analysis of the complexities of Guo's (and, in a larger sense, May Fourth intellectuals' and Chinese Communists') continuity as well as discontinuity with the Confucian tradition.

3. Works on the rise of Chinese Communism include Benjamin I. Schwartz's *Chinese Communism and the Rise of Mao*, Maurice Meisner's *Li Ta-chao and the Origins of Chinese Marxism*, Lee Feigon's *Chen Duxiu: Founder of the Chinese Communist Party*, and Arif Dirlik's *The Origins of Chinese Communism*. While significantly contributing to the understanding of Chinese Communism, these works in general lack attention to the relationship between China's Confucian tradition and the rise of Chinese Communism, one of the subjects on which I focus in my study.

4. Yu Ying-shih (余英時) has recently challenged the analogical use of "enlightenment" to describe the May Fourth intellectual movement. Yu, however, does not disagree that "autonomy of the individual" was part of the May Fourth pursuit. See Yu Ying-shih, "Neither Renaissance nor Enlightenment: A Historian's Reflections on the May Fourth Movement" in *The Appropriation of Cultural Capital: China's May Fourth Project*, ed. Milena Dolezelova-Velingerova and Oldrich Kral (Cambridge, MA, and London: Harvard University Press, 2001), 299–324.

5. Li Zehou, *Zhongguo xiandai sixiangshi lun* (Hefei: Anhui wenyi chubanshe, 1994), 29–45.

6. Guo Moruo, *Wenyi lunji (huijiao ben)*, ed. Huang Chunhao (Hunan: Hunan People's Press, 1984), 67–68; *Hongshui* (Shanghai: Shanghai shudian, 1985), vol. 1, no. 7: 212–219; vol. 1, no. 9: 323–330; vol. 2, no. 14: 71–82.

The use of the Chinese-Western polarity as a scholarly approach, though often relevant and convenient, is not without its limits. Such a polarity, for instance, presupposes profound incompatibility between Chinese tradition and Western modernity. As my book shows, Guo's May Fourth thinking and his early Communist thought suggest that there is not necessarily always an insurmountable gap between tradition and modernity.

Benjamin Schwartz also noticed that there may be similarity between some elements of Chinese traditional thought and modern Western thinking. See Benjamin I. Schwartz, *China and Other Matters* (Cambridge, MA: Harvard University Press, 1996), 55, 58–59.

Also, Li Zehou argues that during the May Fourth period enthusiasm for the modern West led some intellectuals to Marxism while continued faith in Chinese tradition led some others toward the later formation of New-Confucianism, something fundamentally different from Marxism. Contrary to Li's argument, the case of Guo, who clearly verbalized his Communist thinking as a combination of the best of both Western modernity and Chinese tradition, shows that the May Fourth interest in Communism was not without its traditional Chinese background.

Further, as an interesting reference, Guo's endeavor to combine the best of Chinese tradition and Western modernity reminds us of, among others, his May Fourth contemporary Hu Shi's intention to "connect" the best of Chinese civilization with the best of the modern West. See Dolezelova-Velingerova and Kral, eds., *The Appropriation of Cultural Capital*, 306, 313.

7. Wm. Theodore de Bary, *Learning for One's Self—Essays on the Individual in Neo-Confucian Thought* (New York: Columbia University Press, 1991), 4, 8.

8. Benjamin I. Schwartz, *In Search of Wealth and Power: Yen Fu and the West* (Cambridge, MA: Harvard University Press, 1964), 19.

9. Yu Ying-shih, *Neizai chaoyue zhilu*, ed. Xin Hua and Ren Jing (Beijing: Zhongguo guangbodianshi chubanshe, 1992), 12.

10. Guo's keeping the *qi* (regulating the family) part of the Confucian sequence here should be taken as a matter of rhetoric, since, as elaborated later, by 1925 he had long broken with the Confucian concept and social norm of regulating the family.

11. Guo Moruo, *Wenyi lunji (huijiao ben)*, 60.

12. My linking of the Confucian calling for state management here to Guo's modern drive to save his nation obviously differs from Myron L. Cohen's argument that there has been an "iconoclastic nationalism" or "nationalistic antitraditionalism" among modern Chinese (especially May Fourth) intellectuals, who have negated Chinese tradition for the sake of China's present-day national salvation. The nationalist drives of these intellectuals, I argue, were not entirely "iconoclastic," since part of their inspiration came (subconsciously perhaps for many) from the traditional Confucian calling for managing the state. See Myron L. Cohen, "Being Chinese: The Peripheralization of Traditional Identity," *Daedalus* 120: 2 (Spring 1991): 127.

13. Liu Shaoqi, *Lun gongchandangyuan de xiuyang* (Beijing: People's Press, 1949).

14. Guo's individualist confrontation with the Confucian family and *lijiao* society was not always a black-and-white issue of modern Western individualism versus Chinese Confucian tradition. In the struggle to assert himself against the social norms and ethics of *lijiao*, he actually got help from the Confucian personalist emphasis on the development of the self. Functioning within the heavily collective-oriented Confucian system, of course,

such emphasis on the self would hardly amount to serious encouragement for individualist confrontation with society. Under the influence of and cofunctioning with modern Western individualism, however, that Confucian concept of the self became a positive factor in help-ing Guo justify his rebellious behavior against the collective of *lijiao* society. In other words, in his case, the otherwise nonconfrontational tension between the Confucian emphasis on the self and Confucian collectivism turned confrontational due to the outside influence of Western individualism.

Also, Guo's break with the Confucian father-son and husband-wife bonds needs to be viewed in a relative context. While disobeying his Confucian parents on the arranged mar-riage and dishonoring his obligation as a Confucian husband to his arranged wife, he never ceased loving his parents as a son, and he did not develop a total disrespect for the social institution of marriage.

15. On this matter, Chang Hao offers some elaborate analysis. See Chang Hao, *Chang Hao zixuan ji* (Shanghai: Shanghai jiaoyu chubanshe, 2002), 109–125.

16. Leo Ou-fan Lee has recently argued that "much scholarship on the May Fourth has been preoccupied with, hence 'wasted' on, its anti-traditionalism." "In historical hindsight," he writes, "it now seems quite clear that the May Fourth revolution did not destroy Chinese tradition." While my findings on Guo Moruo's significant continuity with the tradition to a substantial extent agree with Lee's criticism, Guo's (and many of his fellow May Fourthians') break with the Confucian family and the *lijiao* society did amount to a destruction of a major portion of the tradition. See Dolezelova-Velingerova and Kral, eds., *The Appropriation of Cultural Capital*, 33.

17. For instance, Chang Hao, in his thesis on what he calls the "Transitional Period" in modern Chinese intellectual history, has elaborately analyzed the changes of the Confu-cian tradition from 1895 to 1920. See Chang Hao, *Chang Hao zixuan ji*, 109–125.

18. Li Zehou notes that the May Fourth "enlightenment" had resulted in some intel-lectuals' interest in anarchism which, among other things, features the goal of achieving "the absolute freedom of the individual." Then some of these intellectuals came to realize that anarchism was, after all, impractical "empty talking." In contrast, Marxism had in reality just succeeded in Soviet Russia. As a result, Li argues, some of those intellectuals turned from anarchism to Marxism, as they had to a certain extent confused Marxism with anarchism and taken Marxism as some kind of a practical alternative to the empty talk of anarchism. Insightful as it is, however, Li's argument is vague and stops short of seeing a direct relation-ship between the May Fourth awakening of individual freedom and the beginning of interest in Marxism in China. See Li Zehou, *Zhongguo xiandai sixiangshi lun*, 29–35.

19. Guo did not confuse Marxism with anarchism here, as Li Zehou would argue, even though Guo was for a while vaguely interested in anarchism. Marxism attracted Guo here because it did clearly promise him a society in which "the free development of each is the condition for the free development of all." See *Chuangzao yuekan* (Shanghai: Shanghai shudian, 1983), vol. I, no. 2: 128, 138; Karl Marx and Frederick Engels, *The Communist Manifesto* (New York: International Publishers, 1948), 31.

Guo's attraction to the Marxist promise of ultimate individual development also can be traced to his influence by Confucian personalism which, as elaborated on later in this book, emphasizes in its own way the importance of the self.

20. Li Dazhao, *Li Dazhao wenji* (Beijing: Renmin chubanshe, 1984), vol. II, 437–438.

21. Ibid., 609.

22. Qu Qiubai, *Qu Qiubai wenji (zhengzhi lilun bian)* (Beijing: Renmin chubanshe, 1988), vol. II, 24–25.

It also should be noted that, like Guo's May Fourth thinking, Mao Zedong's pre-Communist thought around the period 1917–1918 also consisted of a combination of both Confucian personalism and Western individualism. While in a way carrying the Confucian concern for others, Mao's thinking at the time centered on the self, which in his writing sometimes overshadows the interests of others. One can argue that Mao's leap in a few years from such individualist thinking to Communism may not be fully explained with the theories of nationalism overtaking individualism or confusion of anarchism with Marxism. See Mao Zedong, *Mao Zedong zaoqi wengao* (Changsha: Hunan chubanshe, 1990), 116–285.

23. This point can be supported by Cai Hesen's (蔡和森) 1920 statement that he saw Communism and anarchism as sharing common goals and that for him "proletarian dictatorship" is the means, "the only means," to eventually achieve those goals. See Li Zehou, *Zhongguo xiandai sixiangshi lun*, 33.

24. Zhao Shuli, *Zhao Shuli xuanji* (Beijing: Kaiming shudian, 1951). One can in fact easily argue that the popular support that the Communists won because of their anti-*lijiao* social reforms was a major reason for their eventual success in China.

25. Mao Zedong, *Selected Works of Mao Zedong* (Beijing: Renmin chubanshe, 1969), 1002. Later a third "Mountain," "bureaucrat capitalism" (*guanliao zibenzhuyi* 官僚資本主義), was included as a target of the Communist revolution.

26. In this regard, the continuous functioning of the Confucian calling to manage the state can be seen in the fact that many Chinese during and after May Fourth fought against the Confucian family and *lijiao* society not only for themselves as individuals but also for reforming and saving their nation in the modern world.

27. Lydia Liu argues that individualism, which has an "apparent clash with the nation-state," contributed to China's national revolution or, in her words, "contributed to the process of inventing *geren* (individual) for the goals of liberation and national revolution." As I see it, the reason May Fourth individualism could have contributed to the Communist national revolution was because it was limited in its scope: it focused on challenging the Confucian family and *lijiao* society and was not confrontational with the nation-state. See Lydia H. Liu, *Translingual Practice: Literature, National Culture, and Translated Modernity—China, 1900–1937* (Stanford, CA: Stanford University Press, 1995), 91.

Paraphrasing Mark Elvin's argument, Kirk Denton also discusses a "duality at the heart of modern (Chinese) representations of self": a "paradox ... wherein the individual feels at once a powerful desire to assert the self against tradition and society and an equally compelling need to submit to the forces of history or the moral appeal of a collective self. Individual writers may exhibit a paradoxical tendency to both exalt the self and allow the self to succumb to such larger totalities as History, Nation, Epoch, or the Masses." I believe that a major portion of such dualistic phenomena could be better understood by seeing the limited nature of May Fourth Western-inspired individualism, which resulted in the individual's rebellion against the Confucian family and *lijiao* society but at the same time made it possible for an individual to be (continuously) loyal to the nation (and collective causes such as that of Communism). As his or her Confucian devotion to the nation was seldom interfered with by this limited individualism, the Chinese individual often willingly and enthusiastically participated in the nationalist (and other collectivist) cause(s) during and after May Fourth and was not, at least not always, passively "submit(ting)" or "succumb(ing)" to the nation or other collectives. (The individual's passion for China as a nation also was a result of the influence of modern nationalism.) On a related issue, I also would argue that with the limited individualism, the May Fourth individual was mostly "exalt(ing)" the self against the Confucian family and *lijiao* society and was in reality not "asserting" himself or herself against "tradition" in general, of which the Confucian family and *lijiao* society were only a part. See Kirk A. Denton, *The Problematic of Self in Modern Chinese Literature: Hu Feng and Lu Ling* (Stanford, CA: Stanford University Press, 1998), 68.

28. This book is no place to elaborately engage in the contemporary controversy among scholars over the difference between the young and mature Marx on the issue of his humanism and his willingness to use force and violence. As far as this author can see, Marx, at least in his late years, did advocate the use of violence for revolutionary purposes.

Also, the liberation of the nation here is more of an issue and a concern for Leninism than Marxism.

29. He did have to make an effort, though, to adapt to the Marxist/Leninist view that nations will eventually cease to exist in the Communist cosmopolitanist world, since his Confucian sequence of managing the state and harmonizing the world does not necessarily make the nation irrelevant in the cosmopolitan harmony.

30. Guo Moruo, Zong Baihua, and Tian Shouchang, *San ye ji* (Shanghai: Yadong tushuguan, 1923), 145.

Guo's combining the Confucian concept of inner transcendence with Marxism shows that he as a Chinese individual found Marxist materialism lacking what he needed for moral and spiritual guidance. Interestingly, as Gail Lee Bernstein points out, Kawakami Hajime also found that Marxism could not meet his spiritual needs as a Japanese individual. See Gail Lee Bernstein, *Japanese Marxist: A Portrait of Kawakami Hajime 1879–1946* (Cambridge, MA: Harvard University Press, 1990), 169.

31. *Hongshui*, vol. 1, no. 8: 233; Guo Moruo, *Xuesheng shidai* (Hong Kong: Sanlian shudian, 1978), 335–336. Guo's argument here recalls Wang Yangming's Neo-Confucian emphasis on the power of the mind-heart and will.

32. Guo Moruo, *Xinglunan* (Shanghai: Shangwu yinshuguan, 1933), 82, 84–85.

33. Mao and Yun both expressed longing for pastoral ideals in 1919. See Peng Ming, *Wusi yundong shi* (Beijing: Renmin chubanshe, 1984), 509–510. According to Maurice Meisner, Li Dazhao also had strong admiration for rural life and anti-urban sentiments, and Li also had publicly expressed reservations about historical materialism. Unlike Guo Moruo's statement here, however, Li agreed with Marx's insistence on high-level material production as a characteristic of Communism. See Meisner, *Li Ta-chao*, 82–83, 86, 91–95, 149.

It should be noted that while the pastoral/rural mentality of Guo, Mao, Yun, and Li can all be traced to their Confucian (and Taoist) upbringings, Li's rural mentality was also a result of the influence of Russian populism, as pointed out by Meisner. The only thing that may marginally relate Guo to Russian populist influence is his interest in the early 1920s in Turgenev's *Virgin Soil*, which deals with the populist movement.

CHAPTER 1

1. Guo Moruo, *Shaonian shidai* (Hong Kong: Sanlian shudian, 1978), 266.

2. Ibid., 266–268.

3. Ibid., 268–269.

4. Ibid., 270.

5. Ibid., 269–270.

6. Wang Jiquan and Tong Weigang, *Guo Moruo nianpu (1)* (Jiangsu: Jiangsu People's Press, 1983), 44. Guo also said it was January 15 of China's lunar year that year. See Guo Moruo, *Shaonian shidai*, 277.

7. Guo Moruo, *Shaonian shidai*, 276.

8. Ibid., 276–277; Wang and Tong, *Guo Moruo nianpu (1)*, 257.

9. Guo Moruo, *Shaonian shidai*, 281–283.

10. Ibid., 284.

11. Ibid., 284–285.

12. Ibid., 285.

13. Ibid.

14. He was to see his arranged wife only two more times in his lifetime, first during a very short trip back home in July 1913 to say good-bye to his parents before he left Sichuan that year, and then in 1939 when going home to visit his aged father. As for the wife, even though Guo abandoned her, she was to honor the arranged marriage, just as many women did in the traditional Confucian society, and she stayed at Guo's parents' home as his wife. See Guo Moruo, *Shaonian shidai*, 290–292, 304; Zhongguo Guo Moruo yanjiu xuehui, *Guo Moruo yu rujia wenhua* (Jinan: Shandong renmin chubanshe, 1994), 92.

15. Guo Moruo, *Shaonian shidai*, 40–41.

16. Ibid., 79–81.

17. Guo Moruo, *Guo Moruo jiuti shici xinian zhushi*, ed. Wang Guoquan et al. (Harbin: Heilongjiang remin chubanshe, 1982), 39.

18. Guo Moruo, *Shaonian shidai*, 266.

19. Ibid., 297.

20. Ibid.

21. Guo Moruo, *Shaonian shidai*, 297, 316–317. Guo's involvement in the "unhealthy" habits, it should be noted, had been going on for a long time in his early years in Sichuan. With the impact of Western cultures and abolition of the civil service examinations in 1905, China's educational system went through radical and chaotic changes. The old Confucian authority of the school and teachers came to be increasingly challenged by students, sometimes because of the teachers' lack of training to meet the needs of teaching the new (Western) subjects. In reacting to this situation, Guo, dissatisfied with his schools and some teachers, had repeatedly run into trouble in school and ended up involved in activities such as drinking, gambling, causing trouble in theaters, and homosexual behavior, which was considered something "ugly" in Confucian culture. Other factors also had contributed to these habits, such as his adolescent mind-set and the frustration over his parents' refusal to let him leave Sichuan for school abroad or in big cities such as Beijing and Shanghai. Years later, when writing his autobiography in the late 1920s, Guo clearly regretted these "shameful," "degenerate," "disgusting," "stupid," and "meaningless" behaviors in his Sichuan years. It is possible that the memory of this period in his life was part of the reason for the sense of guilt

and inferiority that he had in his pre-1919 years in Japan. See Guo Moruo, *Shaonian shidai*, 91–93, 96–99, 101–106; Guo Moruo, *Xuesheng shidai*, 5.

22. Guo Moruo, *Shaonian shidai*, 308, 316–317.

23. Ibid., 316–319.

24. Ibid., 319–338; Guo Moruo, *Xuesheng shidai*, 9; Wang and Tong, *Guo Moruo nianpu (1)*, 54.

25. Guo Moruo, *Xuesheng shidai*, 10; Guo Moruo, *Yinghua shujian*, ed. Tang Ming-zhong and Huang Gaobin (Sichuan: Sichuan People's Press, 1981), 22–23; Wang and Tong, *Guo Moruo nianpu (1)*, 56.

26. Guo Moruo, *Xuesheng shidai*, 10.

27. Wang and Tong, *Guo Moruo nianpu (1)*, 73, 150.

28. Guo Moruo, Zong Baihua, and Tian Shouchang, *San ye ji*, 36–38; Wang and Tong, *Guo Moruo nianpu (1)*, 62–63, 65.

29. Guo Moruo, *Guo Moruo xuanji* (Hong Kong: Wenxue chubanshe, 1956), 47; Guo Moruo, *Yinghua shujian*, 142.

30. Guo Moruo, *Shaonian shidai*, 295–296.

31. Guo Moruo, *Guo Moruo xuanji*, 47.

32. Ibid., 47.

33. Guo Moruo, *Yinghua shujian*, 22, 44–45, 80, 89, 128, 140, 144–145.

34. Ibid., 79–80.

35. Guo Moruo, *Guo Moruo xuanji*, 47–50; Guo Moruo, *Yinghua shujian*, 142.

36. Guo Moruo, *Wenyi lunji*, 185.

37. Guo Moruo, *Guo Moruo jiuti shici xinian zhushi*, 114.

38. After he noted receiving a letter from his Sichuan home in early November 1917, Guo did not seem to hear from his parents again until March 1918. See Guo Moruo, *Yinghua shujian*, 135–136, 140.

39. Guo Moruo, *Yinghua shujian*, 144.

40. Guo Moruo, *Guo Moruo jiuti shici xinian zhushi*, 117–118. One reason Guo refers to Tomiko here as a "bird without its nest" is probably because their living together without her parents' permission had resulted in her parents' ending their relations with her. This conflict between Tomiko and her family reflects the complexity of Japanese society which, on the one hand, had been Westernized and, on the other, was still very much controlled by Confucian and other traditional morals. The metaphor of a "bird without its nest" in this poem also might refer to the fact that Guo and Tomiko, because of their low income, had to move quite often in order to find rental houses at bargain prices.

41. Guo Moruo, *Guo Moruo xuanji*, 49.

42. This sister was called "Seventh Sister" according to a certain way of naming the children in Guo's family. She was not really the seventh among Guo's sisters.

43. In a letter to home in November 1917, Guo mentioned that this sister had been arranged to be married in 1918. See Guo Moruo, *Yinghua shujian*, 135–136.

44. Guo Moruo, *Yinghua shujian*, 79–81.

45. Guo Moruo, *Guo Moruo xuanji*, 47.

46. Guo Moruo, *Yinghua shujian*, 135–136.

47. Guo Moruo, *Guo Moruo xuanji*, 47.

48. Guo Moruo, Zong Baihua, and Tian Shouchang, *San ye ji*, 37.

49. Guo Moruo, *Guo Moruo jiuti shici xinian zhushi*, 122.

50. Ibid., 128.

51. Guo Moruo, *Wenyi lunji*, 55.

52. Ibid., 186.

53. Guo Moruo, *Nushen (huijiao ben)*, ed. Sang Fengkang (Hunan: Hunan People's Press, 1983), 202.

54. Guo Moruo, *Wenyi lunji*, 184–185; Guo Moruo, *Xuesheng shidai*, 57; Guo Moruo, *Nushen*, 202.

55. Guo Moruo, *Wenyi lunji*, 186.

56. Guo Moruo, *Xuesheng shidai*, 58; Guo Moruo, *Nushen*, 200.

57. Guo Moruo, *Nushen*, 210; Guo Moruo, *Xuesheng shidai*, 57.

58. Guo Moruo, *Wenyi lunji*, 55–56; Wang and Tong, *Guo Moruo nianpu (1)*, 60.

59. For specific methods of quiet sitting he had followed the instructions of a Japanese book. See Guo Moruo, *Wenyi lunji*, 56.

60. Guo Moruo, *Wenyi lunji*, 56.

61. Ibid.

62. Hou Wailu et al., *Zhongguo sixiangshi gang* (Beijing: Zhongguo qingnian chubanshe, 1980–1981), 336.

63. Guo Moruo, *Wenyi lunji*, 56.

64. Ibid., 58, 64.

65. David Roy believes that Guo's *Luo Ye* is evidence that Guo once converted to Christianity. This author, however, does not think that *Luo Ye* is credible evidence in this regard. See Roy, *Kuo Mo-jo*, 188; Guo Moruo, *Guo Moruo quanji (wenxuebian 9)*, ed. Guo Moruo zhuzuo bianji chuban weiyuanhui (Beijing: Remin wenxue chubanshe, 1985), 67.

66. Guo Moruo, *Wenyi lunji*, 185–186.

After he fell in love with Tomiko in 1916, Guo also became interested in Heinrich Heine (1797–1856). With his adventurous experience of loving and living with Tomiko, he found that he could relate to Heine's works and find in them some encouragement for his romantic desires and feelings. With the "rich this-worldliness" that they expressed, he once noted, Heine's poems appealed to him as being "closer to nature" than the "other-worldliness" of Tagore's works. See Guo Moruo, *Nushen*, 203; Guo Moruo, *Xuesheng shidai*, 57–58.

67. Hou Wailu et al., *Zhongguo sixiangshi gang*, 337, 338; Qian Mu, *Yangmingxue shuyao* (Taiwan: Zhengzhong shuju, 1955), 72, 47, 49.

Lao Zi, in whom Guo also was interested, also taught people to free themselves from all desires. See Guo Moruo, *Wenyi lunji*, 20.

68. Guo Moruo, *Nushen*, 204, 141, 210; Guo Moruo, "Guo Moruo nushen jiwai yiwen," ed. Deng Niudun, *Nankai University Journal* 2 (1978): 58; Guo Moruo, *Xuesheng shidai*, 56, 59.

69. Guo still lived in Japan during this period until April 1921, when he started moving back and forth between Japan and China.

70. Guo Moruo, *Xuesheng shidai*, 59; Guo Moruo, *Nushen*, 201–210.

71. Guo Moruo, *Nushen*, 210.

Guo's literary success also meant that he had finally discovered that he was a man of worth and talent (in literature). Previously, his interest in literature had made him indifferent toward medical studies, and his hearing problem (as a sequelae of typhus abdominalis) had made it difficult for him to follow lectures at medical school. With his problems at school, he had experienced self-doubt and a sense of inferiority as an underachiever and painfully considered himself a man without talent. See Guo Moruo, *Guo Moruo jiuti shici xinian zhushi*, 123.

72. The collection was published in May 1920, only eight months after the first publication of his poems and the beginning of what he called the "emancipation" of his feelings. In fact, his first letter to confess his "guilt" to Zong, then editor of *Shi Shi Xin Bao's Xue Deng*, was written on January 18, 1920, just four months after his first publication. See Wang and Tong, *Guo Moruo nianpu (1)*, 99; Guo Moruo, Zong Baihua, and Tian Shouchang, *San ye ji*, 21.

73. Guo Moruo, Zong Baihua, and Tian Shouchang, *San ye ji*, 33–43.

74. Ibid., 57–65.

75. Guo's interest in Goethe seemed to have casually started when he began to be exposed to Goethe's works in his German classes at the Sixth Higher School at Okayama. One of the texts that he read for German in his third year at the higher school, for instance, was Goethe's *Dichtung und Wahrheit*. By about 1918, he also seemed to have read Goethe's *The Sorrows of Young Werther*, for he had by then already thought about translating the novel into Chinese. In the summer of 1919, he also started his intermittent translation of parts of Goethe's *Faust*, some of which were later published in China. See Guo Moruo, *Xuesheng shidai*, 57, 64; Wang and Tong, *Guo Moruo nianpu (1)*, 68–69; Guo Moruo, *Wenyi lunji*, 226–227.

76. Guo Moruo, Zong Baihua, and Tian Shouchang, *San ye ji*, 12, 14–15.

77. Ibid., 14–15.

The complexity that Guo saw in Goethe's life and personality also might have helped him ease his sense of guilt over the "unhealthy" habits that he had developed in his early years in Sichuan. As shown in *San Ye Ji*, he also received help in this regard from Zong Baihua. See Guo Moruo, Zong Baihua, and Tian Shouchang, *San ye ji*, 28, 11, 43.

It needs mentioning that the confessions written and published by St. Augustine (354–430), Jean-Jacques Rousseau (1712–1778), and Count Leo Nikolaevich Tolstoy (1828–1910) also seemed to have inspired Guo to confess his sense of guilt to his friends and to the public and thus make a major step to finally justify his rebellion against the ethics of *lijiao*. Further, Oliver Goldsmith (1728–1774) and Charles Baudelaire (1821–1867) also seemed to have helped Guo get rid of his sense of immorality. With his past and his literary success, Guo seemed to have discovered that he could relate to Goldsmith's "degeneration" and Baudelaire's "decadence," as well as their achievement as established Western literary figures. See Guo Moruo, Zong Baihua, and Tian Shouchang, *San ye ji*, 9, 44, 76.

78. Guo Moruo, Zong Baihua, and Tian Shouchang, *San ye ji*, 73–76.

79. Ibid., 76.

80. Ibid., preface.

81. Ibid., appendix, 1–2.

82. Ibid., 35.

83. Ibid., appendix, 1–2, 4; Guo Moruo, *Xuesheng shidai*, 59.

84. Guo Moruo, Zong Baihua, and Tian Shouchang, *San ye ji*, Zong's postscript, 4.

85. Wang and Tong, *Guo Moruo nianpu (1)*, 16; Guo Moruo, *Wenyi lunji*, 238–243.

86. Guo Moruo, *Wenyi lunji*, 239–240.

87. Wang and Tong, *Guo Moruo nianpu (1)*, 120, 130.

88. It should be noted that Guo still deeply loved his parents. In fact, the knowledge that he had broken his parents' hearts was the most unbearable for him in his rebellion against the arranged marriage. Further, Guo was not without sympathy toward his arranged wife. In his eyes, the woman was just a "pitiful" and an "innocent" "victim" of "the old system." See Guo Moruo, *Ganlan* (Shanghai: Xiandai shuju, 1931), 51–58; Guo Moruo, *Guo Moruo xuanji*, 48.

89. Guo Moruo, *Wenyi lunji*, 13–14.

90. Ibid., 19.

91. Guo's belief was probably based on *Li ji*, which suggests that Confucius had divorced his wife. See *Li Ji* (Taiwan: Yiwen yinshuguan, 1989).

92. Guo Moruo, Zong Baihua, and Tian Shouchang, *San ye ji*, 12–15.

93. Guo Moruo, *Wenyi lunji*, 10–11, 27.

94. Guo here played on two Chinese characters: *si* (silk) and *shi* (poetry).

95. Guo Moruo, *Guo Moruo yiwenji (1)*, ed. Wang Jinhou et al. (Chengdu: Sichuan University Press, 1988), 31–32; Guo Moruo, *Nushen*, 144–146. I have consulted *Selected Poems from the Goddesses* for part of the translation here. See Guo Moruo, *Selected Poems from the Goddesses*, trans. John Lester and A. C. Barnes (Beijing: Foreign Languages Press, 1958).

96. Guo Moruo, *Guo Moruo yiwenji (1)*, 32.

97. Guo Moruo, *Wenyi lunji*, 191–192.

98. Though Tomiko had strongly resisted Guo's attempts at a literary career, believing that medicine would be a more reliable profession for him to pursue in order to provide for the family, she finally gave in to his love for literature. Their original plan was that Guo should go to Shanghai first by himself. Once he found a job there and could support the family, Tomiko and the children would follow him. See Guo Moruo, *Xuesheng shidai*, 75–76; Wang and Tong, *Guo Moruo nianpu (1)*, 112–113.

99. Wang and Tong, *Guo Moruo nianpu (1)*, 120.

100. Guo Moruo, *Xuesheng shidai*, 92, 108.

101. Wang and Tong, *Guo Moruo nianpu (1)*, 116–118, 120; Guo Moruo, *Xuesheng shidai*, 93.

102. Guo Moruo, *Xuesheng shidai*, 115.

103. For a comparison of how much 203 yuan meant at the time, a school in Shanghai once offered a monthly salary of 200 yuan for a position to teach English.

104. Guo Moruo, *Xuesheng shidai*, 84–85, 115.

105. Ibid., 93.

106. Ibid., 115–116.

107. Ibid., 114.

108. Ibid., 85, 93.

109. Ibid., 85, 92–93.

110. Ibid., 114.

111. Wang and Tong, *Guo Moruo nianpu (1)*, 121; Guo Moruo, *Xuesheng shidai*, 122.

112. Guo Moruo, *Xuesheng shidai*, 122–123.

113. Wang and Tong, *Guo Moruo nianpu (1)*, 132, 139; Guo Moruo, *Xuesheng shidai*, 124–129, 150.

114. Guo Moruo, *Xuesheng shidai*, 150.

115. *Chuangzao zhoubao* (Shanghai: Shanghai shudian, 1983), vol. 2, no. 47: 10–14. Guo also once said that the position offered to him by the Red Cross was president of the hospital. See *Chuangzao zhoubao*, vol. 2, no. 41: 6.

116. *Chuangzao zhoubao*, vol. 2, no. 41: 6.

117. Guo Moruo, *Xuesheng shidai*, 150.

118. Ibid., 125, 150, 151. Cheng Fangwu returned to work for Tai Dong in Shanghai in October 1922.

119. Guo Moruo, *Xuesheng shidai*, 152, 156. Yu Dafu at the time also was in Shanghai working at least part time for Tai Dong.

120. Guo Moruo, *Xuesheng shidai*, 165.

121. Ibid., 156, 165. For Tai Dong's treatment of Guo and his friends, also see Yu Dafu, *Yu Dafu zixu*, ed. Zhao Hongmei (Beijing: Tuanjie chubanshe, 1996), 98.

122. Guo Moruo, *Xuesheng shidai*, 167–168.

123. Ibid., 125, 151–152, 167–168.

124. Ibid., 150.

125. Guo's third son was born in January 1923. See Wang and Tong, *Guo Moruo nianpu (1)*, 146; Guo Moruo, *Xuesheng shidai*, 151.

126. *Chuangzao zhoubao*, vol. 2, no. 41: 6.

127. Guo Moruo, *Xuesheng shidai*, 165, 339.

128. *Chuangzao zhoubao*, vol. 2, no. 41: 9.

129. Ibid., 7. Guo never mentioned later what had happened to this plan. Judging from the available information, it seems that Tomiko never actually followed through on this plan.

130. Guo Moruo, *Xuesheng shidai*, 166, 152.

131. Ibid., 181–182.

132. Ibid., 188.

133. Ibid., 165. Guo also once said that he was thinking of working as a teaching or research assistant in the physiology department at Kyushu Imperial University. See *Chuangzao zhoubao*, vol. 2, no. 47: 14.

134. *Chuangzao zhoubao*, vol. 2, no. 41: 12–13.

135. Ibid., 10.

136. Ibid., 6.

137. *Chuangzao zhoubao*, vol. 2, no. 47: 6–7.

138. Ibid., 7–9.

139. In late July 1923 Yu was still working on *Creation Daily* in Shanghai and showed no intention of leaving. By late October of that year, then, Yu had already left for Beijing. The confrontation between Yu and Guo, therefore, should have taken place between late July and late October 1923. See Guo Moruo, *Xuesheng shidai*, 156–157, 160, 162–163.

140. Guo Moruo, *Xuesheng shidai*, 160–161.

141. Ibid., 162–168, 190–191.

142. Ibid., 127, 140–148, 153–155, 122, 86–90, 109, 126–129, 197–198; Guo Moruo, *Wenyi lunji*, 140; *Chuangzao jikan* (Shanghai: Shanghai shudian, 1983), vol. 1, no. 1: 17–18.

143. *Chuangzao zhoubao*, vol. 2, no. 41: 12.

144. Guo Moruo, *Xuesheng shidai*, 170; *Chuangzao zhoubao*, vol. 2, no. 52: 15; Guo Moruo, *Guo Moruo yiwenji (1)*, 126.

145. Guo Moruo, *Xuesheng shidai*, 181–182; Guo Moruo, *Guo Moruo yiwenji (1)*, 126–127; *Chuangzao yuekan*, vol. 1, no. 2: 127.

Guo's leaving for Japan also seemed to be part of his and the Creation Society's break with Tai Dong, whose treatment of them had finally become too much to bear. (Among Creation Society members, Yu Dafu had already broken off relations with Tai Dong about six months earlier). Further, Guo broke with Tai Dong at the time also because he was then ready to give up his literary career and therefore no longer needed to "use" Tai Dong for his literary purposes. See Guo Moruo, *Xuesheng shidai*, 167–168.

146. Guo Moruo, *Xuesheng shidai*, 188. His plan to work as an assistant in the physiology department at Kyushu Imperial University did not materialize either.

147. *Chuangzao yuekan*, vol. 1, no. 2: 130–133; Guo Moruo, *Xinglunan*, 7.

148. Guo Moruo, *Xuesheng shidai*, 197. Guo suggested that he had not sold his work until this period in Japan. This seemed to be true in the sense that previously he had not made it a profession to publish his works directly for money. Besides, he had worked for Tai Dong for a large part of his previous literary career, and Tai Dong certainly had not paid him directly for his writings. See Guo Moruo, *Xuesheng shidai*, 137.

149. Guo Moruo, *Xuesheng shidai*, 197.

150. *Chuangzao yuekan*, vol. 1, no. 2: 132; Guo Moruo, *Xinglunan*, 7.

151. Ruan Wuming, *Zhongguo xinwentan milu* (Shanghai: Nanqiang shuju, 1933), 173; Guo Moruo, *Xuesheng shidai*, 324.

152. Guo Moruo, *Xuesheng shidai*, 202, 204, 230, 247–248; Wang and Tong, *Guo Moruo nianpu (1)*, 195.

153. Guo Moruo, *Xuesheng shidai*, 352, 326.

154. Guo Moruo, *Guo Moruo yiwenji (1)*, 131.

155. *Chuangzao yuekan*, vol. 1, no. 6: 14. Guo's fourth child was born in 1925, making a bigger family for him to support. See Guo Moruo, *Xuesheng shidai*, 416.

156. *Chuangzao yuekan*, vol. 1, no. 2: 130; *Hongshui*, vol. 1, no. 5: 130.

157. *Chuangzao yuekan*, vol. 1, no. 2: 130, 132; *Chuangzao zhoubao*, vol. 2, no. 52: 16; Guo Moruo, *Xuesheng shidai*, 182.

158. *Chuangzao yuekan*, vol. 1, no. 2: 130, 129.

159. *Chuangzao yuekan*, vol. 1, no. 2: 128, 138; Marx and Engels, *The Communist Manifesto*, 31.

160. *Chuangzao yuekan*, vol. 1, no. 2: 128–129, 138.

161. *Hongshui*, vol. 1: 8.

162. *Hongshui*, vol. 1, no. 7: 216.

163. Guo Moruo, *Wenyi lunji*, 5–7.

164. *Hongshui*, vol. 2, no. 16: 140.

165. *Chuangzao yuekan*, vol. 1, no. 2: 128–129.

166. Guo Moruo, *Wenyi lunji*, 58, 70.

167. *Chuangzao yuekan*, vol. 1, no. 2: 138–139.

168. *Hongshui*, vol. 1, vol. 2, no. 16: 139.

169. Guo Moruo, *Wenyi lunji*, 16.

170. Guo Moruo, Zong Baihua, and Tian Shouchang, *San ye ji*, 12–15.

171. In a letter to Zong Baihua, Guo specifically notes that Confucius was not a "religious figure" or "religious founder." See Guo Moruo, Zong Baihua, and Tian Shouchang, *San ye ji*, 14.

172. Guo was trained in middle school by Huang Jinghua, a student of Liao Ping. As Guo put it, Mr. Huang had "a strong tendency to deify Confucius." In primary school, Guo also was taught by another student of Liao Ping, a Mr. Shuai Pingjun, whose teaching was one of the reasons Guo became interested in Confucian learning. See Guo Moruo, *Shaonian shidai*, 111, 64–65.

173. Guo Moruo, *Xuesheng shidai*, 58; Guo Moruo, *Nushen*, 72–73; Guo Moruo, *Selected Poems from the Goddesses*, 25; Wang and Tong, *Guo Moruo nianpu (1)*, 69.

It was largely through the works of Goethe, who had been influenced by Spinoza, that Guo came to be interested in the works and philosophy of Spinoza.

174. Guo Moruo, *Wenyi lunji*, 228–229.

175. Hou Wailu et al., *Zhongguo sixiangshi gang*, 336–339, 309–311.

176. Guo Moruo, *Wenyi lunji*, 185.

177. Buddhist influence on Guo could be traced to his early years in Sichuan. Some of his poems written in those years, for instance, demonstrated his knowledge of Buddhist literature and thinking. In one of those poems he even claims that he has "long been tired of the mundane world" and "often thought of" ridding himself of "this-worldly desires and mundane ideas" in a Buddhist manner. See Guo Moruo, *Guo Moruo jiuti shici xinian zhushi*, 13–14.

178. Guo Moruo, *Wenyi lunji*, 19, 22, 25, 28.

179. Ibid., 25. No further references can be found in this article or Guo's other writings to help make sense of what he means here by "Hebraism's damage to medieval Europe."

180. In fact, one can argue that some of his fellow May Fourthians' celebration of humanity also could be traced to the Confucian concept of inner transcendence.

It also needs mentioning as a reference that Chang Hao has noticed a tendency in twentieth-century China to deify man (Chang Hao, "Playing God: Deification of Man in Twentieth-Century Chinese Thought," unpublished paper).

181. Guo Moruo, *Nushen*, 109; Guo Moruo, *Selected Poems from the Goddesses*, 43. Guo's pantheistic belief in people's godlike power can be traced to the influence of Wang Yangming's emphasis on the moral and spiritual power of human beings, which was an essential part of Wang's Neo-Confucian school of mind-heart learning.

182. Guo Moruo, *Guo Moruo yiwenji (1)*, 71.

183. Ibid., 77. Two points can be made here. First, Guo demonstrated that he had been influenced by certain tendencies in China's tradition to deify man. Second, in his effort to fight against "established religions" and "superstitions" in the May Fourth era, he was to a certain extent referring to China's ancient tradition for justification of his celebration and worship of humanity.

184. Guo Moruo, *Wenyi lunji*, 14.

185. Ibid., 14–15.

186. Ibid., 15; Wm. Theodore de Bary, *Learning for One's Self*, 114. Guo's concept of the restraint of human desires also can be traced to Taoist influence. He agreed, for instance, to the Taoist teaching that people should "learn from nature" and "rid themselves of all desires" so that their spirit would be "clear" and their "creative instinct" would be brought into full play. His influence by the moralistic thinking of Tagore and Kabir also might have played a role in this regard. Further, as he had seriously studied the Bible and had loved and lived with Tomiko, who was a Christian, certain moralistic elements in Western Christian cultures also might have contributed to his attitude against desires. See Guo Moruo, *Wenyi lunji*, 19–20; Guo Moruo, Zong Baihua, and Tian Shouchang, *San ye ji*, 112–116.

187. Guo Moruo, *Wenyi lunji*, 14–15.

188. While attacking *lijiao* in his preface to the new edition of *Romance of the Western Chamber*, Guo suggests that the ethics of *lijiao*, if modified to be nonsuppressive, could have positive functions in "helping with the proper development of people's human nature (*renxing*)," whose "essential basis" are the sexual desires and relations between men and women. So modified, of course, "*lijiao*" will be different than the long-established *lijiao* social practice. See Guo Moruo, *Wenyi lunji*, 239.

189. Guo Moruo, Zong Baihua, and Tian Shouchang, *San ye ji*, 58–59.

190. Ibid., 112–116.

191. Ibid., 111–112.

192. Ibid., 1; Johann Wolfgang von Goethe, *Faust I & II*, ed. and trans. Stuart Atkins (Cambridge, MA: Suhrkamp/Insel, 1984), 30.

193. Guo Moruo, *Nushen*, 165.

194. Guo Moruo, *Guo Moruo yiwenji (1)*, 19–21.

195. Guo Moruo, Zong Baihua, and Tian Shouchang, *San ye ji*, 56–57, 77–78.

196. Guo Moruo, *Wenyi lunji*, 22, 25.

197. Ibid., 20. Guo here obviously was referring to Taoism as a philosophy against self-ishness and material concerns. Later in 1924 he was to reinterpret Taoism and disdain Taoist "practical ethics" as being "selfish." No matter how much his view on Taoism changed, however, he had consistently resented people's selfish pursuit of material gains. See Guo Moruo, *Wenyi lunji*, 67, 60.

198. Guo Moruo, *Wenyi lunji*, 28.

199. *Chuangzao zhoubao*, vol. 1, no. 22: 4.

200. Guo Moruo, *Wenyi lunji*, 15–16.

201. Ibid.; Confucius, *The Analects*, trans. D. C. Lau (New York: Penguin Books, 1979), 128.

202. Guo Moruo, *Xuesheng shidai*, 166.

203. Guo Moruo, *Wenyi lunji*, 59.

204. Ibid., 59–60.

205. The phrase "regulating the family" here had of course lost its traditional meaning for him, as he had already broken with the Confucian family bonds of father-son and husband-wife on the issue of his arranged marriage.

206. Guo Moruo, *Wenyi lunji*, 60–61.

207. Ibid., 57, 55.

208. Ibid., 62.

209. Ibid., 64–65.

210. Ibid., 63–64, 69–70.

211. Guo Moruo, *Nushen*, 203.

212. As he was increasingly committed to the collective action of the Communist revolution, Wang Yangming's idea of "tempering" oneself through "doing things" and Wang's whole concept of uniting knowledge with action also served as part of his mental preparation.

213. In addition to people's material desires, Guo also criticized the desires for fame (*ming* 名) and social and political status. It is interesting to note that when enjoying his literary fame in the early 1920s, he seldom mentioned the desire for *ming* as one that should be restricted. It was not until after he had been profoundly frustrated and disappointed in his literary career that he began to ponder bitterly fame, as painfully expressed in his previously quoted letter to Tomiko in March 1924. See Guo Moruo, *Wenyi lunji*, 59; *Chuangzao zhoubao*, vol. 2, no. 47: 6–7.

214. Guo Moruo, *Wenyi lunji*, 64. Along the line of his May Fourth Confucian thinking, Guo saw that Wang Yangming's greatness lay in the achievement of not only the virtue of *ren* but also the virtues of *yong* (courage) and *zhi* (wisdom). Coping himself with the social and political reality of the mid-1920s, he highly admired the "ultimate courage" and "calmness" that Wang displayed in "constantly struggling against" "ugly," "evil," and "dangerous" environments, especially the political situations of Wang's time.

215. Guo Moruo, *Xinglunan*, 82.

216. Guo Moruo, *Wenyi lunji*, 63–64, 14–15.

217. Ibid., 67.

CHAPTER 2

1. Guo Moruo, *Xuesheng shidai*, 64.

2. Ibid., 64.

3. Guo Moruo, *Nushen*, 64.

4. Ibid., 200.

5. Guo Moruo, *Xuesheng shidai*, 64.

6. This English translation of the poem is basically the version in Guo Moruo, *Selected Poems from the Goddesses*, except for the following: Sentence* in that version is "—Dedicated to my native land," which to a certain extent loses Guo's original meaning. Sentences** in that version read "for her my heart's delight"; using "her" instead of "you," according to this author, is not a good translation. Sentence*** in that version is "today must I see the light of day again," which is a translation of one of Guo's later revisions of the poem and is different than Guo's early version. See Guo Moruo, *Nushen*, 58–59; Guo Moruo, *Selected Poems from the Goddesses*, 19.

7. Guo Moruo, *Xuesheng shidai*, 65; Wang and Tong, *Guo Moruo nianpu (1)*, 98–99.

8. Guo Moruo, *Xuesheng shidai*, 70; Wang and Tong, *Guo Moruo nianpu (1)*, 107; Guo Moruo, *Nushen*, 1–14.

9. Guo Moruo, *Xuesheng shidai*, 77.

10. Guo Moruo, *Nushen*, 164; Guo Moruo, *Selected Poems from the Goddesses*, 64.

11. Guo Moruo, *Xuesheng shidai*, 78.

12. Ibid.

13. Guo Moruo, *Nushen*, 165.

14. Guo Moruo, *Xuesheng shidai*, 79–80.

15. Guo Moruo, *Nushen*, 167–168.

16. Guo Moruo, *Xuesheng shidai*, 80.

17. Ibid., 115

18. Ibid., 114–115.

19. Ibid., 130; Wang and Tong, *Guo Moruo nianpu (1)*, 138. To a certain extent, Guo's interest also was a result of his unpleasant experiences as a Chinese living in Japan, which made him more anxious to change and strengthen his motherland so that Chinese like him would no longer be bullied by others. See Guo Moruo, *Nushen*, 213.

20. Guo Moruo, *Xuesheng shidai*, 137–139; Wang and Tong, *Guo Moruo nianpu (1)*, 139.

21. *Chuangzao zhoubao*, vol. 1, no. 3: 13–14.

22. Guo Moruo, *Guo Moruo yiwenji (1)*, 17.

23. Ibid., 21.

24. Ibid., 17–23.

25. Ibid., 23; Guo Moruo, *Guo Moruo jiuti shici xinian zhushi*, 130–131.

26. Guo Moruo, *Guo Moruo yiwenji (1)*, 5–16.

27. Guo Moruo, *Nushen*, 115–118; Guo Moruo, *Xuesheng shidai*, 64–65.

28. At this time, both Inner and Outer Mongolia were, to different degrees, under China's control. Inner Mongolia had been part of China for quite a long time. As for Outer Mongolia, it came under Chinese control again in 1919, after its independence from China during the 1911 revolution. In 1921, however, Outer Mongolia was to be invaded by the Soviets.

29. Guo Moruo, Zong Baihua, and Tian Shouchang, *San ye ji*, 165.

30. Guo Moruo, *Guo Moruo yiwenji (1)*, 42–66.

31. *Chuangzao jikan*, vol. 1, no. 3: 1.

32. Guo Moruo, *Xinglunan*, 40–47.

33. Guo Moruo, *Xuesheng shidai*, 324.

34. Ibid., 56–57.

35. His giving up medicine was of course also due to his hearing problem, which made it difficult for him to study or practice medicine. Ironically, perhaps his literary career enabled him to serve his country much better than a medical career.

36. The tension in this period between his love for literature and his interest in science would later help develop a tension in his thinking between emotion and reason.

37. Guo Moruo, *Yinghua shujian*, 67, 68.

38. Ibid., 68.

39. Ibid., 74.

40. The convention was called the Sino-Japanese Military Mutual Assistance Convention. It was concluded by Japanese and Chinese governments on March 25, 1918. See Roy, *Kuo Mo-jo*, 70.

41. Guo Moruo, *Xuesheng shidai*, 32–33.

42. Guo Moruo, *Xuesheng shidai*, 33, 54.

43. Guo Moruo, *Guo Moruo jiwai xubaji*, ed. Shanghai Library and Sichuan University (Sichuan: Sichuan People's Press, 1982), 44.

44. Guo Moruo, *Moruo wenji (10)* (Beijing: Renmin wenxue chubanshe, 1959), 403. Guo also once indicated that he had noticed this phenomenon as early as late 1923 and early 1924. See Guo Moruo, *Xuesheng shidai*, 164.

45. Guo Moruo, *Moruo wenji (10)*, 403.

46. Guo's doubt about capitalism, along with his previously shown criticism against foreign capitalists and imperialists as a major source of China's problems at the time, must have contributed to the beginning of his serious interest in Marxist/Leninist theories in 1924. On the other hand, since much of his analysis of the textile industry crisis and much of his criticism of capitalism and imperialism came after reading and translating Kawakami's book, they were certainly also his application of the Marxist/Leninist theories that he had just learned.

47. Guo obviously was here referring to World War I.

48. Guo Moruo, *Moruo wenji (10)*, 404–406. Guo makes similar criticism of capitalism and imperialism in, among others, "Going to Yixing" (written around early 1925 or the end of 1924) and his preface to Qi Shufen's (?–1927) *China under Economic Invasions* (Shanghai: Guanghua shuju, 1931). See Guo Moruo, *Guo Moruo Jiwai xubaji*, 41–44; Guo Moruo, *Xuesheng shidai*, 195, 332–336, 381–382; Wang and Tong, *Guo Moruo nianpu (1)*, 184, 229.

49. Guo Moruo, *Guo Moruo quanji (wenxuebian 6)*, ed. Guo Moruo zhuzuo bianji chuban weiyuanhui (Beijing: Renmin wenxue chubanshe, 1986), 145–146; Guo Moruo, *Xuesheng shidai*, 206–210.

50. Guo Moruo, *Moruo wenji (10)*, 408–410.

51. Guo Moruo, *Guo Moruo yiwenji (1)*, 134.

52. Guo Moruo, *Xuesheng shidai*, 210–212; Guo Moruo, *Guo Moruo quanji (wenxuebian 6)*, 146–148.

53. Guo Moruo, *Moruo wenji (10)*, 407.

54. Guo Moruo, *Xuesheng shidai*, 194–195, 325–326.

55. Ibid., 195.

56. *Chuangzao yuekan*, vol. 1, no. 3: 10; *Hongshui*, vol. 2, no. 16: 136–137.

57. Guo Moruo, *Xuesheng shidai*, 271.

58. Guo Moruo, *Guo Moruo yiwenji (1)*, 157–159.

59. *Chuangzao yuekan*, vol. 1, no. 3: 10.

60. *Chuangzao zhoubao*, vol. 2, no. 44: 8; Mo Moruo, *Xuesheng shidai*, 268.

61. Guo Moruo, *Xuesheng shidai*, 267. Tomiko and their children later joined him in Guangdong in May of that year. See Guo Moruo, *Xuesheng shidai*, 271, 274.

62. Before 1926, Guo seemed to have some hesitation about joining the Chinese Communists, and part of the reason was that he somehow felt that the Communist activists at the time did not fully measure up to his standards of being Communist. In his October 1925 "A Poor Man's Poor Talk," for instance, he writes that he is afraid that the Communists in China do not necessarily measure up to being "not fearful of death" and "not in pursuit of money," his standards of ideal Communists that could be traced to his Confucian concept of *yong* and his Confucian indifference toward material gains. He also indicates in the article that he sees (some of) the Chinese Communists at the time as doing "anti-Communist" things. Possibly to distance himself from those Communists, he claims at the end of the article that he is not one of the practicing Communists. In his December 1925 "The Creation of a New State," he also criticizes that "many of the so-called Communists in China" either do not understand or "misunderstand" Marxism. See *Hongshui*, vol. 1, no. 4: 92–94; no. 8: 232.

63. Xu Binru, "Huiyi Luxun yijiuerqinian zai Guangzhou de qingkuang," *Luxun zai Guangzhou*, ed. Zhongshan da xue zhong wen xi. (Guangzhou: Guangdong People's Press, 1976), 201; Gu Fulin, *Guo Moruo qianqi sixiang ji chuangzuo* (Jinan: Shangdong People's Press, 1983), 45.

64. Xu Binru, "Huiyi Luxun," 201; Gu Fulin, *Guo Moruo*, 45, 56; Guo Moruo, *Xuesheng shidai*, 274.

CHAPTER 3

1. Although he no longer showed it clearly in his May Fourth cosmopolitanist thinking, Guo in his early years sometimes expressed an ambition for a China-centered cosmopolitan empire. Overjoyed by the success of the 1911 revolution, for instance, he wrote in a couplet in 1912 that since China had been liberated from the Manchus and therefore would be strengthened again as a nation, he could not wait to further "make the whole world a Chinese empire," with Europe and Africa as China's "prefectures and counties" and America and Australia as China's "cities." See Guo Moruo, *Guo Moruo jiuti shici xinian zhushi*, 42.

Also worth noting here is that Guo's May Fourth cosmopolitanist transcendence of nationalist concerns might be related to his having stayed away from China in Japan for many years, thus distancing him from his home country. In other words, the international perspective that he had gained by living abroad might have contributed to his being able to go beyond mere nationalist concerns.

2. Guo Moruo, *Nushen*, 64–65.

3. Ibid., 112. In a letter written to Zong Baihua in January 1920, Guo also tells his friend that he and some others intend to organize a medical society in order to contribute to the ultimate goal of "saving the whole of mankind." See Guo Moruo, Zong Baihua, and Tian Shouchang, *San ye ji*, 21.

4. Guo Moruo, *Guo Moruo yiwenji (1)*, 28–29.

5. Guo Moruo, *Nushen*, 119–124. Patriotism in modern Western cultures, as exemplified by MacSwiney's case, also was an inspiration and influence for Guo's nationalist thinking.

6. Guo Moruo, *Nushen*, 122–123; Guo Moruo, *Selected Poems from the Goddesses*, 46–47.

7. Guo Moruo, *Guo Moruo nushen jiwai yiwen*, 67–68.

8. Guo Moruo, *Guo Moruo yiwenji (1)*, 66.

9. Guo Moruo, *Wenyi lunji*, 22. Guo's terminology here clearly shows his gradual influence by modern Western and Japanese Leftist thinking. This influence on Guo seemed to have started in the late 1910s, when Japan was feeling the impact of the 1917 Soviet revolution and the Japanese Leftist movement was getting out of its "winter period." As he later recalled, he was then "very much" influenced by Japanese Leftist journals such as *Kaizo* (Reconstruction), first published in 1919, and *Tane maku hito* (The Sowers), which was published from February 1921 to August 1923. It was probably also during this period that he read Fukui Junzo's *Modern Socialism*. See Guo Moruo, *Nushen*, 201; Zhongguo Guo Moruo yanjiu xuehui, *Guo Moruo yanjiu (7)* (Beijing: Wenhua yishu chubanshe, 1989), 281–285; Fukui Junzo, *Modern Socialism* (Tokyo: 1899).

10. He mentions his goal of "realizing" this ideal society (the Great Harmony), for instance, in "Coal, Iron, and Japan." See Guo Moruo, *Guo Moruo yiwenji (1)*, 66, 58, 65.

11. The phrase "people's contracts" here indicates that he might have been influenced by some contract theories in Western political thought, possibly Rousseau's.

12. Guo Moruo, *Guo Moruo yiwenji (1)*, 72–73, 77, 81.

13. Ibid., 76, 81.

14. Guo's egalitarian discourse here clearly reveals a modern Leftist influence. In the meantime, the modern egalitarian influence also might have inspired him to reconceptualize traditional egalitarianism. In fact, one may argue that it was to a certain degree the egalitarian elements of his traditional thinking that had led him to be attracted to modern Western egalitarian concepts.

Guo's egalitarianism in this period also can be seen in his 1919 poem *Night*, which, like *The Pompeii of Chinese Intellectual History*, depicts democracy with an egalitarian approach:

Night! Dark night!
Only you are "democracy"!
You embrace the whole of mankind:
　　there are no longer differences between:
　　　　the poor and rich,
　　　　the noble and humble,
　　　　the beautiful and evil,
　　　　or the wise and foolish,
　　you are a huge furnace that smelts all:
　　　　poverty and wealth,
　　　　nobility and humbleness,
　　　　beauty and evil,
　　　　and wisdom and foolishness,
　　　　　　—all causes for chaos and suffering.
You are a giant engineer for:
　　emancipation, liberty, equality, and peace,
　　　　—all sources for harmony and happiness.
Dark night! Night!
I truly love you,
I no longer want to leave you.
What I hate is the light that comes from outside:
it causes differences in this world,·
　　　　which used to be without differences. (Guo Moruo, *Nushen*, 128)

15. Guo Moruo, *Guo Moruo yiwenji (1)*, 77.

16. *Chuangzao jikan*, vol. 1, no. 4: 11, 3–4.

17. Whether this is Confucius's saying is controversial.

18. Guo Moruo, *Guo Moruo yiwenji (1)*, 77–78; James Legge, trans., *The Sacred Books of China—The Texts of Confucianism* (Oxford: Clarendon Press, 1885), 364–366. The names here are translated by this author with Pinyin. *Also note:* * "Great Harmony" here is this author's translation.

19. His use of "private ownership" and "public ownership" reveals a Leftist influence.

20. Guo Moruo, *Guo Moruo yiwenji (1)*, 78.

21. Ibid., 81. Guo's description of the ancient society as a "democracy" recalls Kang Youwei's (康有為) belief that Confucius used the times of Yao and Shun, both before the Three Dynasties, as a model of "democracy" for later societies to follow. After all, Kang's thinking was similar to, if not plagiarized from, Liao Ping's, whose thinking was a major influence on Guo in his early years in Sichuan. However, on one issue Guo did seem to have deviated from the *Jinwen* school of thinking of Liao Ping and Kang Youwei: as shown

previously, Guo believed that what Confucius said in *Li Ji* was a historical fact: an ideal society existed in ancient times and collapsed when the Three Dynasties began. Kang and Liao, however, believed that the *Li Ji*, as one of the "Six Classics" of Confucianism, could not be taken as history, because it was made up by Confucius for the purpose of reform in his own times. See Hou Wailu et al., *Zhongguo sixiangshi gang*, 255–256; Wang Fansen, *Gushibian yundong de xingqi: Yige sixiangshi de fenxi* (Taibei: Yunchen wenhua shiye gufen youxian gongsi, 1987), 96–97; Guo Moruo, *Shaonian shidai*, 111.

22. Guo Moruo, *Nushen*, 67; Guo Moruo, *Selected Poems from the Goddesses*, 23.

23. Guo Moruo, *Guo Moruo yiwenji (1)*, 46. It is interesting to note that Guo here praised "chimneys and railway tracks" because he considered and accepted them as an integral part of nature. In other words, for him, the primary concern was nature, and industrialization somehow had to be justified and accepted as something that was in harmony with nature. This approach to industrialization certainly was in contrast to what had been commonly seen in the modern West, at least by the beginning decades of the twentieth century: an industrial drive that featured an aggressiveness to conquer and exploit nature as an object.

24. His passion for pastoral life also reminds us of the fact that he had been brought up in a rural setting in Sichuan, and by the time he went to Shanghai in April 1921, he had lived for about six years in Japan, mostly in areas that were not major urban or industrial centers.

25. Guo Moruo, *Nushen*, 166–173.

26. Guo Moruo, *Guo Moruo yiwenji (1)*, 42–43; Goethe, *Faust*, 60.

27. Guo Moruo, *Guo Moruo yiwenji (1)*, 43–44.

28. Guo Moruo, *Nushen*, 112.

29. Ibid., 208, 72.

30. Guo Moruo, *Guo Moruo nushen jiwai yiwen*, 66.

31. Guo Moruo, *Wenyi lunji*, 230–231.

32. Guo Moruo, *Guo Moruo nushen jiwai yiwen*, 59–61.

33. Guo Moruo, *Nushen*, 79–84; Guo Moruo, *Selected Poems from the Goddesses*, 29–32.

34. Guo Moruo, *Wenyi lunji*, 229–230. Along with Guo's longing for nature and pastoral and primitive life there also was an idealization of children in his May Fourth thinking, which further illustrated his pursuit of an ideal of original, innocent, and pure human existence and a profound discomfort with what seemed to be the alienation from that ideal: the sophistication, noise, and pollution of modern civilization. When praising children, for instance, he once referred to Goethe's belief that adults should take children as models and learn from them, Lao Zi's teaching that people should control their breath "gently like a baby," and Mencius's saying that "a great man is one who retains the heart of a newborn babe." See Guo Moruo, *Wenyi lunji*, 231; Lao Zi, *Dao de jing* (Taiwan: Zhongguo guojiao taibeizongshe, 1956), 9; Lao Zi, *Tao te ching*, trans. Stephen Addiss and Stanley Lombardo (Indianapolis, IN, and Cambridge, MA: Hackett, 1993), 10; Mencius, *Mencius*, vol. 1, trans. D. C. Lau (Hong Kong: Chinese University Press, 1979), 162–163. Guo also referred to the Bible in this regard. See Guo Moruo, *Wenyi lunji*, 231; *The Holy Bible* (New Revised Standard Version) (Nashville, TN: Thomas Nelson, 1989), 641, 19.

35. Guo Moruo, *Guo Moruo yiwenji (1)*, 44–45. In "On Chinese and German Cultures," he also writes that in Confucianism "the development of the self" is eventually meant to benefit China and the world. See Guo Moruo, *Wenyi lunji*, 19.

36. Guo Moruo, *Nushen*, 27.

37. Guo Moruo, *Wenyi lunji*, 228–229.

38. Guo Moruo, Zong Baihua, and Tian Shouchang, *San ye ji*, 54.

39. Guo Moruo, *Guo Moruo yiwenji (1)*, 58.

40. Ibid., 65.

41. Ibid., 42–66.

42. Guo Moruo, *Wenyi lunji*, 94–96.

43. Chang Hao, *Youan yishi yu minzhu chuantong* (Taiwan: Lianjing chuban shiye gongsi, 1989), 204.

44. Guo Moruo, *Guo Moruo yiwenji (1)*, 32–33.

45. Guo Moruo, *Nushen*, 1–13; Guo Moruo, *Selected Poems from the Goddesses*, 1–8.

46. Guo Moruo, *Nushen*, 8; Guo Moruo, *Selected Poems from the Goddesses*, 8.

47. Guo Moruo, *Nushen*, 115–118.

48. Ibid., 100.

49. Ibid., 28.

50. Guo Moruo, *Guo Moruo nushen jiwai yiwen*, 67–68.

51. Chen She (?–208 B.C.) and Wu Guang (?–209 B.C.) were leaders of a major peasant uprising against the Qin Dynasty (221–207 B.C.). See Guo Moruo, *Guo Moruo nushen jiwai yiwen*, 69.

52. Guo Moruo, *Guo Moruo yiwenji (1)*, 28–29.

53. Guo Moruo, *Xuesheng shidai*, 133.

54. *Chuangzao jikan*, vol. 1, no. 4: 4, 11, 15, 18. He also once expressed sympathy to Tolstoy's version of anarchism. See Guo Moruo, *Nushen*, 112.

55. Guo Moruo, *Xuesheng shidai*, 90–91. It is interesting to note here that Zhu, before coming to Shanghai, also was very close to the young Mao Zedong in Beijing. A student at the time in the philosophy department of Beijing University, Zhu often visited Mao, who was working as a librarian at the university from late 1918 to early 1919. As Mao later recalled, Mao "at that time" "favored many" anarchist "proposals," and he and Zhu "often discussed anarchism and its possibilities in China." What is interesting here is that Mao and Guo, who both had been influenced by anarchist thinking and actually shared an anarchist friend in Zhu Qianzhi, later both turned to Communism. See Mao Zedong, *Mao Zedong zishu* (Beijing: People's Press, 1993), 34; Edgar Snow, *Red Star over China* (New York: Grove Press, 1973), 152.

56. Guo Moruo, *Nushen*, 116, 118.

57. Ibid., 110–114.

58. Guo Moruo, *Guo Moruo yiwenji (1)*, 42–66.

59. Guo Moruo, *Nushen*, preface.

60. Guo Moruo, *Guo Moruo quanji (wenxuebian1)*, ed. Guo Moruo zhuzuo bianji chuban weiyuanhui (Beijing: Renmin wenxue chubanshe, 1982), 314–315.

61. *Chuangzao zhoubao*, vol. 1, no. 23: 5.

62. Guo Moruo, *Xuesheng shidai*, 166.

63. *Chuangzao zhoubao*, vol. 2, no. 38: 7–8.

64. Guo Moruo, *Xuesheng shidai*, 133; Guo Moruo, *Nushen*, 213.

65. Guo Moruo, *Xuesheng shidai*, 95–96; Wang and Tong, *Guo Moruo nianpu (1)*, 117.

66. Guo Moruo, *Xuesheng shidai*, 106.

67. Guo Moruo, *Nushen*, 212–213.

68. Ibid., 112. He sometimes also emphasized that all of the causes, including those of saving and reviving China and the world, should start with the individual's effort to achieve inner transcendence through self-cultivation and purification. To "thoroughly reform" mankind ("human society"), he said, there should first be the reform of individual human beings. See Guo Moruo, *Wenyi lunji*, 16, 191.

69. *Chuangzao yuekan*, vol. 1, no. 2: 128, 129, 138.

70. "Marx Enters Confucius's Temple" was written with a bantering style. Using such a style, however, does not mean that Guo was not serious in what he said in his writing about Confucianism and Marxism. For one thing, sufficient evidence shows that Guo since mid-1924 had kept a strong faith in both Confucianism and Marxism. It does not make sense, therefore, if he meant disrespect for Confucius and Marx in "Marx Enters Confucius's Temple." Further, in two open letters that he wrote in December 1925 and March 1926, Guo himself noted the sincerity of his comparison of Confucianism and Marxism in "Marx Enters Confucius's Temple." In those two letters, especially the first one, he seriously elaborated on his view in "Marx Enters Confucius's Temple," that Confucianism and Marxism were similar in several major aspects. See *Hongshui*, vol. 1, no. 7: 212–219; vol. 1, no. 9: 323–330; vol. 2, no. 14: 71–82.

71. *Hongshui*, vol. 1, no. 7: 215; Legge, *The Sacred Books of China*, 364–366. Guo does indicate, however, that Confucius differed from Marx in that Confucius did not have the scientific system of Marx to carry out his idealism. Confucius, Guo suggests, was in modern terms only a "utopian socialist."

Also, Guo, in his "The Creation of a New State," again identifies Marx's ideal of Communist society with the Confucian ideal of Great Harmony. See *Hongshui*, vol. 1, no. 8: 228.

72. *Hongshui*, vol. 1, no. 8: 228, 231. In his October 1925 "A Poor Man's Poor Talk," he also compares the Communist ideal to Great Harmony. See *Hongshui*, vol. 1, no. 4: 93.

73. *Hongshui*, vol. 1, no. 7: 215–216.

74. Guo Moruo, *Wenyi lunji*, 228.

75. His attraction to Marxist cosmopolitanism can be traced to his consistent cosmopolitanist thinking in the past.

76. *Hongshui*, vol. 1, no. 4: 94.

77. Ibid., vol. 1, no. 5: 127–131.

78. Ibid., vol. 1, no. 8: 227–233.

79. Ibid., vol. 1, no. 8: 228; vol. 2, no. 14: 42–44.

80. *Chuangzao yuekan*, vol. 1, no. 3: 4–5.

81. *Hongshui*, vol. 1, no. 1: 5–8.

82. Ibid., vol. 1, no. 10–11: 339.

83. Ibid., vol. 2, no. 16: 138–139. Guo once suggested that some use of force would still be necessary, even in the ideal society of Communism, because in that society there might still be "occasional" evils to be fought against by "all mankind." He did not, though, specify what those "evils" would be. See *Hongshui*, vol. 1, no. 12: 408.

Also, since Guo hardly accepted the Marxist concept of socioeconomic classes, as discussed later, his idea of class struggle sometimes did not carry a clear class consciousness but rather was largely an urge to struggle, often violently, against any enemies that he saw of his Communist cause.

84. Guo Moruo, *Guo Moruo yiwenji (1)*, 165. Guo's enthusiasm for the action of revolution can to a certain extent be traced to the influence of Wang Yangming's emphasis on the "unity of knowledge and action." It also certainly recalled the radical elements, the "mentality of extremes," and the celebration of action in his May Fourth thinking. See Guo Moruo, *Wenyi lunji*, 62; Guo Moruo, *Xuesheng shidai*, 186.

85. *Hongshui*, vol. 1, no. 10–11: 341; Kawakami Hajime, *Shakai soshiki to shakai kakumei* (Kyoto: Kobundo, 1922), 461–472; Kawakami Hajime, *Shehui zuzhi yu shehui geming*, trans. Guo Moruo (Shanghai: Shangwu yinshuguan, 1950), 203–209.

CHAPTER 4

1. Guo's most detailed admiration for the ancient golden age and its thinking was expressed in his 1921 "The Pompeii of Chinese Intellectual History" and his 1922 "The Two Princes of Guzhu."

2. Guo Moruo, *Wenyi lunji*, 16, 9; *Asahi Shimbun* (Osaka), New Year's Day special issue, 1923.

3. Guo Moruo, *Wenyi lunji*, 13–14. Guo's worshiping of Confucius here recalls again his early influence by Liao Ping's school of thinking.

4. Guo Moruo, *Wenyi lunji*, 9.

5. Ibid., 11.

6. Ibid., 25. Guo's depicting Taoism as an active ideology recalls his influence by Goethean activism and Wang Yangming's emphasis on action.

7. Guo Moruo, *Wenyi lunji*, 19–20.

8. Ibid., 27. The influence of Taoism on Guo also could be seen in his love for works by poets of the Six Dynasties period (222–589), many of which convey strong Taoist messages. He was especially attracted to the poems and character of Tao Yuanming (陶淵明) (365–427), who expressed Taoist antimundane ideas in his works and personified Taoist thinking in his carefree lifestyle and in seeking escape from society. See Guo Moruo, *Ganlan*, 204–209; Guo Moruo, *Shaonian shidai*, 307–308, 325; Guo Moruo, *Guo Moruo jiuti shici xinian zhushi*, 5–6, 29, 39.

9. Guo Moruo, *Guo Moruo yiwenji (1)*, 68, 38.

10. Guo Moruo, *Wenyi lunji*, 13–14; Guo Moruo, Zong Baihua, and Tian Shouchang, *San ye ji*, 13.

11. Guo Moruo, *Wenyi lunji*, 25.

12. Ibid., 51, 40.

13. Ibid., 45.

14. Guo Moruo, *Guo Moruo yiwenji (1)*, 37–38.

15. Guo Moruo, *Wenyi lunji*, 20–21, 23–25.

16. Ibid., 25. Guo also later noted that Mo Zi had certain knowledge of mathematics. See Guo Moruo, *Wenyi lunji*, 40, 47.

17. Guo Moruo, *Wenyi lunji*, 47.

18. Ibid., 40, 47.

19. Ibid., 53, 48, 40.

20. Ibid., 25. 48.

21. Ibid., 25, 22.

22. Guo's faith in science could be traced to his training in science, which intensified when he first went to Japan and had to work "desperately" hard on science subjects in order to pass the entrance examinations to qualify for the Chinese government scholarship. In his high school years in Japan, he was thoroughly educated through the Japanese high school system, which had been substantially Westernized in its curriculum of natural sciences. For his premed studies at the Sixth Higher School at Okayama, he was required to do both course and laboratory work for physics, chemistry, zoology, and botany. He also had to learn advanced mathematics, including analytic geometry, advanced algebra, differential calculus, and integral calculus. Then, at the medical school of Kyushu Imperial University, he was solidly educated in what he described as "a serious and complete system of learning." His first two years of medical study at the university focused on preclinical courses such as anatomy, histology, physiology, medical chemistry, pathology, pharmacology, bacteriology, and psychopathology. Even though he was having increasing difficulty with his studies because of his hearing problem, during his first two years at the medical school he had been "very interested" in these courses in preclinical medicine, which had taught him "pure natural sciences" and had enabled him to discover "the secret of the human body." Years after he gave up medicine and became a literary celebrity in China, he still noticed that, due to his medical training in Japan, he felt that the "foundation" of his knowledge of medical science was better than the foundation of his literary knowledge. "I am a person," he said in the 1940s, "who wholeheartedly respects medical science." See Guo Moruo, *Xuesheng shidai*, 10, 11, 12–13, 63–64.

23. Guo Moruo, *Guo Moruo yiwenji (1)*, 42, 46.

24. Guo Moruo, *Wenyi lunji*, 23, 26, 28.

25. Ibid., 23, 28.

26. Guo's influence by Goethe's proactive mentality can be seen in his preface to his translation of *The Sorrows of Young Werther*, in which he specifically notes that he is attracted to Goethe's active spirit and approach. See Guo Moruo, *Wenyi lunji*, 229.

27. Guo Moruo, Zong Baihua, and Tian Shouchang, *San ye ji*, 14.

28. Guo Moruo, *Guo Moruo yiwen ji (1)*, 86–88.

29. Guo Moruo, *Wenyi lunji*, 227–228. Guo's attraction to Goethe's celebration of emotion and intuition could be traced to his influence by Wang Yangming's subjectivist emphasis on the mind-heart.

30. Guo Moruo, *Wenyi lunji*, 127–129. To a certain extent, Guo's literary sentiment against science recalled the fact that despite his overall faith in science, he even resented scientific studies briefly during the difficult time when he was choosing literature over medicine as a career. See Guo Moruo, *Xuesheng shidai*, 64.

31. Guo's faith in reason, it should be noted, could be traced to his influence by the Taoist concept of an objective law of nature (*dao*).

32. Guo Moruo, Zong Baihua, and Tian Shouchang, *San ye ji*, 44–45.

33. Ibid., 15–16.

34. While Confucianism, Taoism, science, and Goetheanism largely formed the essence of Guo's May Fourth synthesis, other elements also existed in his May Fourth thinking. These elements, for instance, included the increasing influence of Leftist radicalism, as well as the influence of Kant. Guo had, for instance, compared Kant's concept of ethics to Confucius's concept of "*li*." He also once noted that he "believed in Kant's concept of ethics" and considered people's "conscience" the "guidance" of all their actions. For some time Guo also showed an interest in Nietzsche. He once noted that he had found no "fundamental differences" between the thinking of Nietzsche and that of his then-favorite philosopher, Lao Zi. Nietzsche, he said, "mirrored" Lao Zi. Guo's interest in Nietzsche also could be seen in the fact that from May 1923 to January 1924, he had translated much of Nietzsche's *Thus Spake Zarathustra*, published intermittently in *Creation Weekly*. Shelley for a while also was an attraction for Guo. In December 1922, for instance, he noted that Shelley was one of the poets he "admired the most." Shelley, he delighted, was a "favorite of nature, a believer of pantheism, and a valiant fighter of revolutionary thinking." "I love Shelley," he wrote, "I can feel his heart and I can understand him." See Guo Moruo, *Wenyi lunji*, 15, 27–28; *Chuangzao zhoubao*, vol. 1 and vol. 2 (especially vol. 1, no. 9: 15, vol. 1, no. 1: 12–13, and vol. 2, no. 30: 1–4); Wang and Tong, *Guo Moruo nianpu (1)*, 152, 168; *Chuangzao jikan*, vol. 1, no. 4: 19–20.

35. One reference point may be needed here concerning the relationship between the Romanticist and Taoist elements in Guo's synthesis. Arthur Lovejoy once pointed out that one of the factors that helped result in European Romanticism was the influence of Chinese art. Since traditional Chinese art had been heavily influenced by Taoist philosophies, a point can be made that European Romanticism can be traced to certain Chinese Taoist influences. This historical link between Taoism and Romanticism may in a sense help us understand why Guo, with his Taoist background, was attracted to the Romanticist thinking of Goethe. See Arthur O. Lovejoy, *Essays in the History of Ideas* (Baltimore, MD: Johns Hopkins University Press, 1948), 99–135.

36. It should be noted that in his search for the best of the East and West Guo had made conscious efforts to identify certain parts of Chinese tradition with parts of Western civilization. He had, for instance, identified Confucius's "talent," "character," and thinking with those of Goethe and Kant and compared the thinking of Lao Zi to that of Nietzsche. He also had identified the "spirit" of Chinese tradition with the thinking of ancient Greece. In "The Pompeii of Chinese Intellectual History," he specifically compares China's ancient thinking to ancient Greek "Hellenism." In ancient Chinese thinking, he writes, it was "man"

who "created all the million things and man himself was god." The figures in China's mythology, such as Pan Gu, Tian Huang, Di Huang, Ren Huang, You Chao Shi, and Sui Ren Shi, were all "fictitious figures" who were "half humans and half gods." Such Chinese thinking "fully demonstrated" China's "spirit of liberty and original creation" and was "very similar" to ancient Greek culture, whose gods possessed such "human characteristics" as being able to "love," to "be jealous," and even to "commit adultery." In the same article, he also states that the ancient Chinese idea of "one developing into two," "two developing into four," and "four developing into eight" reminds him of the concept of the "multiple division of cells" in modern Western science. The ancient Chinese idea, he says, could be considered a "hypotheses of multiple division" before the modern Western discovery of cells. See Guo Moruo, Zong Baihua, and Tian Shouchang, *San ye ji*, 12–15; Guo Moruo, *Wenyi lunji*, 13, 15, 27–28, 19, 20–21; Guo Moruo, *Guo Moruo yiwenji (1)*, 70–71, 75.

37. Guo Moruo, *Guo Moruo yiwenji (1)*, 87. The term *Jingshen kexue* is used here to refer to what is otherwise known as the social sciences.

38. Guo Moruo, *Xuesheng shidai*, 182.

39. Guo Moruo, *Wenyi lunji*, 18–28, 22 n. 3, 66–69.

40. Guo Moruo, *Xuesheng shidai*, 166.

41. *Chuangzao zhoubao*, vol. 1, no. 15: 5.

42. Ibid., vol. 1, no. 15: 5. Guo, in "Wang Yangming: A Great Spiritualist," again criticized such contradiction in Lao Zi's thinking. See Guo Moruo, *Wenyi lunji*, 60.

Guo also showed here that despite his criticism of Taoism, he was still to a certain extent interested in the Taoist concept *dao*. In fact, a point can be made that his interest in the Taoist "purposeless" "*dao*" and his criticism of the Taoist "selfish" "*de*" were both consistent with his Confucian moral view against people's selfish purposes and their desires for material gains.

43. *Chuangzao zhoubao*, vol. 1, no. 15: 4, 1–6.

44. Guo Moruo, *Wenyi lunji*, 66–67. Guo finished "Wang Yangming: A Great Spiritualist" on June 17, 1924, around the time he was finishing his translation of *Social Organization and Social Revolution*. This helps show that he was clearly continuing his faith in Confucianism, as expressed in the article, when he was converting to Marxism through the translation of Kawakami's book. See Guo Moruo, *Wenyi lunji*, 70; Guo Moruo, *Xuesheng shidai*, 182, 185–186; Wang Yangming, *Yangming quanshu* (Shanghai: Taidong tushuju, 1925), vol. 1, no. 2: 130, 132; *Chuangzao zhoubao*, vol. 2, no. 52: 16.

45. Guo Moruo, *Wenyi lunji*, 67. This was the only time Guo noted that he believed in Confucianism as a "religion." Even though this was rare, it was consistent with his deification of Confucius in the past years.

It also is interesting to note that much of Guo's interest in Marx developed after his interest in a series of German figures: Goethe, Heine, Kant, and Nietzsche.

46. Guo Moruo, *Wenyi lunji*, 68.

47. Part of the Confucian inadequacy here is what Guo continued to see as Confucianism's lack of a "scientific spirit." In "Marx Enters Confucius's Temple" he notes again that because Confucius lived in a time when sciences were still not "invented," his thinking was not "systematic," and he "did not understand logic." See *Hongshui*, vol. 1: 213, 217.

Also, Guo's reservation here about Marxism's (as a social science) lack of a transcendental perspective is consistent with his May Fourth belief that science alone does not explain everything in people's lives.

48. Guo Moruo, *Wenyi lunji*, 67.

49. Ibid., 67.

50. *Hongshui*, vol. 1, no. 7, 214–215.

51. Ibid., 215; Legge, *The Sacred Books of China*, 364–366.

Guo, in his "The Creation of a New State," again identifies Marx's ideal of a Communist society with the Confucian ideal of Great Harmony. See *Hongshui*, vol. 1, no. 8: 228.

52. *Hongshui*, vol. 1, no. 7: 216; Wang Zichen, *Sishu duben* (Beijing: Zhongguo shudian, 1986), 307; Confucius, *The Analects*, 138.

53. *Hongshui*, vol. 1, no. 7: 216–217; Wang Zichen, *Sishu duben*, 238, 216; Confucius, *The Analects*, 119–120, 113.

Guo, in "Wang Yangming: A Great Spiritualist," also notes that Confucianism "strove for" material development. Confucius, Guo writes, mentioned that moral cultivation came after material prosperity. See Guo Moruo, *Wenyi lunji*, 67.

54. *Hongshui*, vol. 1, no. 9: 328.

55. Ibid., 329. Guo does admit in the letter that Confucius's thinking was somewhat "limited" by his time. See *Hongshui*, vol. 1, no. 9: 329.

56. *Hongshui*, vol. 1, no. 9: 327.

57. Ibid., 326. Guo here is in a sense equating proletarians with the Confucian "men of virtues."

58. *Hongshui*, vol. 1, no. 9: 326, 328; for reference, also see *Hongshui*, vol. 1, no. 8: 228–229.

59. Here again, with his break with the Confucian family bonds of father-son and husband-wife on the issue of his arranged marriage, the concepts of "filial piety" and "family" had largely lost their traditional meaning for him.

60. *Hongshui*, vol. 1, no. 9: 326–327. Guo also notes in the letter that the nine-square land system (*jingtian zhi*) that Mencius advocated was actually a Communist system. See *Hongshui*, vol. 1, no. 9: 327.

61. Traces of Goetheanism and Taoism from his May Fourth synthesis could still be seen here and there in Guo's thinking since the mid-1920s. As late as 1926, for instance, he spent some time editing his old translation of Goethe's *The Sorrows of Young Werther*, indicating that by then he still liked that book. In general, however, elements of Goetheanism and Taoism were overshadowed by his new Confucian/Marxist/Leninist synthesis. See Guo Moruo, *Xuesheng shidai*, 166; *Hongshui*, vol. 2, no. 20: 365–366.

62. It needs to be mentioned that Guo's May Fourth interest in natural sciences continued in his new Communist synthesis in the mid-1920s.

63. *Chuangzao yuekan*, vol. 1, no. 2: 130.

64. Guo Moruo, *Xuesheng shidai*, 182; *Chuangzao yuekan*, vol. 1, no. 2: 128.

65. *Chuangzao yuekan*, vol. 1, no. 2: 128; *Hongshui*, vol. 1, no. 7: 216–217. Guo's progressive worldview of Confucianism actually might also have contributed to his interest in

historical materialism. Consistent with his 1923 "The Traditional Spirit of Chinese Culture," he writes in "Wang Yangming: A Great Spiritualist" that Confucianism considers "noumenon" (*benti*) to be "moving" "naturally" with "a certain order," "along a certain course," and ultimately in a "progressive" manner toward "perfection." Such Confucian thinking, though primarily moralistic by nature and in that regard fundamentally different than historical materialism, might have made him feel that he could relate to historical materialism's belief that human society progresses through stages of development toward the ultimate ideal of Communism. See Guo Moruo, *Wenyi lunji*, 62–63.

66. Gail Lee Bernstein, *Japanese Marxist: A Portrait of Kawakami Hajime 1879–1946* (Cambridge, MA: Harvard University Press, 1990), 117–123.

67. Kawakami, *Shakai soshiki to shakai kakumei*, 497–511; Kawakami, *Shehui zuzhi yu shehui geming*, 222–228.

68. Kawakami, *Shakai soshiki to shakai kakumei*, 404–412, 433–435, 509–530, 550–556; Kawakami, *Shehui zuzhi yu shehui geming*, 180–181, 191–192, 228, 229–236, 246; Bernstein, *Japanese Marxist*, 106, 109–128; Nikolai Lenin, *The Soviets at Work* (New York: Rand School of Social Science, 1919), 6–10, 38–39.

69. Kawakami, *Shakai soshiki to shakai kakumei*, 435–472; Kawakami, *Shehui zuzhi yu shehui geming*, 192–209; Bernstein, *Japanese Marxist*, 119–123; *Hongshui*, vol. 1, no. 10–11: 339.

70. *Hongshui*, vol. 1, no. 10–11: 337–339.

71. Ibid., 338–339; Marx and Engels, *The Communist Manifesto*, 44.

72. *Hongshui*, vol. 1, no. 10–11: 341; Karl Marx and Frederick Engels, *Karl Marx, Frederick Engels: Collected Works*, vol. 9 (New York: International Publishers, 1977), 453. The emphasis here was originally made by Marx.

73. Guo does note that while dualistically existing with historical materialism, Marx's activism is still "based" on the scientific study of historical materialism. See *Hongshui*, vol. 1, no. 10–11: 337–341.

74. *Hongshui*, vol. 1, no. 10–11: 339; Karl Marx and Frederick Engels, *Karl Marx, Frederick Engels: Collected Works*, vol. 35 (New York: International Publishers, 1996), 10.

75. *Hongshui*, vol. 1, no. 10–11: 341, 337–338.

76. Guo's knowledge of Kawakami's thinking was basically limited to his reading of *Social Organization and Social Revolution*. In other words, he did not seem to be aware of the details of Kawakami's intellectual development that Gail Lee Bernstein discusses in her book. See Bernstein, *Japanese Marxist*.

77. *Hongshui*, vol. 1, no. 10–11: 335, 333–334.

78. Ibid., 342, 339; Marx and Engels, *Collected Works*, vol. 35, 10.

79. *Chuangzao yuekan*, vol. 1, no. 2: 137.

80. Ibid., 129.

81. Guo Moruo, *Xinglunan*, 82, 84–85.

82. His description here also reminds us of his early poems that refer to *taohuayuan* (桃花源), a utopian village depicted by Tao Yuanming as a simple farming community isolated

from society that offered a peaceful and harmonious life. See Guo Moruo, *Guo Moruo jiuti shici xinian zhushi*, 29, 39.

83. *Hongshui*, vol. 1, no. 1: 5–8.

84. Ibid., vol. 2, no. 16: 137–138.

85. When Guo in his May Fourth description of pantheism stated that all nature is the expression of God, or him, his pantheism merged into an idealism that saw spirit, mind, ideas, and morals as being superior to the reality of matter. His May Fourth idealism also could be seen in his statement that "as the ultimate products of the liberal spirit of human beings," "ideas should transcend all reality and guide people's life. . . . When life in reality is the true expression of progressive ideas, the people who live in that reality enjoy the ultimate happiness." He once wrote that he wanted to use his "inner light to shine all over the world." He had admired Goethe's heart and emotion as the light that could produce "various pictures on a blank wall" and "create a universe with feelings" out of "death and ruins." He also had praised what he saw as Confucius's celebration of "the independence and self-reliance of spirit." See Guo Moruo, *Guo Moruo yiwenji (1)*, 67; Guo Moruo, *Nushen*, 84; Guo Moruo, *Wenyi lunji*, 228, 14.

Guo's May Fourth idealism tended to be subjective, and his emphasis on the primary importance of minds (mind-hearts) and their ideas over reality recalls his influence by the subjectivist thinking of Wang Yangming's Neo-Confucianism. Such a tendency, however, had already existed in his early Sichuan years before his influence by Wang, recalling a fundamental influence by the overall Confucian emphasis on human moral concerns over material matters. For instance, when in middle school in Chengdu, criticizing the incompetence and corruption of his teachers, he blamed nothing but the teachers' "lack of moral conscience," the corruption of "social morals," and, above all, the "degeneration" of China's "spiritual civilization." "The only way" to cure these problems, he believed, was to have people "purify their souls." Another example was his criticism of his oldest brother, who after the 1911 revolution became Sichuan's provincial minister of communications. In his eyes, his brother, who had influenced him with new ideas, became demoralized after joining the establishment. Among other things, he was shocked to find that this fairly modern brother had picked up the habit of smoking opium, one of the evils of the old days! Since his "corrupted" brother was in charge of Sichuan's railway industry after the revolution and this industry was having various problems, he moralized the issue by blaming the problems on his brother's "indulgence in a corrupt life." See Guo Moruo, *Shaonian shidai*, 172, 296–298.

86. *Hongshui*, vol. 2, no. 16: 139–140.

87. Ibid., vol. 1, no. 8: 233.

88. Guo Moruo, *Xuesheng shidai*, 335–336.

89. *Hongshui*, vol. 1, no. 9: 326.

CONCLUSION

1. Wang Jiquan and Tong Weigang, *Guo Moruo nianpu (2)* (Jiangsu: Jiangsu People's Press, 1983), 431–433.

Bibliography

Asahi Shimbun (Osaka) 大阪<<朝日新聞>>. New Year's Day special issue, 1923.

Bernstein, Gail Lee. *Japanese Marxist: A Portrait of Kawakami Hajime 1879–1946.* Cambridge, MA: Harvard University Press, 1990.

Chan Wing-Tsit. *A Source Book in Chinese Philosophy.* Princeton, NJ: Princeton University Press, 1963.

Chang Hao 張灝. *Liang Ch'i-ch'ao and Intellectual Transition in China: 1890–1907.* Cambridge, MA: Harvard University Press, 1971.

———. *Chinese Intellectuals in Crisis, Search for Order and Meaning, 1890–1911.* Berkeley: University of California Press, 1989.

———. *Youan yishi yu minzhu chuantong* 幽暗意識與民主傳統 (Sense of evil and democracy and tradition). Taiwan: Lianjing chuban shiye gongsi, 1989.

———. "Xingxiang yu shizhi—zairen wusi sixiang" 形像與實質: 再認五四思想 (Image and reality: A reexamination of May Fourth thinking). In *Ziyou minzhu de sixiang yu wenhua* 自由民主的思想與文化 (The liberal and democratic thinking and culture), ed. Wei Zhengtong et al., 23–57. Taiwan: Ziliwanbaoshe, 1990.

———. "Playing God: Deification of Man in Twentieth-Century Chinese Thought." Unpublished paper.

———. *Chang Hao zixuan ji* 張灝自選集 (Selected essays). Shanghai: Shanghai jiaoyu chubanshe, 2002.

Chenbao fukan 晨報副刊 (Morning paper supplement). Beijing, February 28, 1925.

Chow Tse-tsung. *The May Fourth Movement: Intellectual Revolution in Modern China.* Cambridge, MA: Harvard University Press, 1960.

Chuang Tzu 庄子. *Chuang tzu.* Translated by Burton Watson. New York: Columbia University Press, 1964.

Chuangzao jikan 創造季刊 (Creation quarterly). (A reprint of the originals, published by Shanghai Taidong tushuju from 1922 to 1924). Shanghai: Shanghai shudian, 1983.

Chuangzao yuekan 創造月刊 (Creation monthly). (A reprint of the originals, published by Shanghai Chuangzaoshe from 1926 to 1929). Shanghai: Shanghai shudian, 1985.

Chuangzao zhoubao 創造周報 (Creation weekly). (A reprint of the originals, published by Shanghai Taidong tushuju from 1923 to 1924). Shanghai: Shanghai shudian, 1983.

Cohen, Myron L. "Being Chinese: The Peripheralization of Traditional Identity." *Daedalus* 120: 2 (Spring 1991).

Cohen, Paul A., and Merle Goldman, eds. *Ideas across Cultures.* Cambridge, MA: Harvard University Press, 1990.

Confucius. *The Analects.* Translated by D. C. Lau. New York: Penguin Books, 1979.

De Bary, Wm. Theodore. *Learning for One's Self—Essays on the Individual in Neo-Confucian Thought.* New York: Columbia University Press, 1991.

Denton, Kirk A. *The Problematic of Self in Modern Chinese Literature: Hu Feng and Lu Ling.* Stanford, CA: Stanford University Press, 1998.

Dirlik, Arif. *The Origins of Chinese Communism.* New York: Oxford University Press, 1989.

Dolezelova-Velingerova, Milena, and Oldrich Kral, eds. *The Appropriation of Cultural Capital: China's May Fourth Project.* Cambridge, MA, and London: Harvard University Press, 2001.

Duiker, William. *Ts'ai Yuan-p'ei: Educator of Modern China.* University Park and London: Pennsylvania State University Press, 1977.

Feigon, Lee. *Chen Duxiu: Founder of the Chinese Communist Party.* Princeton, NJ: Princeton University Press, 1983.

Fogel, Joshua A., ed. and trans. *Recent Japanese Studies of Modern Chinese History.* (A special issue of *Chinese Studies in History,* Fall-Winter 1984–85/Vol. XVIII, No. 1–2). New York: M. E. Sharpe, 1984.

Fukui Junzo 福井準造. *Kinsei shakai shugi* 近世社會主義 (Modern socialism). Tokyo: Yuhikaku Shobo, 1899.

Furth, Charlotte, ed. *The Limits of Change.* Cambridge, MA: Harvard University Press, 1976.

Goethe, Johann Wolfgang von. *Faust I & II.* Edited and translated by Stuart Atkins. Cambridge, MA: Suhrkamp/Insel, 1984.

Gu Fulin 谷輔林. *Guo Moruo qianqi sixiang ji chuangzuo* 郭沫若前期思想及創作 (Guo Moruo's early thinking and writing). Jinan: Shangdong People's Press, 1983.

Guo Moruo 郭沫若. *Ta* 塔 (Tower). Shanghai: Guwenshuju, 1926.

———. *Xingkong* 星空 (Star skies). Shanghai: Taidong tushuju, 1928.

———. *Ganlan* 橄欖 (Olives). Shanghai: Xiandai shuju, 1931.

———. *Moruo shiji* 沫若詩集 (Poems of Guo Moruo). Shanghai: Xiandai shuju, 1931.

———. *Moruo shuxinji* 沫若書信集 (Letters of Guo Moruo). Shanghai: Taidong tushuju, 1933.

———. *Xinglunan* 行路難 (A hard journey). Shanghai: Shangwu yinshuguan, 1933.

———. *Jinxi pujian* 今昔蒲劍 (Rush sword, past and present). Shanghai: Haiyan shudian, 1947.

———. *Tiandi xuanhuang* 天地玄黃 (Black heaven and yellow earth). Shanghai: Dafu chubangongsi, 1947.

———. *Guo Moruo xuanji* 郭沫若選集 (Selected works of Guo Moruo). Hong Kong: Wenxue chubanshe, 1956.

———. *Moruo wenji (1)* 沫若文集 (一) (Works of Guo Moruo 1). Hong Kong: Sanlian shudian, 1957.

———. *Selected Poems from the Goddesses.* Translated by John Lester and A. C. Barnes. Beijing: Foreign Languages Press, 1958.

———. *Moruo wenji (10)* 沫若文集 (十) (Works of Guo Moruo 10). Beijing: Renmin wenxue chubanshe, 1959.

———. *Moruo wenji (16)* 沫若文集 (十六) (Selected works of Moruo 16). Beijing: Renmin wenxue chubanshe, 1962.

———. *Moruo zixuanji* 沫若自選集 (Moruo's self-selected works). Hong Kong: Xinyue chubanshe, 1962.

———. "Guo Moruo nushen jiwai yiwen" 郭沫若女神集外佚文 (Guo Moruo's writings uncollected in the *Goddesses*). Edited by Deng Niudun. *Nankai University Journal* 2 (1978): 58–69.

———. *Shaonian shidai* 少年時代 (My younger years). Hong Kong: Sanlian shudian, 1978.

———. *Xuesheng shidai* 學生時代 (My school years). Hong Kong: Sanlian shudian, 1978.

———. *Guo Moruo shaonian shigao* 郭沫若少年詩稿 (Guo Moruo's early poems). Edited by Leshan shiguansuo. Chengdu: Sichuan remin chubanshe, 1979.

———. *Wenyi lunji xuji* 文藝論集續集 (Collected literary essays continued). Beijing: Renmin wenxue chubanshe, 1979.

———. *Yinghua shujian* 櫻花書簡 (Letters from Japan). Edited by Tang Mingzhong and Huang Gaobin. Sichuan: Sichuan People's Press, 1981.

———. *Guo Moruo jiuti shici xinian zhushi* 郭沫若舊體詩詞系年注釋 (An annotated chronological collection of Guo Moruo's old-style poems, Vol. I). Edited by Wang Guoquan et al. Harbin: Heilongjiang remin chubanshe, 1982.

———. *Guo Moruo jiwai xubaji* 郭沫若集外序跋集 (Unpublished prefaces and postscripts written by Guo Moruo). Edited by Shanghai Library and Sichuan University. Sichuan: Sichuan People's Press, 1982.

———. *Guo Moruo quanji (lishibian 2)* 郭沫若全集(歷史編二) (Complete works of Guo Moruo—history 2). Edited by Guo Moruo zhuzuo bianji chuban weiyuanhui. Beijing: Remin wenxue chubanshe, 1982.

———. *Guo Moruo quanji (wenxuebian 1)* 郭沫若全集(文學編一) (Complete works of Guo Moruo—literature 1). Edited by Guo Moruo zhuzuo bianji chuban weiyuanhui. Beijing: Renmin wenxue chubanshe, 1982.

———. *Guo Moruo quanji (wenxuebian 2)* 郭沫若全集(文學編二) (Complete works of Guo Moruo—literature 2). Edited by Guo Moruo zhuzuo bianji chuban weiyuanhui. Beijing: Renmin wenxue chubanshe, 1982.

———. *Nushen (huijiao ben)* 女神 (匯校本) (The *Goddesses*, an annotated text). Edited by Sang Fengkang. Hunan: Hunan People's Press, 1983.

———. *Guo Moruo quanji (lishibian 3)* 郭沫若全集(歷史編三) (Complete works of Guo Moruo—history 3). Edited by Guo Moruo zhuzuo bianji chuban weiyuanhui. Beijing: Remin wenxue chubanshe, 1984.

————. *Guo Moruo quanji (wenxuebian 5)* 郭沫若全集(文學編 五) (Complete works of Guo Moruo—literature 5). Edited by Guo Moruo zhuzuo bianji chuban weiyuanhui. Beijing: Remin wenxue chubanshe, 1984.

————. *Wenyi lunji (huijiao ben)* 文藝論集(匯校本) (Collected literary essays, an annotated text). Edited by Huang Chunhao. Hunan: Hunan People's Press, 1984.

————. *Guo Moruo quanji (wenxuebian 9)* 郭沫若全集(文學編 九) (Complete works of Guo Moruo—literature 9). Edited by Guo Moruo zhuzuo bianji chuban weiyuanhui. Beijing: Remin wenxue chubanshe, 1985.

————. *Guo Moruo quanji (wenxuebian 10)* 郭沫若全集(文學編 十) (Complete works of Guo Moruo—literature 10). Edited by Guo Moruo zhuzuo bianji chuban weiyuanhui. Beijing: Remin wenxue chubanshe, 1985.

————. *Guo Moruo quanji (wenxuebian 6)* 郭沫若全集(文學編 六) (Complete works of Guo Moruo—literature 6). Edited by Guo Moruo zhuzuo bianji chuban weiyuanhui. Beijing: Renmin wenxue chubanshe, 1986.

————. *Guo Moruo yiwenji (1)* 郭沫若佚文集(上) (Guo Moruo's uncollected works 1). Edited by Wang Jinhou et al. Chengdu: Sichuan University Press, 1988.

————. *Guo Moruo yiwenji (2)* 郭沫若佚文集(下) (Guo Moruo's uncollected works 2). Edited by Wang Jinhou et al. Chengdu: Sichuan University Press, 1988.

"Guo Moruo zhuyi jinian" 郭沫若著譯紀年 (A chronology of works written or translated by Guo Moruo). Edited by Shanghai Library. In *Guo Moruo yanjiu ziliao (xia)* 郭沫若研究資料(下) (References for the study of Guo Moruo, vol. 3), ed. Wang Xunzhao et al., 334–861. Beijing: Zhongguo shehuikexue chubanshe, 1986.

Guo Moruo, Zong Baihua, and Tian Shouchang 郭沫若，宗白華，田壽昌. *San ye ji* 三葉集 (Cloverleaf). Shanghai: Yadong tushuguan, 1923.

The Holy Bible (New Revised Standard Version). Nashville, TN: Thomas Nelson, 1989.

Hongshui 洪水 (Flood). (A reprint of the originals, published by Shanghai Chuangzaoshe from 1924 to 1927). Shanghai: Shanghai shudian, 1985.

Hou Wailu 侯外廬 et al. *Zhongguo sixiangshi gang* 中國思想史綱 (An outline of Chinese intellectual history). Beijing: Zhongguo qingnian chubanshe, 1980–1981.

Jin Guantao 金觀濤. "Zhongguo wenhua de lixing jingshen jiqi quexian" 中國文化 的理性精神及其缺陷 (The rational elements in Chinese culture and their defects). *The Chinese Intellectual* (quarterly) 17 (1989): 87–96.

Kaizo 改造 (Reconstruction). Tokyo: Kaizosha, 1919–1955.

Kawakami Hajime 河上肇. *Shakai soshiki to shakai kakumei* 社會組織ㄉ社會革命 (Social organization and social revolution). Kyoto: Kobundo, 1922.

————. *Shehui zuzhi yu shehui geming* 社會組織與社會革命 (Social organization and social revolution). Translated by Guo Moruo. Shanghai: Shangwu yinshuguan, 1950.

Lao Zi 老子. *Dao de jing* 道德經 Annotated by Wang Hansheng. Taiwan: Zhongguo guojiao taibeizongshe, 1956.

————. *Tao te ching.* Translated by Stephen Addiss and Stanley Lombardo. Indianapolis, IN, and Cambridge, MA: Hackett, 1993.

Larson, Wendy. *Literary Authority and the Modern Chinese Writer.* Durham, NC, and London: Duke University Press, 1991.

Lee, Leo Ou-fan. *The Romantic Generation of Modern Chinese Writers.* Cambridge, MA: Harvard University Press, 1973.

Legge, James, trans. *The Sacred Books of China—The Texts of Confucianism.* Oxford: Clarendon Press, 1885.

Lenin, Nikolai. *The Soviets at Work.* New York: Rand School of Social Science, 1919.

Levenson, Joseph R. *Confucian China and Its Modern Fate.* Berkeley and Los Angeles: University of California Press, 1968.

Li Dazhao 李大釗. *Li Dazhao wenji* 李大釗文集 (Collected works of Li Dazhao). Beijing: Renmin chubanshe, 1984.

Li ji 禮記 (Book of rites). (As part of the Shihsanjing zhushu). (The 1815 Nanchang fuxue edition, reprinted in 1989.) Taiwan: Yiwen yinshuguan, 1989.

Li Zehou 李澤厚. *Zhongguo jindai sixiangshi lun* 中國近代思想史論 (Essays on modern Chinese intellectual history). Hefei: Anhui wenyi chubanshe, 1994.

———. *Zhongguo xiandai sixiangshi lun* 中國現代思想史論 (On contemporary Chinese intellectual history). Hefei: Anhui wenyi chubanshe, 1994.

Liao Ping 廖平. *Guxue kao* 古學考 (On the "ancient text" learning). Annotated by Zhang Xitang. Hong Kong: Taipingshuju, (reprinted) 1962.

Lin Yusheng. *The Crisis of Chinese Consciousness: Radical Anti-Traditionalism in the May Fourth Era.* Madison: University of Wisconsin Press, 1979.

Liu, Lydia H. *Translingual Practice: Literature, National Culture, and Translated Modernity—China, 1900–1937.* Stanford, CA: Stanford University Press, 1995.

Liu Shaoqi 劉少奇. *Lun gongchandangyuan de xiuyang* 論共產党員的修養 (On the cultivation of a Communist). Beijing: People's Press, 1949.

Lovejoy, Arthur O. *Essays in the History of Ideas.* Baltimore, MD: Johns Hopkins University Press, 1948.

Mao Dun 茅盾. *Ziye* 子夜 (Midnight). Hong Kong: Lingnan chubanshe, 1966.

Mao Zedong 毛澤東. *Selected Works of Mao Zedong.* Beijing: Renmin chubanshe, 1969.

———. *Mao Zedong zaoqi wengao* 毛澤東早期文稿 (Early writings of Mao Zedong: June 1912–November 1920). Changsha: Hunan chubanshe, 1990.

———. *Mao Zedong zishu* 毛澤東自述 (Mao Zedong talks). Beijing: People's Press, 1993.

Marx, Karl, and Frederick Engels. *The Communist Manifesto.* New York: International Publishers, 1948.

———. *Karl Marx, Frederick Engels: Collected Works.* Vol. 9. New York: International Publishers, 1977.

———. *Karl Marx, Frederick Engels: Collected Works.* Vol. 35. New York: International Publishers, 1996.

Meisner, Maurice. *Li Ta-chao and the Origins of Chinese Marxism.* Cambridge, MA: Harvard University Press, 1967.

———. *Marxism, Maoism, and Utopianism.* Madison: University of Wisconsin Press, 1982.

Mencius. *Mencius.* Translated by D. C. Lau. Hong Kong: Chinese University Press, 1979.

Metzger, Thomas A. *The Western Concept of the Civil Society in the Context of Chinese History.* (Hoover Essays, No. 21). Stanford, CA: Hoover Institution, Stanford University Press, 1998.

———. *Tang Chun-i's Rejection of Western Modernity.* Unpublished manuscript.

Moore, Barrington Jr. *Soviet Politics: The Dilemma of Power.* Cambridge, MA: Harvard University Press, 1956.

Nietzsche, Friedrich. *Thus Spoke Zarathustra.* Translated by R. J. Hollingdale. Baltimore, MD: Penguin Books, 1961.

Peng Ming 彭明. 1984. *Wusi yundong shi* 五四運動史 (A history of the May Fourth movement). Beijing: Renmin chubanshe, 1984.

Prusek, Jaroslav. *The Lyrical and the Epic: Studies of Modern Chinese Literature.* Edited by Leo Ou-fan Lee. Bloomington: Indiana University Press, 1980.

Qi Shufen 漆樹芬. *Jingjiqinluexia zhi zhongguo* 經濟侵略下之中國 (China under economic invasions). (As *Minguo congshu* 民國叢書 I, 34). Shanghai: Guanghua shuju, 1931.

Qian Mu 錢穆. *Yangmingxue shuyao* 陽明學述要 (The essence of Wang Yangming's thinking). Taiwan: Zhengzhong shuju, 1955.

———. *Zhongguo jinsanbainian xueshushi* 中國近三百年學術史(A history of Chinese scholarship in the past three hundred years). Taiwan: Shangwu yinshuguan, 1964.

Qu Qiubai 瞿秋白. *Qu Qiubai wenji (zhengzhi lilun bian)* 瞿秋白文集 (政治理論編) (Collected works of Qu Qiubai—the part on political theories). Beijing: Renmin chubanshe, 1988.

Roy, David. *Kuo Mo-jo: The Early Years.* Cambridge, MA: Harvard University Press, 1971.

Ruan Wuming 阮無名. *Zhongguo xinwentan milu* 中國新文壇秘錄 (Secret records of China's new literary circle). Shanghai: Nanqiang shuju, 1933.

Schram, Stuart. *Mao Tse-tung.* New York: Simon and Schuster, 1966.

———. *The Thought of Mao Tse-tung.* Cambridge: Cambridge University Press, 1989.

Schwarcz, Vera. *The Chinese Enlightenment: Intellectuals and the Legacy of the May Fourth Movement of 1919.* Berkeley: University of California Press, 1986.

Schwartz, Benjamin I. *Chinese Communism and the Rise of Mao.* Cambridge, MA: Harvard University Press, 1951.

———. *In Search of Wealth and Power: Yen Fu and the West.* Cambridge, MA: Harvard University Press, 1964.

———. *China and Other Matters.* Cambridge, MA: Harvard University Press, 1996.

Shimada Kenji. *Pioneer of the Chinese Revolution: Zhang Binglin and Confucianism.* Translated by Joshua A. Fogel. Stanford, CA: Stanford University Press, 1990.

Snow, Edgar. *Red Star over China.* New York: Grove Press, 1973.

Spinoza, Benedict De. *The Chief Works of Benedict De Spinoza.* Translated by R. H. M. Elwes. London: George Bell and Sons, 1891.

Tagore, Rabindranath. *The King of the Dark Chamber.* New York: Macmillan, 1914.

———. *The Gardener.* New York: Macmillan, 1915.

———. *Songs of Kabir.* New York: Macmillan, 1916.

Tane maku hito 種蒔く人(The sowers). (A reprint of the originals, published from 1921 to 1923). Tokyo: Japan Modern Literature Society, 1961.

The Thirteen Principal Upanishads. Translated by Robert Ernest Hume. London: Geoffrey Cumberlege: Oxford University Press, 1951.

Trotzky, Leon. *Our Revolution: Essays on Working-Class and International Revolution, 1904–1917.* Collected and translated, with biography and explanatory notes, by Moissaye J. Olgin. New York: Henry Holt and Company, 1918.

Waley, Arthur. *Three Ways of Thought in Ancient China.* London: George Allen & Unwin, 1939.

Wang Fansen 王汎森. *Gushibian yundong de xingqi: yige sixiangshi de fenxi* 古史辨運動的興起：一個思想史的分析 (The Rise of the Gushibian Movement: An Intellectual Historical Analysis). Taibei: Yunchen wenhua shiye gufen youxian gongsi, 1987.

Wang Jiquan and Tong Weigang 王繼權，童焯鋼. *Guo Moruo nianpu (1)* 郭沫若年譜 (上) (A chronicle of Guo Moruo-1). Jiangsu: Jiangsu People's Press, 1983.

———. 王繼權，童焯鋼. *Guo Moruo nianpu (2)* 郭沫若年譜 (下) (A chronicle of Guo Moruo-2). Jiangsu: Jiangsu People's Press, 1983.

Wang Yangming 王陽明. *Yangming quanshu* 陽明全書 (Collected works of Wang Yangming). Shanghai: Taidong tushuju, 1925.

Wang Zichen 王淄塵. *Sishu duben* 四書讀本 (A text of the Four Classics). Beijing: Zhongguo shudian, 1986.

Whitman, Walt. *The Collected Writings of Walt Whitman.* Edited by Gay Wilson Allen and Sculley Bradley. New York: New York University Press, 1965.

Xiao Yanzhong and Zhu Yi 蕭延中，朱藝, ed. *Qimeng de jiazhi yu juxian* 啟蒙的价值與局限 (The value and limits of enlightenment). Taiyuan: Shenxi renmin chubanshe, 1989.

Xu Binru 徐彬如. "Huiyi Luxun yijiuerqinian zai Guangzhou de qingkuang" 回憶魯迅一九二七年在廣州的情況 (Recollections on Luxun in 1927 in Guangzhou). In *Luxun zai Guangzhou* 魯迅在廣州(Luxun in Guangzhou), ed. Zhongshan da xue zhong wen xi, 199–208. Guangzhou: Guangdong People's Press, 1976.

Yu Dafu 鬱達夫. *Yu Dafu zixu.* Edited by Zhao Hongmei. Beijing: Tuanjie chubanshe, 1996.

Yu Ying-shih 余英時. "Wusi yundong yu zhongguo chuantong" 五四運動與中國傳統 (The May Fourth movement and Chinese tradition). In *Qimeng de jiazhi yu juxian* 啟蒙的价值與局限 (The value and limits of enlightenment), ed. Xiao Yanzhong et al., 74–85. Taiyuan: Shenxi renmin chubanshe, 1989.

———. *Neizai chaoyue zhilu* 內在超越之路 (The path of inner transcendence). Edited by Xin Hua and Ren Jing 辛華，任菁. Beijing: Zhongguo guangbodianshi chubanshe, 1992.

———. "Neither Renaissance nor Enlightenment: A Historian's Reflections on the May Fourth Movement." In *The Appropriation of Cultural Capital: China's May Fourth Project,* ed. Milena Dolezelova-Velingerova and Oldrich Kral, 299–324. Cambridge, MA, and London: Harvard University Press, 2001.

———. et al. *Zhongguo lishi zhuanxing shiqi de zhishifenzi* 中國歷史轉型時期的知識分子 (Chinese intellectuals during the transitional period). Taiwan: Lianjing, 1992.

Zeng Leshan 曾樂山. *Makesi zhu yi zhexue de zhongguo hua ji qi li cheng* 馬克斯主義哲學的中國化及其歷程 (The Sinification of Marxism and its historical development). Shanghai: Huadong shifan daxue chubanshe, 1991.

Zhang Zhidong 張之洞. *Zhangwenxianggong quanji* 張文襄公全集 (The complete works of Zhang Zhidong). Taiwan: Wenhai chubanshe, 1963.

Zhao Shuli 趙樹理. *Zhao Shuli xuanji* 趙樹理選集 (Selected works of Zhao Shuli). Beijing: Kaiming shudian, 1951.

Zhongguo Guo Moruo yanjiu xuehui 中國郭沫若研究學會 (Chinese Guo Moruo Research Society). *Guo Moruo yanjiu (2)* 郭沫若研究 (2) (Study on Guo Moruo-2). Beijing: Wenhua yishu chubanshe, 1986.

———. *Guo Moruo yanjiu (3)* 郭沫若研究(3) (Study on Guo Moruo-3). Beijing: Wenhua yishu chubanshe, 1987.

———. *Guo Moruo yanjiu (7)* 郭沫若研究(7) (Study on Guo Moruo-7). Beijing: Wenhua yishu chubanshe, 1989.

———. *Guo Moruo bainian danchen jinian wen ji* 郭沫若百年誕辰紀念文集 (Collected writings in celebration of the 100th anniversary of Guo Moruo's birth). Beijing: Shehui kexue wenxian chubanshe, 1994.

———. *Guo Moruo yu rujia wenhua* 郭沫若與儒家文化(Guo Moruo and the Confucian culture). Jinan: Shandong renmin chubanshe, 1994.

———. *Guo Moruo yu dongxifang wenhua* 郭沫若與東西方文化(Guo Moruo and Eastern and Western cultures). Beijing: Dangdai zhongguo chubanshe, 1998.

Index

Page numbers in italics refer to illustrations.

Guo Moruo
adherence to Marxism/Leninism,
4–5, 6, 7, 8, 9, 10, 31, 37–39, 48,
51–52, 61–62, 64, 71–90, 98–
107, 115n19, 117n28, 117n29,
117n30, 129n46, 130n62,
131n9, 136n83
alcohol abuse, 15, 118–119n21
ambitions for China: 131n1, 134n35,
135n68
approach to industrialization, 75–76,
105, 133n23
arranged marriage, 1, 5, 7–8, 11–22,
24, 26, 27, 33, 42, 44, 80, 91, 92,
114, 115n14, 118n14, 122n88,
140n59
brothers and sisters of, 18–20, 67, 142n85
Buddhist influence on, 18, 125n77
childhood, 84, 142n85
children with Sato Tomiko, 16–17,
19, 21, 34–36, 59, 61, 70, 110,
123n125, 125n155, 130n61
and Christianity, 24, 45, 120n65,
126n186
and common-law marriage, 16–22, 61
continuity with Confucian tradition, 4,
10, 13, 17, 29, 37, 46, 48, 51–52,
53, 92–94, 99, 105, 115n16,
139n45
conversion to Communism, 1–10,
38–39, 47, 48–52, 84–85, 98,
109, 130n62
criticism of capitalism, 62, 129n46,
130n48
enthusiasm for revolution, 89–90, 104,
136n84
financial difficulties of, 34–35, 37, 39,
48, 99
first published as a poet, 1, 24
and freedom of expression, 34
hearing impairment of, 33, 121n71,
129n35, 137n22
influenced by Western-style romance,
13, 14, 16, 17, 21, 25, 26–27, 43,
46, 91, 120n66
life in Japan, 16–22, 26, 59, 105, 131n1,
133n24, 137n22

literary career, 34–35, 37, 51, 57, 59,
122n98, 124n148, 125n168,
127n213, 137n22
medical education of, 15, 16, 32, 33, 34,
37, 60, 68, 137n22
neurasthenia of, 22, 23
and pantheism, 41–42, 79–80, 87,
96–97, 142n85
parents of, 15, 16, 17, 18, 19, 20, 28, 32,
33, 60, 66, 67, 122n88
and passion for pastoral life, 75–77,
133n24, 133n34
rejection of Confucian social values,
14, 15, 22–31, 41–47, 114n10,
115n16
Russian populist influence on, 117n33
"Seventh Sister" of, 19–21, 119n42,
119n43
and social science, 98, 102, 139n37
suicidal thoughts, 18–19, 35–36, 43
and tension between China and Japan,
57, 58, 59, 72, 80, 128n19
and tension between Confucian moralism and Marxist historical materialism, 2, 5, 10, 46–47, 50, 102,
105, 110, 139n42, 140n65
Guo Moruo (works)
"Appendicitis and Capitalism," 39, 89
"The Awakening of Writers and Art-
ists," 39, 40, 90, 106
Coal in the Grate—My love for my coun-
try, 54–55
"Coal, Iron, and Japan," 59, 73, 75, 76,
79, 80, 84, 95, 131n10
"The Character and Thinking of Hui
Shi," 94
"The Creation of a New State," 87, 88,
106, 130n62
Dawn, 78
"A Dialogue between the Yellow River
and the Yangzi River," 85
Estuary of the Huangpu, 55
A Fragrant Noon, 77–78
"From Economic Struggle to Political
Struggle," 90
Ganlan, 122n88
"Going to Yixing," 106, 130n48